Simulating Computer Systems

MIT Press Series in Computer Systems
Herb Schwetman, editor

Simulating Computer Systems
Techniques and Tools

M. H. MacDougall

The MIT Press
Cambridge, Massachusetts
London, England

PUBLISHER'S NOTE

This format is intended to reduce the cost of publishing certain works in book form and to shorten the gap between editorial preparation and final publication. Detailed editing and composition have been avoided by photographing the text of this book directly from the author's prepared copy.

This book was printed and bound in the United States of America

Library of Congress Cataloging-in-Publication Data

MacDougall, M. H. (Myron H.)
    Simulating computer systems.

    Bibliography: p.
    Includes index.
    1. Computer simulation. I. Title
QA76.9.C65M335 1987   004.2'1   87-3880
ISBN 0-262-13229-X

Contents

Contents

Contents

Series Foreword

This series is devoted to all aspects of computer systems. This means that subjects ranging from circuit components and microprocessors to architecture to supercomputers and systems programming will be appropriate. Analysis of systems will be appropriate as well. System theories are developing, theories that permit deeper understandings of complex interrelationships and their effects on performance, reliability, and usefulness.

We expect to offer books that not only develop new material but also describe projects and systems. In addition to understanding concepts, we need to benefit from the decision making that goes into actual development projects; selection from various alternatives can be crucial to success. We are soliciting contributions in which several aspects of systems are classified and compared. A better understanding of both the similarities and the differences found in systems is needed.

It is an exciting time in the area of computer systems. New technologies mean that architectures that were at one time interesting but not feasible are now feasible. Better software engineering means that we can consider several software alternatives, instead of "more of the same old thing," in terms of operating systems and system software. Faster and cheaper communications mean that intercomponent distances are less important. We hope that this series contributes to this excitement in the area of computer systems by chonicling past achievements and publicizing new concepts. The format allows publication of lengthy presentations that are of interest to a select readership.

Herb Schwetman

Preface

1. Nature of the Tools

This book is intended for computer and communication system designers who want to analyze the performance of their designs using simulation. It provides an introduction to discrete-event simulation, including model building and output data analysis, and presents a discrete-event simulation "language" called **smpl**.[1] Simulation modeling with **smpl** is discussed, using a variety of models as examples. The design of **smpl** and a C language implementation are described, and various modifications are considered.

smpl is a functional extension of a general-purpose programming language called the *host* language. This extension takes the form of a set of library functions (the **smpl** simulation subsystem) which, together with the host language itself, compose an event-oriented simulation language. A **smpl** simulation model is implemented as a host language program: simulation operations are performed via calls on the functions of the simulation subsystem. This approach to discrete-event simulation is a venerable one. It provides a simulation capability suitable for small-to-medium scale models (process-oriented simulation languages are preferable for large-scale models) which can be implemented in most languages on most machines.

The **smpl** simulation subsystem is part of a simulation environment called **SMPL**. **SMPL** provides additional tools, including debugging, data collection and plotting, and simulation output analysis functions, together with an interactive interface to simulation model execution called **mtr**. With the aid of **mtr**, the user can, at execution time, display and modify

---

[1]Throughout this book, subsystem and module names appear in bold (e.g., **smpl**, **mtr**), file names appear in italics (*smpl.c*, *math.h*), and identifiers such as function and variable names appear in fixed-space type (`smpl()`, `busy`); function names are distinguished by appended parentheses.

simulation parameters, set breakpoints and control tracing, display any simulation report or plot, initiate and monitor simulation output analysis, and initiate various graphics displays. An overview of the design of **SMPL** is given, and design details of some of its facilities are presented.

2. Implementation

Versions of **smpl** have been implemented in languages including Basic, C, Fortran, Pascal, and PL/I on machines ranging from a microprocessor with 32K bytes of memory through an Amdahl 580 mainframe up to CRAY super-computers. The **C** implementation described in this book runs on both microcomputers and mainframes: only the basic random number generator differs between systems. You should be able to take the **smpl** source code in the appendix, enter it in your system, and get it working with few changes.[2]

A version of the **SMPL** system, **SMPL/PC**, has been implemented for the IBM Personal Computer and compatible personal computers (PCs). The reader interested in simulation on a personal computer should be aware that the basic PC is of limited use: it is just too slow. To obtain meaningful results, each simulation run (i.e., each instance of model execution) may require simulation of anywhere from several thousand to hundreds of thousands of events. A simulation study may involve dozens of runs; on the basic PC, the execution time required can be measured in days. The availability of a floating point arithmetic coprocessor such as the Intel 8087 Numeric Data Processor significantly changes the situation. As an illustration, consider the execution time of the following statement:

```
z = -x*log(ranf());
```

which is used to generate a random variate z from a negative exponential distribution with mean x. On a basic PC (a PC without an 8087), 20,000 executions of this statement required approximately 700 seconds; plugging in an 8087 reduced this time to 20 seconds. (These times reflect a specific implementation of the log and random number generator functions in addition to the code generation characteristics of the compiler used.) For any particular program, the performance improvement provided by the 8087 will dependent on the relative frequency and type of floating point instructions in the program. However, the 8087 does transform the PC into a viable tool for

---

[2]Source code for the programs in this book, including **smpl**, is available on diskette. For information, write the author at P. O. Box 2089, Sunnyvale, CA 94087-2089.

a variety of small- to medium-scale simulations; this viability is enhanced by later model PCs with faster CPUs.

3. Organization of the Book

This book is divided into two parts. The first part, Chapters 1-6, provides an introduction to discrete-event simulation using **smpl**. The second part, Chapters 7-9, gives an overview of the **SMPL** simulation environment, describes the implementation of **smpl,** and presents various extensions. A source code listing of **smpl** is given in the appendix.

Chapter 1 begins with a brief discussion of simulations and systems. Representation of work in a simulation model and methods for generation of simulation input parameters are reviewed. A simple queueing system simulation model is developed, and performance measures and operational laws are introduced in considering instrumentation for this model. In Chapter 2, **smpl** simulation operations are introduced, and a **smpl** model of a queueing network is presented and discussed. The development, debugging, verification, and validation of simulation models are discussed in Chapter 3, together with hybrid modeling and the use of analytic models in verification. Chapter 4 describes methods of simulation output analysis with emphasis on replication and batch means methods. This is followed by a brief review of other aspects of problem analysis, such as the comparison of alternative designs. In Chapters 5 and 6, two simulation models are studied in detail: a multiprocessor system model and an Ethernet model. These examples emphasize the joint use of simulation and analytic models, and further illustrate the use of **smpl**.

Each of the chapters in the first part of this book concludes with problems. In several cases, solutions to problems in one chapter are needed in attacking problems in later chapters. The problems of Chapters 5 and 6 take the form of modeling projects; developing, debugging, and validating the models for these projects involves a fair amount of work. As in real-world design environments, no answers are provided.

The second part of this book is concerned with tools. Chapter 7 gives an overview of the simulation run-time interface and reporting and debugging tools of the **SMPL** simulation environment. Chapter 8 provides a detailed description of the implementation of **smpl**: data structures are described, and the various simulation functions are discussed with reference to the **smpl** source listing. This description, coupled with the source listing itself, should be sufficient to implement **smpl** on any system. Chapter 9 discusses various extensions and modifications to **smpl**, and sketches the design of **mtr**, the interactive interface module of **SMPL**.

4. Performance Analysis Tools and Texts

Computer performance analysis draws its tools from a number of fields, including probability, statistics, and queueing theory. Simulation modeling requires some knowledge of each of these subject areas, and this book assumes that the modeler is supported by appropriate references in these areas. There are a number of texts available covering these subjects in various combinations. Some of these are briefly discussed below (omissions are due to ignorance, not lack of recommendation).[3] The modeler's library will need several of these: selections are inter-dependent because of differences in coverage and emphasis, so carefully review the contents of each potential acquisition. Subjects important to the beginning modeler are basic probability, basic statistics, statistical aspects of simulation, analysis of single queues, and analysis of queueing networks, together with the application of these subjects in performance evaluation of computer and communication systems.

Two books on probability, statistics, and queueing theory with a computer orientation are *Probability, Statistics, and Queueing Theory,* [Allen 1978], and *Probability & Statistics with Reliability, Queueing, and Computer Science Applications* [Trivedi 1982]. Both provide analysis of individual queues and some discussion of queueing networks, and either would be an adequate reference to basic probability and statistics, and analysis of individual queues. (There are numerous non-computer-oriented texts on these subjects. Some of these, particularly those with an engineering bent, are very good). Allen provides a very useful appendix of formulas for a number of queueing systems (but makes up for it with a collection of APL programs for queueing system analysis). Trivedi provides a more extensive introduction to queueing networks, a useful chapter on regression analysis, and lots of good examples. *Modeling and Analysis: An Introduction to System Performance Evaluation Methodology* [Kobayashi 1978] includes, among other topics, brief introductions to probability, statistics (including regression), analysis of individual queues, and queueing network analysis. Kobayashi covers a lot of ground; one would like to see this book updated and doubled in size. A comprehensive treatment of the analysis of individual queues is *Queueing Systems. Vol. I: Theory, Vol. II: Computer Applications* [Kleinrock 1975].

In the last few years, there have been many advances in the analysis and application of networks of queues. Developments in mean value analysis (MVA) and in decomposition and approximation methods have substan-

---

[3]Full citations are given in the References at the end of this book.

tially enhanced the utility and applicability of queueing network analysis. Recency of publication is important in selecting a text in this area. *Quantitative System Performance* [Lazowska et al 1984] provides a readable, practical discussion of MVA-based queueing network analysis with algorithms and applications, together with an introduction to operational laws and the analysis of performance bounds. It is strongly recommended for several reasons, including its operational approach to network analysis. *Metamodeling* [Agrawal 1985] summarizes approximation methods for queueing network analysis and provides a view of the state of the art in this area. Other sources include the *Computer Performance Modeling Handbook* [Lavenberg 1983] and *Computer Systems Performance Modeling* [Sauer and Chandy 1981].

For a number of years, the standard text on simulation — at least on the statistical aspects — was *Principles of Discrete Event Simulation* [Fishman 1978]; it continues to be a valuable reference. In recent years, several new books on the subject have appeared, including *Simulation Modeling and Analysis* [Law and Kelton 1982], *A Guide to Simulation* [Bratley et al 1983], and *Discrete-Event System Simulation* [Banks and Carson 1984]. Each provides good subject coverage with particular strengths. Law and Kelton is very readable and has good chapters on selecting input distributions, and on output data analysis. Bratley et al provide Fortran listings of random variate generators, and Banks and Carson provide summary descriptions of various queueing systems. All four are within easy reach of the author's chair and are frequently referenced. Kleijnen [1975] provides a comprehensive discussion of the statistical aspects of simulation. While dated in a few areas, this is a useful text; unfortunately, it is vastly over-priced.

There are a number of books on computer performance evaluation, several of which have already been mentioned. Kobayashi [1978] covers a wide range of subjects, including probability, statistics, queueing, and simulation. *Computer Systems Performance Evaluation* [Ferrari 1978] emphasizes performance measurement methods and workload characterization in addition to simulation and analysis; its view is oriented toward the practioner, rather than the theorist. *Measurement and Tuning of Computer Systems* [Ferrari et al 1983] is the best available reference on computer system workload characterization, also is good in the area of measurements, and provides a nice introduction to queueing network analysis. Lavenberg [1983] covers probability theory, individual queues, exact and approximate methods of queueing network analysis, and simulation. This book combines contributions from several authors; it is not very well unified but has several strong chapters, including a good presentation on statistical analysis of simulation results by Welch. Sauer and Chandy [1981] focus on queueing network models, and provide a comprehensive description of the implementation of a queueing network simulator. *A Computer & Communications Network Performance Analysis Primer* [Stuck and Arthurs 1985] discusses estimation of performance and performance bounds for a variety of systems (and could be improved by better indexing).

The major source of information on performance analysis methods and applications is technical journals and conferences, particularly those of the ACM (Association for Computing Machinery) and the IEEE (Institute of Electrical and Electronic Engineers) Computer Society and Communications Society. The Winter Simulation Conference, jointly sponsored by the ACM, IEEE, and several other professional societies, covers a wide range of simulation methods and applications. Proceedings for this and a number of other conferences are available through ACM and IEEE book services. *Operations Research*, the journal of ORSA (Operations Research Society of America), frequently publishes papers on statistical aspects of simulation.

Acknowledgements

The author gratefully acknowledges the support of Bill Harding, who provided the initial impetus for this book, the help of Makoto Kobayashi and Bill McCormack, whose careful reading of the manuscript caught many errors and helped improve the presentation, and the many contributions of Yung-Li Lily Jow to the models and methods discussed here.

M. MacDougall
Sunnyvale, California

Simulating Computer Systems

1. Introduction

1.1 Simulations and Systems

A variety of types, levels, and forms of simulation are used in computer and communication system design. We'll begin with a brief look at some of the terms used in describing simulations, systems, and simulation languages.

Simulations. The type of simulation which is our subject is called *discrete-event system-level simulation*. Discrete-event systems change state at discrete points in time, as opposed to continuous systems, which change state over time. (Although not our concern, a variety of fascinating continuous-time simulation models are used in computer system design to analyze such things as heat dissipation, ink drop formation for ink jet printers, and the acceleration profile for voice-coil-driven disk actuators.)

Computer systems are modeled at several levels of detail: circuit-level, gate-level, register-transfer-level, and system-level. Each level represents a higher level of abstraction. At the circuit-level, continuous-time simulation is used to analyze state switching behavior. The components — transistors, resistors, etc. — of a circuit are aggregated into a single element in gate-level simulation. At the register-transfer-level, sets of gates are aggregated into elements such as registers, multiplexors, and adders. System-level simulation begins at a level somewhere above the register transfer level. Gate-level, register-transfer-level, and system-level simulation all are forms of discrete-event simulation. Gate- and register-transfer-level models are developed to analyze the behavior of the system from a functional standpoint, and represent the complete system design at different levels of abstraction. System-level models are developed to analyze the system from a performance standpoint, and represent only those elements of the system pertinent to the performance issue of concern.

Determining which elements of the design are to be represented in the system-level model and the level of abstraction with which these elements are to be represented is a matter of judgement.

Simulation input data may be generated probabilistically within the simulation program, or it may be generated externally. In *trace-driven* simulation, simulation input is obtained from a trace of actual system execution. Various kinds of traces are useful in computer performance evaluation: instruction traces are used to drive pipeline models, address traces to drive cache models, and IO traces to drive disk subsystem models. System accounting data has been used to drive computer system scheduling models. Our discussion deals only with internally-generated simulation input data; for a discussion of trace-driven simulation and further references, see Kobayashi [1978] or Ferrari [1978].

A *hybrid simulation* model combines a discrete-event simulation model and an analytic (e.g. queueing) model so as to reduce computational time while preserving model accuracy. (The term also is used to describe a combination of digital computer and analog computer simulation.) This is an important concept: we'll return to it in Chapter 3.

Systems. In modeling a system, we need to describe its dynamic composition, the way it accomplishes work, not just its static structure. The dynamic composition of a system can be described in terms of activities, processes, and events [MacDougall 1975].

Performance measures relate to the rate at which systems accomplish work, and so have time as an independent variable. Work is accomplished through the execution of activities. An *activity* is the smallest unit of work in our view of a system. Since it is a unit of work, every activity has an associated execution time. A logically-related set of activities constitutes a *process*. The execution time of a process is (ignoring concurrency) the sum of the execution and delay times of its activities. A process may, in turn, be viewed as an activity of a higher- level process. For example, execution of a program may be viewed as a process comprising compute and input/output activities; execution of an input/output activity may be viewed as a process comprising seek, latency, and data transfer activities. The distinction depends on our level of view.

Systems are composed of both active and passive entities; we can view the work-performing facilities of a system as simple passive objects which assume one of two states — busy or idle — as the result of actions of activities. Such objects also are decomposable. At one level of view, a CPU may be represented as single passive entity made busy or idle by compute activities. At a more detailed view, compute activities can be decomposed into instruction execution processes comprising instruction fetch, operand fetch, execute, and result store activities. Correspondingly, the CPU is decomposed into instruction fetch, cache, pipeline, execution, and mainstore units. Also, a passive entity at one level of view may decompose into a combination of active and passive entities at another level of view.

The initiation of activities is triggered by events. An *event* is a change of state of some system entity, active or passive; this change of state results from the action of an activity. The termination of an activity is an event. The initiation of an activity is distinguished from the start of its execution; for example, termination of a task's compute activity may initiate its input/output activity, but execution of the latter cannot begin until the disk is free. An activity whose execution is delayed because the requisite conditions do not exist can be viewed as waiting for the event(s) which will give rise to those conditions. Activity termination events are local to the process to which the activity belongs; events representing a state change in a passive system entity may have a wider scope.

These entities — activities, processes, and events — are the constructs used to describe the dynamic behavior of discrete systems and on which simulation languages for these systems are based. A system is viewed dynamically as a collection of interacting processes, with the interactions controlled and coordinated by the occurrence of events. This process view is a hierarchical one; a system is described at a given level of abstraction by a set of process descriptions, each specifying the activities of that process. This description can be expanded into a lower level of abstraction by decomposing activities into processes; description of these processes, together with those of the previous level, form the expanded description of the system. This hierarchical view can substantially ease the task of model construction for complex systems.

A hierarchical approach (sometimes different in nature) is important in other kinds of modeling. Lazowska et al [1984] describe how complex queueing network models are solved by decomposing the network into a set of submodels, evaluating each submodel separately, and combining these individual solutions in a higher-level models to obtain a solution for the whole system. MacDougall [1984] applies decomposition at the instruction level to the evaluation of pipelined processors.

Simulation languages. Simulation languages are classified as *activity-oriented*, *event-oriented*, or *process-oriented*, based on the procedural organization of simulation programs written in that language. A procedural section of a simulation program may describe an activity, an event, or a process, depending on the language used. Correspondingly, a model of a system is viewed as a set of activity descriptions, event descriptions, or process descriptions; each language tends to impose a particular view of the system on the modeler.

Almost all present-day simulation languages are event- or process-oriented. Process-oriented languages such as ASPOL [MacDougall 1975], CSIM [Schwetman 1986], or SIMULA [Birtwhistle et al 1973] are strongly recommended for implementing large-scale simulation models. Simulation programs written in these languages can be constructed as straightforward descriptions of actual system operation. This similitude of model and system makes it much easier to insure that the model is a valid representation of the system, particularly in a development environment where the system design is undergoing constant change. The hierarchical nature of process-oriented languages also is important in the development environment.

Event-oriented simulation languages such as **smpl** are best suited to small- and medium-scale models. They tend to impose a single-level, global view of the system on the modeler. There is a tendency to collect actions of logically unrelated activities in a single event routine; as a consequence, the model can lose all identity with the structure of the system and become difficult to modify. This problem can be minimized by careful structuring of the model — taking a process-oriented view of the system and organizing the model accordingly.

1.2 Representing Work

Developing a model involves two tasks: developing a representation of the system, and developing a representation of the work done by the system. These are inter-related: the level of abstraction at which work is represented must correspond to that at which the system is represented. Before building a very detailed model of a system, we should ask two questions. Do we really need to work at this level of detail to solve the problem? Do we have data to represent work at this level?

The task of describing the work performed by a system is called *workload characterization*; it is a key step in several areas of performance evaluation, including simulation modeling, analytic modeling, and benchmarking. Ferrari [1978] discusses system-level, source-program-level, and instruction-level workload characterization, and is the best of our referenced texts in this subject area. In this section we will look at some considerations in representing work in a simulation model.

Variability. Most of the problems we want to analyze center around contention for system resources; this contention causes work to be queued for or blocked from execution, and system performance may suffer as a result.

Contention arises because of variability in some aspect of system behavior: in the way work arrives at the system, in its execution time, or both. Suppose tasks arrive at a system at an average interval of 10 units, and each task requires an average service time of 6 time units. If there is no variability in inter-arrival or service times, so that they are the same for all tasks, no queueing delays occur, since every arriving task will find the system idle. If there is variability in either or both of these times, then delays may occur; their magnitude depends on the amount of variability and on the extent to which these times may be correlated. In describing the work of a system, then, we need to consider the distributions of the associated variables, not just their mean values. We also need to examine behavior patterns to determine if and how these variables are correlated.

Choosing a distribution. Determining what distribution to use to represent a model variable is one of the most difficult aspects of simulation modeling. When the system being modeled exists, we may be able to measure it, obtain actual distributions, and use these in our model. There are two ways to do this; we can tabulate values of the distribution and do a table look-up to obtain a sample value, or we can fit a theoretical distribution to the actual distribution and use an algorithm to generate a sample value. Common probability distributions, their parameters, and the estimation of parameters from data are discussed in Banks and Carson [1984], Bratley et al [1983], and Law and Kelton [1982]. The discussion in Law and Kelton is the most comprehensive of the three. This subject also is covered in most applications-oriented statistics texts.

At one time, fitting a distribution to data often involved transforming the data into various forms and plotting it on probability paper appropriate to the distribution of interest. Computer programs now are available which substantially reduce the time and effort required. An example is UNIFIT [Law and Vincent 1983], which permits a variety of data transformations, fits up to nine different distributions simultaneously using any of several different goodness-of-fit tests, and provides a number of graphics displays of the results.

If we're modeling a new design and there is no system to be measured: what then? One possibility is to adapt a distribution measured on some existing system -- assume the shape of the distribution will be similar on the new system and adjust the values to reflect system differences. Suppose we are modeling a new computer system and need to specify the distribution of CPU execution intervals; if measurements of this distribution on the current system are available, we can rationalize that the number of instructions executed per interval will be about the same on both systems, and adjust the interval by the ratio of instruction execution rates for the two systems. This may be our best course, but it shouldn't be followed blindly: we need to examine carefully our assumption that the distributional characteristics of the work won't change when the system changes.

We frequently will find ourselves in a situation where we have very little data and no idea what the actual distribution of the data looks like. In order to proceed, we'll have to do some guessing (and, when the model is complete, do some experimentation to determine how sensitive the results are to our guesswork). Suppose the variable of interest is the processing time at some facility. We first try to specify an interval bounded by the best-case and worst-case times a and b. Next, we try to visualize how times may be skewed in this interval. One way to do this is to quarter the interval and guess what proportion of times are likely to fall in each quarter, or quartile. We can then fit a distribution with approximately the same quartile proportions. (Our understanding of the nature of the process may suggest a different division.) If we have no reason to believe that times are more likely to fall in one quartile than another, the best we can do is assume that processing times are uniformly distributed in $[a,b]$. If we can estimate the mode, as well as upper and lower bounds, we can use a triangular distribution (see Law and Kelton [1982], p205, or Banks and Carson [1984], p157).

The exponential distribution. The most important distribution in the analysis of queueing systems is the negative exponential or, simply, the exponential distribution. When we talk about random arrivals or random service, we mean that the inter-arrival times or the service times are exponentially distributed. Equivalently, because of the relationship between the Poisson and exponential distributions, we might talk about Poisson arrivals or service (if the number of events occurring in an interval is Poisson-distributed, the time between events is exponentially distributed).

A important property of the Poisson process is that it is *memoryless*; the probability of an arrival in interval t depends only on the duration of t, and not on when the previous arrival occurred. Equivalently, for Poisson service, the probability that service completes in an interval s is independent of when service started. This memoryless property is the key to obtaining analytic solutions for many queueing problems; consequently, there exists considerable rationalization for the exponential assumption ("*there is no virtue like necessity*").

Another useful property of the Poisson process is that the superposition of Poisson processes is itself a Poisson process. Suppose we are modeling a transaction processing system with a number of terminals: if transactions are generated at each terminal according to a Poisson process, then the composite transaction stream seen by the system also is a Poisson process (see [Kobayashi 1978]). In fact, the individual transaction sources don't necessarily have to be Poisson: if the sources are independent and no one source dominates (and certain other conditions hold), the superposition of the individual transaction streams approaches a Poisson process as the number of sources increases. Inter-arrival times, then, frequently are assumed to be exponentially distributed; we'll probably make the same assumption whenever we can't discern any pattern to the arrival process.

Other important distributions include the Erlang and hyperexponential distributions, both of which are related to the exponential distribution. A k-Erlang distribution can be represented as the sum of k identical exponentially-distributed random variables. A k-stage hyperexponential distribution is a mixture of k different exponential distributions. These are discussed in the referenced simulation and performance evaluation texts.

Sampling from distributions. A particular value of a model variable is determined by generating a random sample from the distribution specified for that variable. A particular sample value usually is called a random variate.[1] There are numerous techniques for generating these samples, all of which employ a uniform random number generator. A uniform random number generator is a numerical algorithm which produces a deterministic sequence of values distributed between 0 and 1. There are a number of desirable characteristics for this sequence: uniformity, independence, long period (length of the sequence before it begins to repeats), etc. The design and testing of random number generators is discussed at length in the referenced texts on simulation; also, see Knuth [1981]. A word of caution: don't use the random number generator in your system's math function library until you've verified that it is a reasonable algorithm.

The generation of random variates from a variety of distributions also is discussed in our simulation texts. For a variety of common distributions, Fortran implementations can be found in Bratley et al [1983], and outlines of sampling algorithms in Fishman [1978]. Hastings and Peacock [1974] give brief descriptions of generators for a number of distributions. We'll consider two examples of variate generators here: one using a empirical distribution, and one using a theoretical distribution.

Suppose modeling task execution in a microcomputer system simulation requires generating sample values of the lengths of the files associated with each task. We'll assume that measurements of system operation have produced the file length distribution shown in Figure 1.1. This is a discrete distribution: the possible values of the variate are 1, 2, . . . , 10. To generate a random file length, we first convert the distribution to cumulative form,

---

[1] The term "psuedo-random" sometimes is used to emphasize that the underlying process actually is deterministic..

length in tracks	proportion of files
1	.060
2	.170
3	.238
4	.223
5	.156
6	.087
7	.040
8	.016
9	.007
10	.003

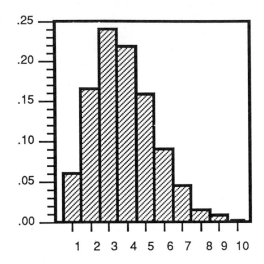

Figure 1.1. Distribution of File Lengths

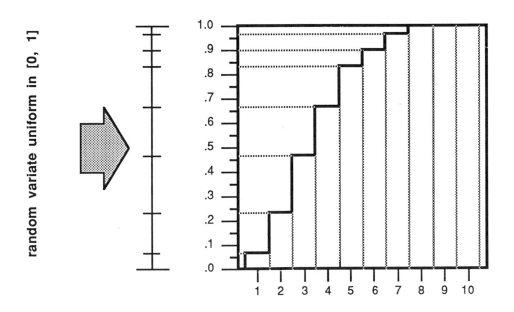

Figure 1.2. Sampling the File Length Distribution

obtaining the proportions P[$l{\le}L$] of files whose lengths are equal to or less than L. Next, we generate a random number r and find the value of L for which P[$l{\le}L$-1] $< r \le$ P[$l{\le}L$]: that value is our sample value.

This process is illustrated in Figure 1.2. The cumulative distribution of file lengths is plotted on the right; the vertical bar to the left of the plot shows the values of the cumulative proportions. Imagine a set of random numbers are generated; the values of these numbers would fall uniformly across the bar; a value falling between the marks corresponding to P[$l{\le}L$-1] and P[$l{\le}L$] generates a sample value of L. If we generate a large enough set of numbers, the proportion of these falling in this interval will approach a value P[$l{\le}L$] - P[$l{\le}L$-1]; this value is the proportion of files of length L.

A C function `flength()` to generate a random file length might be written as follows.

```
flength()
  {
    static double p[10]=
      {.06,.23,.468,.691,.847,.934,.974,.99,.997,1.0};
    int i=0; double r,ranf();
    r=ranf(); while (r>p[i]) i++;
    return(i+1);
  }
```

where `ranf()` is the uniform random number generator function.

There are several points about this process worth noting. First, in this example, we can directly compute the sample value from the index to array `p[]` (by adding 1). Sometimes we can do this, and sometimes we'll have to define an array of sample values and use the index to obtain a value from the array. Second, suppose at some place in our model we need to randomly select 1 of n alternatives, and each alternative has a different probability associated with it. The random selection function would look very much like the function above, except it would return alternative numbers rather than file lengths (but if alternatives are equiprobable, we'd probably just use an expression such as "1+n*ranf()" to pick one).

A similar approach can be used to generate sample values from continuous distributions. For example, suppose measurements of disk seek times give the proportions p(t_{i-1},t_i) of seek times falling in intervals t_{i-1}, t_i. To implement our sampling function, we define two arrays, one containing the interval endpoints t_0, t_1, t_2, ... , the other containing the cumulative proportions 0, P[$t{\le}t_1$], P[$t{\le}t_2$], ... To generate a sample value, we generate a random number r and use it to find the entry in the array for which $P[t{\le}t_{i-1}] < r \le P[t{\le}t_i]$. The sample seek time is determined by interpolation between the corresponding entries in the seek time interval endpoint array. The sample-generating statements might look like this:

```
r=ranf(); while (r>p[i]) i++;
t=t[i-1]+(t[i]-t[i-1])*(r-p[i-1])/(p[i]-p[i-1]);
```

There are several things we can do (in addition to coding changes) to make sample generation more efficient. If there are more than a few entries. we can use a binary, rather than a linear, search of p[]. The intervals used to divide the distribution don't have to be the same width; we can use short intervals where the distribution changes shape rapidly and long intervals where the rate of change is slow to optimize the number of entries.

In both examples, we tabulated the cumulative distribution function $p = F(x)$, generated a random value of p, and used the tabulation to obtain the corresponding value of x; in effect, we generated values of the inverse function $x = F^{-1}(p)$. In some cases, it is possible to determine directly the inverse of the distribution function of a theoretical distribution. For example, suppose inter-arrival times are exponentially distributed with mean T; the probability that an arrival time x is equal to or less than t is given by

$$\Pr[x{\le}t] = 1 - e^{-t/T} \tag{1.1}$$

Let r represent $\Pr[x{\le}t]$; to sample this distribution, we want to generate a random value of r and use it to determine the corresponding value of t. By taking the natural logarithm of both sides of (1.1), with some transpositions before and after, we can obtain the inverse distribution function

$$t = -T \ln(1 - r) \tag{1.2}$$

where $\ln(x)$ denotes the natural logarithm of x. Since r is a random variate uniformly distributed in [0,1], $1 - r$ is identically distributed; therefore, we can rewrite (1.2) as

$$t = -T \ln r \tag{1.3}$$

We can use (1.3) to write a **C** function to generate sample values from the exponential distribution. The following function is one of the **smpl** random variate generation functions.

```
double expntl(t)
  double t;
    {
      double ranf();
      return(-t*log(ranf()));
    }
```

Unfortunately, direct inversion of the distribution function is possible only for a few distributions; other techniques for generating variates frequently are needed. For most of our simulation work, we'll manage with the **smpl** sampling functions supplemented by those presented in our simulation texts. Nevertheless, familiarity with random variate generation techniques is useful; among other things, it provides ideas for incorporating analytic results in our simulation models. Of course, if pressed, we can tabulate values of the distribution function for any discrete or continuous distribution, and generate samples as we did in our earlier examples.

There are a few things to keep in mind when sampling theoretical distributions. First, do the values returned by your random number generator include 0? If so, you will have to be sure that your sampling functions don't attempt to take the logarithm of a zero value. Theoretical distributions may have tails extending to infinity on one or both sides, and samples may need to be clipped. Most variables in computer system simulations don't have negative values: when sampling from the normal distribution, inspect samples and discard negative values. Generators for distributions such as the exponential distribution can return very large values; you may want to truncate the sample distribution to reflect the maximum value realizable in the actual system. The mean value of samples from (for example) a truncated exponential distribution may differ from the exponential distribution's mean unless the latter is adjusted. Section 6.8 discusses computation of an adjusted mean for a truncated exponential distribution.

Correlation. There are two kinds of correlation that may need be represented in a model. One is *autocorrelation*, where successive values from a distribution are not independent but reflect some underlying relationship. This is a difficult subject in terms of both workload characterization and model representation. Fishman [1978] describes two ways of generating autocorrelated sequences.

The second kind of correlation is that between *jointly-distributed* variables: variables from different distributions representing different aspects of work. For example we would expect compiler execution times and compiler input file lengths to be correlated, in which case a functional relationship could be obtained via regression analysis of measurement data. To generate attributes of a particular compilation in a simulation model, we could generate a sample input file length and use its value to compute a sample compilation time. Modeling such relationships mostly involves common-sense tradeoffs between model accuracy and complexity. Developers of synthetic workloads face similar problems and have developed sampling approaches: see, for example, Hughes [1984], and Sreenivasan and Kleinman [1974].

1.3 A Simple Queueing Simulation

This section presents a simulation model of a simple queueing system written in C without the use of **smpl**. We'll review some of the performance measures of interest in queueing system analysis and discuss basic simulation operations. First, let's look at how queueing systems are described.

Queueing notation. A standard notation (called Kendall notation after its originator) is used to describe queueing systems with a single queue and one or more parallel servers. This notation is commonly used in the literature, so it's useful to be familiar with it. Using this notation, a queueing system is described by a descriptor of the form $A/S/c/k/m$, where A represents the inter-arrival time distribution, S represents the service time distribution, c is the number of servers, k is the maximum number of customers allowed in the system, and m is the number of customers available at the source.[2] Among the symbols commonly used to describe distributions are

D	constant inter-arrival or service time
M	exponential distribution
Ek	k-Erlang distribution
Hk	k-stage hyperexponential distribution
G	general (arbitrary) distribution

When the customer population is assumed to be infinite, m usually is omitted; similarly, when the system capacity is assumed to be infinite, k is omitted. The queueing discipline may be appended to the descriptor; if not, it can be assumed to be first-in, first-out. Using this notation, a queueing system with exponential inter-arrival times, constant service times, and a single server is described as an **M/D/1** queue; a system with exponential

---

[2]Use of the term "customer" to describe a system's work-bearing entities and "server" to describe its work-performing entities is traditional. Also, "queueing system" frequently is shortened to "queue".

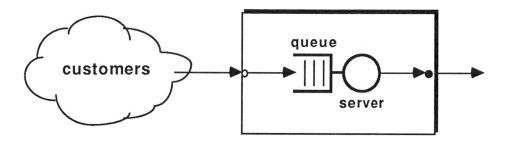

Figure 1.3. A Single Server Queueing System

inter-arrival times, general service times, 2 servers, and a queue capacity of k customers is described as an **M/G/2/k** queue.

The queueing system model. The system to be simulated is the single server queueing system shown in Figure 1.3. Work for the system comes from an infinite population of customers; the inter-arrival times of customers at the system are exponentially distributed with mean *Ta*. On arrival, a customer begins service if the server is free or joins the queue if the server is busy. The queue capacity is unlimited, and the queueing discipline is first-in, first-out; whenever one customer completes service, the next customer to begin service is the one at the head of the queue. Service times are exponentially distributed with mean *Ts*. (This, then, is an **M/M/1** queue.)

The C program of Figure 1.4 is a simulation model of this system, and is about as simple as we can get. It uses the `expntl()` function discussed in the last section to generate inter-arrival and service times. The mean inter-arrival time `Ta` is 200 time units, the mean service time `Ts` is 100 time units, and the period of time to be simulated, `te`, is 200000 time units (so we would expect to simulate approximately 1000 arrivals). `time` represents simulated time, and `n` is the number of customer in the system at any point in time. There are two events: event 1 represents arrivals and event 2 represents service completions. Associated with events 1 and 2 are the event occurrence times `t1` and `t2`; these are the times at which the next instance of the event will occur.

The model advances through time in variable intervals, rather than constant "ticks". At any instant, `t1` is the time of the next arrival and `t2` is the time of the next completion; to determine which event occurs next, these times are compared. If `t1<t2`, then the next event is an arrival. `time` is advanced to the arrival time, the count of the number of customers in the system is incremented, and the time at which the next arrival is to occur is

```
main()
  {
    double Ta=200.0,Ts=100.0,te=200000.0,t1,t2,time;
    double expntl();
    int n;
    n=0; t1=0.0; t2=te; time=0.0;
    while (time<te)
      {
        if (t1<t2)
          { /* event 1:  arrival */
            time=t1; n++; t1=time+expntl(Ta);
            if (n==1) t2=time+expntl(Ts);
          }
        else
          { /* event 2:  completion */
            time=t2; n--;
            if (n>0) t2=time+expntl(Ts); else t2=te;
          }
      }
  }
```

Figure 1.4. Queueing System Simulation Model

computed. If the system was empty when this customer arrived, the time at
which its service will complete is computed.

If t1>t2, then the next event is a service completion: time is advanced
to the completion time and the number of customers in the system is
decremented. If there are still customers in the system after this completion,
then the time of the next service completion is computed. (This implicitly
represents dequeueing of the customer at the head of the queue and the start
of its service.) If the current completion empties the system, t2 is set to te to
insure that the next event to occur will be an arrival; note that this also was
done during initialization to insure that the first event would be an arrival.

Figure 1.5 graphically illustrates the behavior of the simulated system.
Suppose we observe the system for a period of 600 time units, during which
customers arrive at intervals (i.e., inter-arrival times) of 20, 30, 25, 65, 80,
and 80 time units. The service times of these customers are, respectively, 80,
150, 90, 60, 80, and 90 time units. Figure 1.5(a) shows the sequence of arrivals,
waiting times, and service times in the period; Figure 1.5(b) shows the
corresponding changes in the number of customers in the system. If we

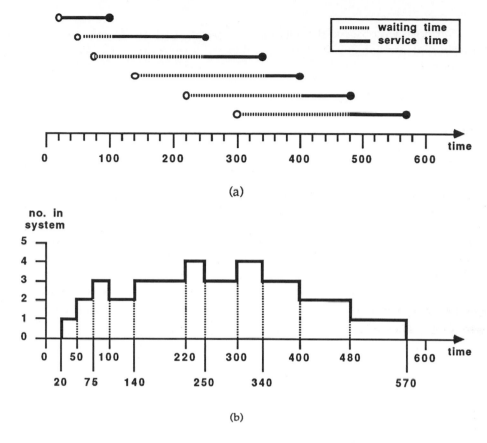

(a)

(b)

Figure 1.5. Queueing System Behavior

manually step through the simulation program using the above inter-arrival and service times, we can see how the model generates this behavior.

1.4 Performance Measures

While the program of Figure 1.4 may successfully model the behavior of an M/M/1 queueing system, it isn't of much use until we add instrumentation to collect the performance measures of interest to us. We can collect just about anything; mostly we'll be interested in mean values, but on occasion we may want distributions as well. We'll begin this section with a look at certain fundamental mean value performance measures and their relationships. Because these relationships apply widely and hold under very general conditions, some have come to be called *laws*.

Suppose we observe the system for a period of time T and measure the number of arrivals, A, and the number of completions, C. We then can compute the

$$\text{arrival rate: } \lambda = A/T \qquad\qquad (1.4)$$

and the

$$\text{throughput rate: } X = C/T. \qquad\qquad (1.5)$$

In measuring a real or simulated system, there may be customers in the system queued for or receiving service both at the start and at the end of the observation period. However, if the period is sufficiently long, the number of arrivals observed should be approximately equal to the number of completions $(C \approx A)$, in which case we can assume $\lambda = X$. This assumption is called the *flow balance* assumption: the flow of work out of the system is balanced by the flow of work into it. When we make this assumption, we only need to count arrivals or completions, whichever is easier, not both.

Suppose we also measure the mean server busy time, B. Now we can compute the

$$\text{server utilization: } U = B/T, \qquad\qquad (1.6)$$

and the

$$\text{mean service time per customer: } T_s = B/C. \qquad\qquad (1.7)$$

Utilization Law. Through simple algebra, we can combine (1.5), (1.6) and (1.7) to obtain the *Utilization Law*:

$$U = XT_s \qquad\qquad (1.8)$$

or, assuming flow balance,

$$U = \lambda T_s \qquad\qquad (1.9)$$

In words, the utilization of a server is the product of its throughput rate and the average service time per customer.

Little's Law. Let L be the average number of customers in the system during the observation period, and let W be the average time these customers spend in the system. Define w_i as the time spent in the system by the ith customer: then $W = \Sigma wi / C$. Look back at Figure 1.5(b) for a moment; this is a graph of the number of customers in the system versus time. The average number of customers in the system is the average height of the graph; this is equal to the area under the graph divided by the length of the observation period. Each customer, while in the system, contributes one unit of height to the graph, and so contributes $1 \times wi$ to the area under the graph. The total area is the sum Σwi of the contributions of the C customers completing service during the observation period, which is equal to WC. The average number in the system is this area divided by the observation time: $L = WC/T$. Since, from (1.5), $C/T = X$, we can write

$$L = XW \tag{1.10}$$

or, assuming flow balance,

$$L = \lambda W \tag{1.11}$$

In words, the average number of customers in the system is the product of the system's throughput rate and the average time a customer spends in the system.[3]

The preceding paragraph gave an informal derivation of *Little's Law*, named for J. D. C. Little, who presented the first formal proof [Little 1961]. This law is one of the most important results in queueing theory (the mnemonic of "law" for $L = \lambda W$ makes it easy to remember). It doesn't depend on the form of the inter-arrival or service time distributions or on the queue discipline. Little's Law can be applied at various levels of a system and in various ways at a given level. For example, let L_q be the average number of customers queued in the system (not receiving service), and let W_q be the mean queueing time. We can use the same approach as before to show that

$$L_q = \lambda W_q . \tag{1.12}$$

Note that $L = L_q + U$ and $W = W_q + T_s$. We can consider the Utilization Law to be another application of Little's Law by viewing U as the average

---

[3]In queueing theory literature, the time a customer spends in the system — including service time — usually is called "waiting time". (This isn't intuitive to the designer, who separates working time and waiting time.) Similarly, the term "queue length" is used to describe the number of customers in the system, including those in service. (Always read the definition of terms carefully.) We'll call the time a customer spends in the system its <u>system residence time</u> or its <u>response time,</u> and the time it spends in the queue (not receiving service) its <u>queueing time.</u>

number of customers receiving service. When a system provides service for customers of different classes (e.g., priorities), Little's Law can be applied to classes individually as well as collectively.

Response Time Law. This law commonly is stated in the context of a timesharing system. Let N be the number of terminals in the system, let Z and R be, respectively the mean think time and mean response time at a terminal, and let X be the system throughput. Then,

$$R = (N/X) - Z. \tag{1.13}$$

An example of the use of this law in a different context is given in Section 5.3.

Let's apply some of these relationships to the queueing system whose behavior is represented in Figure 1.5. There are $C = 6$ completions in the observation period of $T = 600$ time units. (Arrival, service start, and service completion times can be obtained by reference to the event times along the time axis of Figure 1.5(b)).

throughput: $X = 6/600 = 0.01$

total busy time: $B = (100\text{-}20)+(250\text{-}100)+ \ldots +(570\text{-}480) = 550$

mean service time: $T_s = 550/6 = 91.7$

utilization: $U = 550/600 = 0.917$, or $U = 0.01 \times 91.7 = 0.917$

residence time sum: $\Sigma w_i = (100\text{-}20)+(250\text{-}50)+ \ldots +(570\text{-}300) = 1335$

mean residence time: $W = 1335/6 = 222.5$

mean queueing time: $W_q = 222.5 - 91.7 = 130.8$

mean number in system: $L = 1335/600 = 2.225$

mean number in queue: $L_q = 2.225 - 0.917 = 1.308$

Little's Law, the Utilization Law, and other important relationships can be derived under relatively pragmatic assumptions by taking an operational view of system behavior. This view was pioneered by J. P. Buzen [Buzen 1976] and by P. J. Denning. Careful reading of their tutorial paper [Denning and Buzen 1978] and of the discussion by Lazowska et al [1984] is recommended strongly.

1.5 Instrumenting the Model

In a simulation model, the observation period T often corresponds to the simulation period, although it will be less when the first part of a simulation run is discarded to eliminate "warm-up" effects (discussed in Chapter 4). For each server in our model, we need to maintain a count C of the number of service completions and a sum B of the server busy times. When the simulation completes, the throughput, utilization, and mean service time of each server can be computed from T, C, and B.

There are two ways we can instrument the model to get the mean number in queue and service L, and the mean residence time W. One way is to accumulate the residence times of customers as they complete service; when the simulation completes, this sum is divided by C to obtain the mean residence time, and then Little's Law is used to compute L. This has one drawback; it requires that each customer be timestamped as it arrives at each server, and this can add unwanted complexity to the model (our **M/M/1** queue doesn't even distinguish customers from one another).

Another approach is to compute L directly. Once again, look back at Figure 1.5(b). The average number of customers in this system is the area under this graph divided by the observation period. Earlier, we computed this area by summing the residence times of each customer. However, this area also is the sum of the areas of a set of rectangles; the height of each rectangle is the number of customers in the system, and the base is the time interval between changes in this number. This suggests an algorithm for computing L. Define variables s and tn, and assume n represents the number of customers in the system. At the start of the observation period, set s to 0 and set tn to the current simulation time, time. Each time a customer arrives in the system, perform

```
s+=n*(time-tn); n++; tn=time;
```

and each time a customer completes service, perform

```
s+=n*(time-tn); n--; tn=time;
```

to compute and sum the areas of the individual rectangles. When the simulation completes, the average number in the system is computed by dividing s by the observation period length, and the average residence time then computed using Little's Law.

This approach is used in the instrumented version of the **M/M/1** queue simulation model shown in Figure 1.6. Most of the variables added in this version are named in accordance with the measures they represent: e.g., C is used to count service completions. Variables B and tb are used to accumulate total server busy time. A server busy period begins when an arriving customer finds the system empty and immediately begins service; the event 1 section

```
main()
  {
    double Ta=200.0,Ts=100.0,te=200000.0,t1,t2,time;
    double B,C,L,s,tb,tn,U,W,X,expntl();
    int n;
    n=0; t1=0.0; t2=te; time=0.0;
    B=s=0.0; C=0; tn=time;
    while (time<te)
      {
        if (t1<t2)
          { /* event 1:  arrival */
            time=t1; s+=n*(time-tn); n++; tn=time;
            t1=time+expntl(Ta);
            if (n==1) {tb=time; t2=time+expntl(Ts);}
          }
        else
          { /* event 2:  completion */
            time=t2; s+=n*(time-tn); n--; tn=time; C++;
            if (n>0) t2=time+expntl(Ts);
            else {t2=te; B+=time-tb;}
          }
      }
    X=C/time; printf("throughput = %f\n",X);
    U=B/time; printf("utilization = %f\n",U);
    L=s/time; printf("mean no. in system = %f\n",L);
    W=L/X;    printf("mean residence time = %f\n",W);
  }
```

Figure 1.6. Instrumented Queueing System Simulation Model

computes its service completion time and sets tb to the current simulation time. A server busy period ends when a customer completes service and there is no other customer in the system; the event 2 section computes the length of the busy period just ended and adds it to B.

1.6 Basic Simulation Operations

The model of Figure 1.6 can be extended in certain ways without difficulty. We can change inter-arrival and service time distributions, limit system capacity, and so on. However, if we try to extend this approach to systems with several servers, next event selection by direct comparison of event occurrence times quickly gets unwieldy; an *event list* scheduling mechanism provides a simpler and yet more general approach.[4]

The event list scheduling mechanism comprises a procedure for scheduling events, a procedure for selecting — "causing" — the next event, a variable representing the current value of simulated time, and the event list data structure itself. When an event, such as the arrival of the next customer, is to be scheduled, the *schedule* procedure is called to create and add an entry to the event list. This entry includes the event occurrence time, the identity of the event to occur, and often the identity of the associated customer. The event list is ordered in ascending values of event occurrences times; the new entry is linked into the list at a position determined by its event occurrence time. Whenever the simulation program completes all processing at a given instant in simulation time, it calls the *cause* procedure to determine which event is to occur next. *cause* removes the entry at the head of the event list, advances simulation time to the event occurrence time contained in the entry, and returns the identity of the event (and of the customer, if included). The simulation program then initiates execution of that event.

Since the event list mechanism is a general one, we implement it to be reusable and place it in a simulation function library — which probably got its start with our random variate generation functions.

The system being simulated frequently comprises a number of facilities, such as disks, channels, and processors. While these differ physically, their model representations have much in common. Each can be set busy or non-busy, each can have requests queued for it, and each requires similar performance measures. Consequently, we are led to develop a generic model of facilities, and provide functions for facility creation and manipulation; these also are added to the library. The need for report generation, debugging aids, and similar capabilities results in further additions, and we eventually end up with a simulation library, or subsystem, something like **smpl**. Although we may not have the power of some of the current simulation languages, we can do our modeling in a language of our choice, and we can tailor our simulation functions to suit our needs.

---

[4]Lists in general and event lists in particular came into common use in the early 1960s. Event selection by direct comparison of event times was described in one of the first books on discrete-event simulation, "The Art of Simulation", by K. D. Toucher [1963].

1.7 A smpl Queueing Simulation

We'll conclude this chapter and preview the next with a look at a **smpl** simulation model version of the **M/M/1** queue; the simulation program is shown in Figure 1.7. The names of **smpl** functions are underlined for emphasis. Floating point variables are declared as `real`, which the user can define as either `float` or `double` (via a `typedef` in *smpl.h*), based on space and possibly time considerations.

There are three initialization steps: `smpl()` is called to initialize the simulation subsystem and name the model, `facility()` to create and name a facility representing the queueing system's server, and `schedule()` to schedule the first customer arrival. (This model doesn't distinguish customers; the value of `customer` remains unchanged during model execution.) The `schedule()` function adds the specified inter-event time — 0, in this case — to the current simulation time (which is initially 0) to obtain the event occurrence time, and creates an event list entry containing the event occurrence time, the event number, and the customer number. The period of the simulation is controlled by the `while` statement; the `time()` function returns the current simulation time.

The `cause()` function removes the entry at the head of the event list, advances simulation time to the event occurrence time of that entry, records the event number as the current event, and returns the event and customer numbers. The program uses the event number to select the next event to be executed.

This model is divided into three events (our earlier model had two events). Event 1 represents a customer arrival; it schedules the server request of the arriving customer for immediate occurrence, and schedules the next arrival. Event 2 is a server request. If the server is free, the `request()` function reserves it for the requestor, returning 0 to indicate that the request was successful, and the customer's service completion is scheduled. If the server is busy, `request()` queues the request and returns 1 to indicate its action. The queue entry includes the customer and the current event.

Event 3 represents a service completion: `release()` is called to release the server. If a request has been queued, `release()` dequeues it, creates an event list entry for it, and puts this entry at the head of the event list. This entry has an event occurrence time equal to the current time, and its event number and customer are those recorded when the request was queued. The next call to `cause()`, then, will result in the execution of event 2 for the dequeued request. This implicit invocation of an event is the reason for the separation of the arrival and server request events in this model.

```
#include <smpl.h>

main()
  {
    real Ta=200.0,Ts=100.0,te=200000.0;
    int customer=1,event,server;
    smpl(1,"M/M/1 Queue");
    server=facility("server",1);
    schedule(1,0.0,customer);
    while (time()<te)
      {
        cause(&event,&customer);
        switch(event)
          {
            case 1:  /* arrival */
              schedule(2,0.0,customer);
              schedule(1,expntl(Ta),customer);
              break;
            case 2:  /* request server */
              if (request(server,customer,0)==0)
                schedule(3,expntl(Ts),customer);
              break;
            case 3:  /* completion */
              release(server,customer);
              break;
          }
      }
    report();
  }
```

Figure 1.7. smpl Queueing System Simulation Model

When the simulation completes, `report()` is called to generate the simulation report. The data given in this report includes the period of the simulation, server utilization, server mean busy period, mean queue length, number of requests completed, and the number of times requests were queued. The model parameters specified in Figure 1.7 result in the simulation of 1025 customer service completions; the reported utilization is 0.5301, the mean busy period is 103.482, and the mean queue length is 0.659.

1.8 Problems

Some of these problems require a random number generator. You can use the one provided in your **C** library, or you can use the **smpl** ranf() function described in Chapter 8: code for this function is given in the Appendix.

1. In modeling program behavior, the number of instructions executed from consecutive memory locations, beginning with the target of a taken branch instruction and ending with (and including) a taken branch instruction, sometimes is called the *headway* between branches. Measurement data collected during the execution of a particular system workload provided the following distribution of inter-branch headways; p_h is the proportion of headways of length h.

h	p_h	h	p_h	h	p_h	h	p_h
1	.0659	9	.0261	17	.0108	25	.0020
2	.1713	10	.0432	18	.0151	26	.0023
3	.1106	11	.0169	19	.0069	27	.0045
4	.1054	12	.0311	20	.0144	28	.0018
5	.0978	13	.0113	21	.0113	29	.0015
6	.0758	14	.0179	22	.0025	30	.0018
7	.0660	15	.0093	23	.0044	31	.0005
8	.0502	16	.0108	24	.0032	≥32	.0074

Headways of length 1 indicate that the target of a taken branch is itself a taken branch; this results from some procedure call protocols and from trans- fers via branch vector tables. The proportion of headways greater than 127 can be assumed to be 0. The mean headway **H** is 6.957 instructions (the reciprocal of **H** is the proportion of instructions which are taken branches).

Plot a histogram of the headway distribution, and write a function to generate random variates from this distribution. (In deciding how to generate headways in the range 32–127, consider the shape of the distribution and the difference between **H** and $\Sigma h\,p_h$, $1 \le h \le 31$.) Generate 5000 sample headway values and compare their distribution with that of the measured headways.

2. The histogram of the headway distribution suggests that it can be modeled as a *mixed* distribution, composed of a constant distribution for headways of 1 and a geometric distribution for headways greater than 1. Assuming this form, the following model can be derived.

$$\Pr[h=i] = p_1, \qquad\qquad i = 1$$
$$= (1 - p_1)p(1 - p)^{i-2}, \qquad i \ge 2 \qquad (1.14)$$

where $p = (1 - p_1)/(H - 1)$

p_1 is the proportion of headways equal to 1 (0.0659). The geometric distribution parameter p is determined from the contribution of the geometric part of the mixed distribution to the mean:[5]

$$(1 - p_1) \sum_{h=2}^{\infty} hp(1 - p)^{h-2} = H - p_1$$

(a) Visually check how well this model matches the headway distribution by overlaying a plot of (1.14) on the headway distribution histogram. To compare the tails of the measured and modeled distributions, compute and plot the log survivor function $\ln \{Pr[h>i]\}$ versus i for each distribution.

(b) Determine, quantitatively, how well the distribution defined by (1.14) matches the measurement data. Refer to a statistics text for methods.

(c) For the geometric distribution $p_k = p(1 - p)^k$, $0 \leq k \leq \infty$, $0 < p < 1$, a sample variate k can be generated from (see, for example, Law and Kelton [1982])

$$k = \lfloor \ln r / \ln(1 - p) \rfloor \tag{1.15}$$

where $\lfloor x \rfloor$ denotes the floor function of x — the largest integer equal to or less than x — and r is a uniform random variate. Using (1.15), write a function to generate sample headway values from the distribution defined by (1.14). Generate 5000 sample headway values and compare their distribution with that of the measured headways. (Save this function for use in the pipeline analysis project of Chapter 5.)

3. If all we know about a variable X is that its values fall within a range [a,b], we'll probably use a uniform distribution to generate values of X. Given an estimate of the most likely value (mode) of X, we can use a triangular distribution to model X. The triangular distribution is defined by its range [a,b] and mode c; its mean is $(a + b + c)/3$. Figure 1.8 shows a sketch of the density function of this distribution and gives its distribution function F(x) = $Pr[X \leq x]$.

Sketch the distribution function for the triangular distribution. What is the value of F(x) at x = c? Let p = F(X), and determine the inverse of the distribution function $F^{-1}(p)$. Use this inverse function to write a random vari-

---

[5]There are other ways to fit the parameters of this model to the measurement data; the choice depends on what characteristics of the data it is desired to preserve.

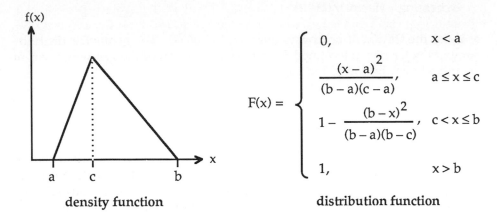

$$F(x) = \begin{cases} 0, & x < a \\ \dfrac{(x-a)^2}{(b-a)(c-a)}, & a \le x \le c \\ 1 - \dfrac{(b-x)^2}{(b-a)(b-c)}, & c < x \le b \\ 1, & x > b \end{cases}$$

density function   distribution function

Figure 1.8. Triangular Distribution

ate generator for the triangular distribution. Check the generator by picking values for a, b, and c, generating a large number of sample values, and comparing the sample and theoretical distributions. (Save the function for use in the timesharing model of problem 3, Chapter 2).

4. A small timesharing system (Figure 1.9) has 16 user terminals connected to a minicomputer system with two disks. A user "thinks" for a time z and, at the end of that time, sends a request to the computer system and waits for the system to respond. When the response is received, the user thinks again and then initiates another request.

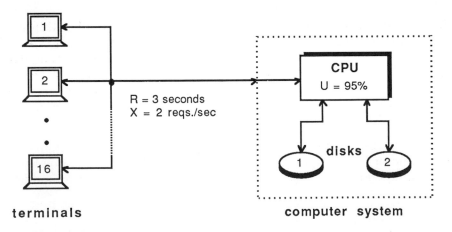

Figure 1.9. Timesharing System

Operating system instrumentation shows that the system processes 2 terminal requests per second with a average response time per request of 3 seconds; the CPU utilization is 95 percent.

(a) What is the mean user think time?

(b) On average, how many users are thinking and how many are waiting for requests to be processed by the computer system?

(c) Each terminal request generates an average of 12 CPU-disk operations. What is the mean CPU execution time for each such operation?

(d) Measurements show that the average CPU queue length is 4.25. Assuming that requests either are competing for CPU service or for disk service (i.e., no memory queueing), what is the mean disk residence time per disk operation?

(e) How would you instrument the system to obtain data to estimate the mean disk operation queueing time?

5. Our modeling work usually will focus on queueing systems of various kinds. However, you'll sometimes find it handy to use simulation to analyze other types of problems and as a check on analytic solutions. This and the following two problems provide simple examples of this use of simulation.

The graph of Figure 1.10 represents a computer program. Diamonds represent branch instructions; each branch path is labeled with the probability of its being taken on any given execution of the branch instruction. This probability is independent of the path taken on previous branches. Rectangles represent non-branch instructions. Write a simulation model of this program to determine the average number of instructions executed; simulate 1000 program executions.

6. A certain allocation mechanism allocates elements from two lists. Whenever an allocation request is received, one of the two lists is selected at random and an element allocated from that list. Write a simulation program to determine the average number of elements remaining in one list at the instant the other list is empty, assuming that each list initially contains 16 elements. Simulate 1000 list emptyings.

7. A table comprising a set of records organized in increasing order of key field values, $K_1 < K_2 < \ldots < K_N$, is searched for a key value A using a *binary search* algorithm (see, e.g., Knuth [1973]). This algorithm first compares A to the value in the middle of the table. The result of this comparison is used to determine which half of the table to examine next, and A is compared with the middle key of the selected half. This process is repeated until the

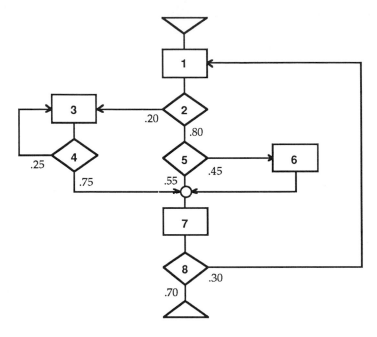

Figure 1.10. Program Graph

desired record is found (or until it has been determined that the record is not in the table). The number of comparisons required for a successful search is in the range [1,m], where $2^{m-1} \leq N < 2^m$; the average is about ln N – 1. Write a simulation program to determine the distribution of the number of compari-sons required for a successful search as well as the mean number. Assume that N = 63 and that A equiprobably is one of the key values K1, K2, ..., KN (so that A always is found in the table). Simulate 1000 searches.

2. smpl

2.1 The smpl View of Systems

At the start of the previous chapter, we discussed the dynamic and static composition of systems in general terms. In this section, we'll discuss a more specific view appropriate to the nature of our tools. In the **smpl** view of systems, there are three kinds of entities: *facilities, tokens,* and *events.*

Facilities. In static form, a system comprises a collection of interconnected facilities. A facility typically represents some work-performing resource of the system being modeled, such as the CPU in a computer system or the bus in an local area network model. Facilities also may represent resources other than hardware, such as a software lock in an operating system. **smpl** provides functions to define facilities, reserve, release, and preempt them, and interrogate their status. The interconnection of facilities is not explicit, but rather is determined by the model's routing of tokens between facilities.

Tokens. Tokens represent the active entities of the system; the dynamic behavior of the system is modeled by the movement of tokens through a set of facilities. A token may represent a task in a computer system model, a packet in a communications network model, or a memory access in a memory bus subsystem model. **smpl** provides two basic kinds of operations for controlling the flow of tokens through the simulated system; a token may reserve (or preempt) facilities, and it may schedule activities of various durations. If a token attempts to reserve an already-busy facility, it is queued until the facility becomes available to it. From a timing standpoint, the flow of a token through the system can be described by its sequence of delay (queueing) and activity times.

What a token represents is up to the modeler; as far as the **smpl** simulation subsystem is concerned, a token is just an integer. The only attribute of a token which the simulation subsystem knows about is its priority. In some models it is not necessary to distinguish between instances of work, as in the queueing model of Figure 1.7; in this model, the token represented indistinguishable customers and was a simple variable whose value remained unchanged over the course of the simulation. In other models, tokens may be indexes to arrays whose elements contain attributes of the work, such as the compute time, memory size, and number of IO requests for a task in a computer system model.

Events. A change of state of any system entity, active or passive, is an event. Suppose a task (or process) completes a CPU execution interval and releases the CPU. Two events have occurred: an activity of the task ended, and the CPU changed state. The termination of one activity of the task may cause initiation of another of the same task; release of the CPU may result in execution of some earlier-initiated activity of some other task. In event-oriented simulation languages such as **smpl**, we usually collect together actions which take place at any one instant in time, and tend to think of this collection as an event. This casual view isn't much of a problem in building small models; however, in developing complex models, an amazing number of problems can be avoided by distinguishing individual events and organizing the model accordingly. We'll revisit this subject in Chapter 3.

smpl provides functions for scheduling events and for selecting — "causing" — events in order of their event occurrence times. From the standpoint of the simulation subsystem, an event is identified by its number, the simulation time at which it is to occur, and possibly the identity of a token involved with the event. What the event represents is up to the modeler; it frequently will correspond to several system events.

A **smpl** simulation program comprises an initialization routine, a control routine, and some number of event routines. A "routine" may range in size from a single statement to a large subprogram, depending on the model's complexity. The control routine selects the number of the next event to occur and transfers control to the appropriate event routine which, typically, schedules one or more other events and then returns to the control routine. When talking about simulation programs, we'll sometimes become even more casual in our terminology, and refer to event routines simply as events.

2.2 Function Descriptions

The functions provided by **smpl** for simulation modeling, testing, and experimentation are described in following sections. First, we'll discuss initialization, facility, event scheduling, and random variate generation functions, and use these to develop a queueing network simulation model.

Next, using this model as an example, we'll review **smpl**'s debugging and report generation functions.

    smpl function descriptions begin with a two-line synopsis. The first line shows the function and its formal parameters. When a function returns a value, it is shown assigning a value to a dummy parameter as, for example, in `n=inq(f)`. The second line of the synopsis shows the types of the parameters. Real-valued parameters are of type `real`, which can be defined as either `float` or `double`. Generally, **smpl** systems and models define `real` as `double`, but space considerations sometimes might dictate its definition as `float`. In either case, definition is accomplished via `typedef` declarations in **smpl** subsystem source programs and in the *smpl.h* file.

    smpl.h contains external declarations for **smpl** functions, `#include`'s for *stdio.h* and *math.h*, the `typedef` declaration for `real`, and the `#define` for the psuedo-keyword `then`. *smpl.h* should be included in all **smpl** simulation programs. (A listing of *smpl.h* appears in the Appendix.)

    Function descriptions tend to be dry reading in any event, and those of following sections are intended to be detailed enough for your use as reference to **smpl**. So, give them a quick first reading, see how the functions are used in the queueing network simulation model, and reread the descriptions of those functions about which you have questions. When you start coding your first model, read through the descriptions once again. A short tabulation of the most commonly-used **smpl** functions appears at the end of this chapter.

2.3 Model Initialization

```
smpl(m,s);
  int m; char *s;
```

```
reset();
```

    The `smpl()` function initializes the simulation subsystem for a simulation run. `m` is 1 if **mtr** is to be activated, and 0 if it is not. When using the implementation of **smpl** presented in this book, `m` should always be 0. **mtr**, part of the **SMPL** simulation environment, provides an interactive interface to model execution; some of its facilities are described in Chapter 7. While its implementation isn't included here, an overview of its design is given in Chapter 9, and you may want to add a similar capability in your system. The "hooks" between **smpl** and **mtr** — there are only a few — have been left in place to keep the **smpl** source code given in the appendix identical to that in the **SMPL** system.) `s` is a pointer to the model's name; the name (limited to 50 characters) appears as a heading on the simulation report.

  `smpl()` initializes and clears data structures, and sets both simulation time and the start of the current measurement interval to zero. **smpl** accumulates measurement data continuously during model execution. Normally, the simulation interval (the period of time simulated) and the measurement interval coincide. and the performance measures given in the simulation report are averaged over the complete simulation run. However, executing a `reset()` function clears all accumulated measurements; the time at which this function is called becomes the start of the measurement interval, and the reported measures represent model activity only from that time to the time at which the report is generated. We may want to use this capability to discard data collected while the model is "warming up" in order to eliminate initialization bias from the model's estimates.

  It often is convenient to make multiple simulation runs during one instance of simulation program execution. We may want to collect perform-ance measures for different values of a model parameter; for example, we might want to see how the mean response time varies as the transaction rate is increased. We can structure the simulation model as a subprogram and execute the subprogram repeatedly, incrementing the transaction rate each time. On each execution of the subprogram, a call to `smpl()` will reinitial-ize the simulation subsystem. Alternatively, we can make multiple runs without reinitialization, except of measurements, by calling `reset()` rather than `smpl()`: this provides another way of dealing with initialization bias.

  Another application of multiple runs is the collection of a set of sample values of a particular performance measure, using identical model parameters in each run, to explore the variability of the measure (for example, to estimate confidence limits for the mean response time). In this case, the runs are *replicated*. Each run uses the same set of parameters; to provide statistical variation from run to run, different samples from distributions of model variables are needed. smpl provides several functions for sampling distributions, all of which use a common random number generator. The sequence, or stream, of values produced by a random number generator is determined by a starting value, called the *seed*. Different seeds generate different streams, resulting in different distribution sample values. **smpl** provides seeds for 15 streams. The first time the simulation program calls `smpl()`, stream 1 is selected; each subsequent call increments the stream number, so a different set of random variates is generated in each run. Conversely, when varying a model parameter from run to run, we may want to use the same stream for each run; the `stream()` function can be used to specify the stream number.

Dealing with model warmup effects, and using replicated simulation runs to compute confidence limits, are discussed in Chapter 4.

2.4 Facility Definition and Control

```
f=facility(s,n);
    char *s; int n;
```

This function creates and names a facility, and returns a facility descriptor `f` used to specify the facility in other operations. `s` is a pointer to the facility name, used to identify the facility in the simulation report and in trace and error messages. Names are limited to 14 characters for multi-server facilities, 16 characters for single-server facilities. `n` is the number of servers in the facility.

A facility comprises a single queue and n parallel servers.[1] When reservation of a facility is requested, servers 1 through n are examined in turn; if a free server is found, it is reserved for the requesting token. If all the servers of the facility already are reserved, the request is entered in the facility's queue. When one of the reserving tokens releases the facility and frees a server, the queued request is reissued. A facility is busy when all servers are reserved; it is not busy when one or more servers are free.

All facility definitions must precede any other facility operations or any event operations, or an error exit will occur. The maximum number of facilities and total number of servers which may be defined is limited by the size of **smpl** data structures. These are described in Chapter 8; you can easily redimension them to meet the needs of your environment.

```
r=request(f,tkn,pri);
    int f,tkn,pri;
```

This function requests that a server of facility `f` be reserved for the token designated by `tkn`. `f` is the facility descriptor returned by the `facility()`

---

[1]In queueing system terms, a facility with n>1 servers is a multi-server queue; facilities with n=1 (our most common case) are single-server queues.

function when the facility was created. The requesting token's priority is given by `pri`; the larger the value of `pri`, the higher the priority. If the facility is not busy, a server is reserved for the requesting token and 0 is returned. If the facility is busy, the request is queued and 1 is returned. The simulation program uses the returned value to determine if the facility has been reserved. If it has, then subsequent operations are executed; typically, these include scheduling completion of the token's execution on that facility. Otherwise, the program selects and executes an event for some other activity.

A server is reserved by marking it with the reserving token. Consequently, a token must always be non-zero, even when tokens are indistinguishable as in the M/M/1 queue model of Figure 1.7. In this model, the token value was fixed at 1.

Each facility has a queue. When a request finds the facility busy, a queue entry is constructed for the request. (A request which initially finds the facility busy is called a *blocked* request to distinguish it from a preempted request.) This entry contains the token and its priority (the values of `tkn` and `pri`), and the current event number (established on the most recent call to `cause()`). Queues are ordered on the basis of priority; equal-priority entries are ordered first-in, first-out. When a `release()` function frees a server, the entry at the head of the queue is dequeued, and the event from that entry, together with the token from the original request, is rescheduled for the current simulation time. When the simulation program calls `cause()` to select the next event, it will return control to the event routine which initially executed the `request()` function, and the request will be reissued.

Model priorities may represent actual system priorities. More generally, they can be used to implement a variety of queueing disciplines. For example, by providing a function to map real-valued service times to integer-valued priorities, a shortest-service-first discipline can be approximated. Setting a request's priority to the facility's current queue length results in last-in, first-out service. Use care when trying this kind of thing with preemptable facilities.

Note that the event number recorded in enqueueing a request is that of the current event established by `cause()`; smpl assumes this identifies the event routine currently being executed by the simulation program. Consequently, the simulation program should not itself transfer control directly between event routines, even though the associated events are to occur at the same instant in time; control should always be transferred by `schedule()` calls.

In structuring event routines, remember that dequeueing of a request causes reentry to an event routine, so that statements in that routine up through the `request()` call will be reexecuted. An activity ending with the release of one facility often is followed by an activity which begins by requesting another facility. If the release and request operations are placed in the same event routine, a queued request will cause the routine to be reexecuted, and reexecution of the release operation will result in an error.

Implicit versus explicit queueing. In most event-oriented simulation languages, queueing and dequeueing are explicit operations. In requesting a facility, the simulation program must check the status of the facility and, if busy, enter the request in a queue. Whenever a facility is released, the program must examine the queue and, if it is not empty, remove the entry at the head of the queue, reserve the facility for it, and schedule its next event. Facility preemption involves even more operations.

In **smpl**, queueing is implicit: the simulation subsystem queues blocked or preempted requests, and dequeues them and reschedules their events when the facility becomes available. Implicit queueing substantially reduces the number of simulation operations that you have to code. However, it does have two drawbacks. There is some loss of generality in representing queueing and facility scheduling algorithms, and you have to be careful in structuring event routines. The pros and cons depend on the kind of system being modeled; we'll examine some situations in which explicit queueing is needed in Chapter 9.

```
r=preempt(f,tkn,pri);
    int f,tkn,pri;
```

`preempt()` requests that a server of facility `f` be reserved for token `tkn`; `pri` is the token's priority. If the facility is not busy, a server is reserved for the requesting token and 0 returned. If the facility is busy, the server with the lowest-priority reserving token is located. If this priority is equal to or greater than that of the requestor, the request is queued and 1 returned. Thus, when a facility is either not busy or has all its servers reserved by tokens of higher priority than the requesting token, `preempt()` executes just like `request()`. A blocked preemptive request is queued, dequeued, rescheduled, and reexecuted in exactly the same manner as a non-preemptive request.

If the facility is busy and the priority of the lowest-priority reserving token is less than that of the requestor, the former is preempted and queued, and its server reserved for the requestor. Preemption takes place as follows.

smpl assumes that the token chosen for preemption has an event scheduled marking the end of its current use of this facility. The event list is searched for an entry for the preempted token. When the entry is found (an error exit occurs if it isn't), smpl removes the entry from the event list and computes the remaining event time — the difference between the time at which the event was scheduled to occur and the current time. A facility queue entry is constructed for the preempted request: this entry contains the token, its priority, the event number of the suspended event, and the remaining event time. This entry is placed on the queue before entries of the same priority, rather than after, so it will be the first of its priority class assigned to a server when one becomes free. Once the preempted token has been queued, the freed server is reserved for the preempting token.

When release() frees one of the facility's servers, smpl dequeues the entry at the head of the queue. If this entry is for a preempted token, the server is reserved for the token and the suspended event is rescheduled to occur at a time equal to the current time plus the remaining event time. Servers are indistinguishable; the current server may or may not be the same one previously reserved by this token. Note that dequeueing of a preempted request and resuming its execution does not involve reexecution of any part of the event routine, but is done entirely within the simulation subsystem.

Because of the way in which preemption is done, a token using a preemptable facility should have one and only one event scheduled for it at a time. This usually is not a problem. Preemptable facilities tend to be limited to CPUs and similar processors, whose users generally do not use another facility at the same time (or, when they do, have the highest priority and can't be preempted). Facilities which need to be reserved simultaneously for a single token, such as the disk, control unit, and data channel composing an IO transfer path, usually are not preemptable. When simultaneous reservation of preemptable facilities is a problem, you'll have to assign separate tokens for the separate facility activities and coordinate these activities in the model.

———————————

```
release(f,tkn);
  int f,tkn;
```

This function releases the server of facility f reserved by token tkn. In releasing a facility, smpl locates the server reserved for the specified token; if it can't find one, an error exit occurs. The server is freed and facility measurement data updated. Next, the facility queue is examined and, if it isn't empty, the entry at its head is dequeued. If this entry is for a blocked request (preemptive or non-preemptive), the event associated with the entry is rescheduled to occur at the current time. If the entry is for a preempted request, the server just released is reserved for the dequeued token, and the associated event is rescheduled to occur at a time equal to the current time plus the remaining event time.

```
n=inq(f)
r=status(f)
u=real U(f)
b=real B(f)
l=real Lq(f)
    int f;
```

These five functions are used to obtain status and performance data for facility f. The inq() function returns the number of tokens currently in queue (only, not including those in service) at the facility. The status() function returns 1 if the facility is busy or 0 if one or more servers is free. The U(), B(), and Lq() functions return, respectively, the mean facility utilization, mean busy period, and mean queue length for the current measurement interval; you can use these to develop a simulation report tailored for a particular model. Since utilization is the average number of busy servers, the value returned by U() may be greater than 1 for a multi-server facility. The current measurement interval starts at the time the last reset() function was executed (if none was executed, it starts at simulation time 0) and continues to the current time.

2.5 Scheduling and Causing Events

```
schedule(ev,te,tkn);
   int ev,tkn; real te;
```

This function is called to schedule an event; ev is the event number, te is the inter-event time, and tkn is a token associated with the event. schedule() checks te to verify that it is not negative (an error exit occurs if it is) and adds it to the current simulation time to obtain the event occurrence time. It then constructs an event list entry containing the event number, the event occurrence time, and the token, and schedules the event by linking this entry on the event list.

The event list is ordered in ascending values of event occurrence times; entries with the same event occurrence time are ordered on the basis of arrival (first-in, first-out). Events with the same occurrence time usually happen because events are scheduled with an inter-event time of 0. The event number is used by the simulation program to select the next event routine to execute. The program may (and should) call `schedule()` to transfer control between event routines, usually with an inter-event time of 0. Release of a facility may result in dequeueing of a request and rescheduling it with an inter-event time of 0. As a consequence, several events may be scheduled for the same simulation time. Very rarely is this a problem. However, "race' conditions can arise; if they do, take a close look at the ordering of request and release operations. Sometimes a very small, but non-zero, inter-event time will help achieve the desired order.

An event which represents initiation or completion of an activity usually has a token associated with it. Other events do not, and the value of `tkn` may be 0 in these cases. For example, an event representing the next arrival in the system may be scheduled with `tkn = 0` because a token is not allocated until the event occurs.

```
cause(ev,tkn);
   int *ev,*tkn;
```

`cause()` removes the entry at the head of the event list, advances simulation time to the event occurrence time of that entry, and returns the event number `ev` and token `tkn`. If the event list is empty, an error exit occurs. (Note that the parameters here are pointers; we need to return two values, and a structure would be unnecessarily complex.) `ev` is saved as the current event. If a facility request in the corresponding event routine is blocked, **smpl** queues the request together with its token and the current event. When a server becomes free, the request is dequeued and that event rescheduled: see the `request()` function description.

```
tkn=cancel(ev);
    int tkn;
```

`cancel()` searches the event list for event `ev`; if found, the corresponding entry is removed from the event list and the token number associated with that entry is returned. If the event is not found, -1 is returned. If multiple instances of event ev exist in the event list, only the first — earliest-occurring — is cancelled. The Ethernet model of Chapter 6 provides examples of the use of `cancel()`.

```
t=real time();
```

`time()` returns the current simulation time. The simulation time is set to 0 during **smpl** initialization and thereafter advanced by `cause()`. The unit of time is established implicitly by the values used in the simulation, so you have to be careful that all times are specified in the same units. It's easy to make mistakes when dealing with both rates and times. For example, a common error in IO subsystem modeling is to specify arrival rates in requests per second and disk service times in milliseconds; fortunately, the magnitude of this error makes it easy to spot.

2.6 Random Variate Generation

```
r=real ranf();
```

`ranf()` is the **smpl** random number generator function. It returns a psuedo-random variate uniformly distributed in the range 0, 1. (More precisely, $0 < r < 1$.) It is used by other random variate generation functions as well as by the simulation program.

Random number generation is the one machine-dependent function in **smpl**. The generator used to produce the simulation model results presented at various points in this book is described in Chapter 8; if you use the same generator, you should obtain identical results. A different generator may produce slightly different results.

```
i=stream(n);
    int n;
```

smpl provides 15 different random number streams by providing 15 different initial values, or seeds, for the random number generator. For the implementation used in this book, these seeds are samples from the generated sequence, spaced 100,000 samples apart.[2] stream() is used to select a stream or to identify the selected stream. If n is in the range 1-15, the corresponding stream is selected (and its number returned); If n is 0, the currently-selected stream remains selected and its number is returned. A value of n less than 0 or greater than 15 causes an error exit.

The stream number is set to 1 on the simulation program's first call to smpl() and incremented on subsequent calls (see the smpl() function description).

```
r=real expntl(x);
r=real erlang(x,s);
r=real hyperx(x,s);
    real x,s;
```

These functions generate random variates from the exponential, Erlang, and hyper-exponential distributions. These distributions are related; the exponential and Erlang distributions are particular cases of the gamma distribution, and the hyperexponential distribution is a composite of exponential distributions. They are used in similar situations, with the specific choice depending on the variability of the distribution being represented. The standard deviation of the Erlang distribution is less than or equal to its mean, the standard deviation of the exponential distribution is equal to its mean, and the standard deviation of the hyperexponential distribution is equal to or greater than its mean.

The expntl() function generates a random variate from an exponential distribution with mean x. The erlang() function generates a random variate from a k-Erlang distribution with mean x and standard deviation s; s must be less than x, or an error exit occurs. k is taken to be the next smallest integer to $(x/s)^2$, so the standard deviation of the generated values may be somewhat less than s. The hyperx() function generates a random variate from a 2-stage hyperexponential distribution with mean x and standard deviation s. s must be greater than x, or an error exit occurs.

---

[2]Sometimes you may want to save the current seed of a stream and later restore it, as when interrupting a simulation which is to be restarted later: this can be done using the seed() function described in Section 7.9.

```
r=real uniform(a,b);
    real a,b;
```

This function returns a random variate from a continuous uniform distribution; r is uniformly distributed in the range a, b. If a is greater than b, an error exit occurs.

```
k=random(i,j);
    int i,j;
```

random() generates random variates from a discrete uniform distribution; it returns an integer equiprobably selected from the set of integers i, i+1, ..., j. If i is greater than j, an error exit occurs.

```
r=real normal(x,s);
    real x,s;
```

normal() returns a random variate from a normal distribution with mean x and standard deviation s. Remember that this function can generate negative values and may need its tail clipped.

The implementation of these generators is described in Section 8.9.

Other distributions. The needs of most computer and communication system models are met with uniform (both continuous and discrete), exponential, Erlang, and hyperexponential random variate generation functions, together with empirical distribution sampling functions. The normal distribution is used infrequently. On occasion, we may need sampling functions for other distributions, such as the Poisson distribution; the referenced simulation texts describe generators for most standard distributions.

The range of behavior encompassed by the exponential, Erlang, and hyperexponential distributions can be represented by the gamma distribution with appropriate parameters. Consequently, gamma variate generation is an important subject in simulation literature. The three individual functions are used in smpl because of their relationship to analytic modeling approaches (see Kobayashi [1978], Chapter 3).

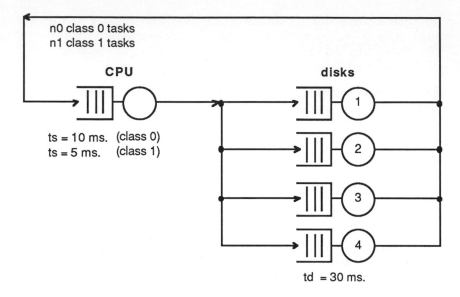

Figure 2.1. Central Server Queueing Network

2.7 A Queueing Network Simulation Model

To see how the functions described in preceding sections are used, we'll look at a high-level model of a hypothetical computer system. This system is represented by the queueing network of Figure 2.1. Networks with this structure are called *central server* networks.[3]

The system comprises a CPU and four disks. A fixed number of tasks of two different classes execute in the system, alternating between CPU and disk activities. There are n0 class 0 tasks, which have a mean CPU execution time of 10 ms. (milliseconds), and n1 class 1 tasks, which have a mean CPU execution time of 5 ms. CPU execution times for both classes are exponentially distributed. CPU requests of class 1 tasks have preemptive priority over those of class 0 tasks. If a class 1 task requests the CPU when it is being used by a class 0 task, the latter is preempted and queued, and the CPU is assigned to the class 1 task. The interrupted task resumes CPU execution when there are no more class 1 tasks requesting the CPU.

---

[3]Buzen's development of efficient computational algorithms for analyzing central server queueing networks [Buzen 1973] triggered a series of advances in queueing network analysis methods.

The disk requests of both classes are distributed randomly and uniformly across all four disks, with the same mean disk service time of 30 ms. Disk service times are assumed to be Erlang-distributed with a standard deviation equal to 1/4 of the mean service time.

Open and closed systems. The M/M/1 queueing system simulated in Chapter 1 is an *open* system; customers arrive from someplace outside the system, are serviced, and leave the system. The source of customers presumably is unlimited: the probability of a new customer arriving in the system is not influenced by the number of customers already in the system, so queues in an open system potentially can grow without limit. The central server queueing network is a *closed* system; tasks receive service at the CPU, at a disk, and then recirculate to request service at the CPU once again. (The time-sharing system of problem 4, Chapter 1, also is a closed system.) The maximum queue length at any facility is bounded by the number of tasks in the system. We can look at this closed network as representing a fixed-level multiprogramming system with a queue of tasks large enough so that, whenever a task leaves the system, it is immediately replaced; the number of tasks executing in the system always remains the same.

Let's assume that the objective of the simulation is to estimate the mean tour time, or cycle time, for each class. A tour time is the interval between two successive CPU requests of a task. If we know the mean tour time of a class and the mean number of tours it makes (mean number of disk requests), we can easily compute the mean time a task spends in the system.

The simulation program. Figure 2.2 shows a **smpl** implementation of this model.[4] **smpl** function names are underlined in this figure. Preprocessor directives (lines 2-6) define the number of tasks, the number of disks, and a symbolic representation (qd) for the value returned by a request or preempt function when a facility reservation request is queued.

Tokens, in this model, represent tasks. Lines 7-12 define a structure array of task attributes: these are a task's class, the unit number for the task's current IO disk request, and the starting time of its current tour. Token values in **smpl** function calls in this model are indexes of the element of this array. Note the array dimensioning: the first element is unused so that we won't have a token with a 0 value.

---

[4]A simulation model of a system is defined by the level of abstraction with which the system is viewed. This definition encompasses both static entities (facilities, in our case) and dynamic entities (activities and events, together with activity parameter values and distributions). Although we often ignore the distinction, a particular simulation program is just one particular implementation of a simulation model.

The declarations of lines 13-19 define variables used to save descriptors returned by facility definition functions, to specify the number of tours to be simulated, and to hold CPU and disk service time distribution parameters.

The first statements of `main()` initialize variables used to accumulate tour counts and times for each class. Line 24 sets the class of each task. Lines 25-28 are initialization operations common to all **smpl** simulation programs: `smpl()` is called to initialize the simulation subsystem, facilities are defined, and the initial events are scheduled. Note that the effect of this last initialization step is to begin the simulation with all tasks scheduled for event 1: the simulated system is otherwise empty. This probably is an unusual system state; we would expect to find tasks distributed throughout the system (unless there was a major "bottleneck" at some point). This state will be reflected in measurement data collected during the first part of the simulation run, biasing estimates of steady-state system performance.

```
1    #include <smpl.h>

2    #define n0 6            /* no. class 0 tasks    */
3    #define n1 3            /* no. class 1 tasks    */
4    #define nt n0+n1        /* total no. of tasks */
5    #define nd 4            /* no. of disk units    */
6    #define qd 1            /* queued req. return */

7    struct token
8      {
9         int cls;           /* task's class (& priority) */
10        int un;            /* unit for current IO req.   */
11        real ts;           /* tour start time stamp       */
12      } task[nt+1];

13  int
14     disk[nd+1],           /* disk facility descriptors */
15     cpu,                  /* cpu facility descriptor    */
16     nts=10000;            /* no. of tours to simulate   */
17  real
18     tc[2]={10.0,5.0},     /* class 0,1 mean cpu times    */
19     td=30.0,sd=7.5;       /* disk time mean, std. dev. */
```

Figure 2.2. Queueing Network Simulation Program

```
20 main()
21    {
22      int i,j,event,n[2]; real t,s[2]; struct token *p;
23      n[0]=n[1]=0; s[0]=s[1]=0.0;
24      for (i=1; i<=nt; i++) task[i].cls=(i>n0)? 1:0;
25      smpl(0,"central server model");
26      cpu=facility("CPU",1);
27      for (i=1; i<=nd; i++) disk[i]=facility("disk",1);
28      for (i=1; i<=nt; i++) schedule(1,0.0,i);
29      while (nts)
30        {
31          cause(&event,&i); p=&task[i];
32          switch(event)
33            {
34              case 1:  /* begin tour */
35                p->ts=time(); schedule(2,0.0,i);
36                break;
37              case 2:  /* request cpu */
38                j=p->cls;
39                if (preempt(cpu,i,j)!=qd) then
40                  schedule(3,expntl(tc[j]),i);
41                break;
42              case 3:  /* release cpu, select disk */
43                release(cpu,i); p->un=random(1,nd);
44                schedule(4,0.0,i);
45                break;
46              case 4:  /* request disk */
47                if (request(disk[p->un],i,0)!=qd) then
48                  schedule(5,erlang(td,sd),i);
49                break;
50              case 5:  /* release disk, end tour */
51                release(disk[p->un],i); j=p->cls;
52                t=time(); s[j]+=t-p->ts; p->ts=t; n[j]++;
53                schedule(1,0.0,i); nts--;
54                break;
55            }
56        }
57      printf("class 0 tour time = %.2f\n",s[0]/n[0]);
58      printf("class 1 tour time = %.2f\n",s[1]/n[1]);
59 }
```

Figure 2.2. Queueing Network Simulation Program (continued)

It is possible to devise more elaborate initialization schemes, but this is seldom done because of the extra programming effort required Usually we'll either discard measurement data collected early in the run or make the run long enough so that this initialization bias has negligible effects on results. We'll discuss this problem at some length in Chapter 4.

The length of the simulation run is controlled by nts. When the program is initialized, this variable is set to the number of tours to be simulated; it is decremented on each tour completion (line 53) and tested by the while statement of line 29. Simulation run lengths typically are controlled either by specifying the simulation time period, as we did in the M/M/1 queue simulation in Chapter 1, or by specifying an execution count for some activity. (Also, for certain output analysis methods, runs are terminated when a specified system state is reached.) Termination on count, rather than time, is recommended since sample counts are needed in the statistical analysis of simulation output. We'll usually have a better idea of how many samples we need than of how much time it will take to collect them.

The cause() function call of line 31 gets the next event together with the index of the task for which the event is to be executed. This event is then used to select the appropriate event "routine" to execute. Note that a pointer to the array element for the task is set on line 31.

Event 1 is the start of a tour; the current simulation time is saved as the tour start time, and event 2 scheduled for immediate occurrence. Event 2 represents a task's CPU request. Remember that a task's class corresponds to its priority in this model. The preempt() function call requests that the CPU be reserved for this task. If the CPU currently is reserved by a task of the same or higher priority, the request is queued, a queued response is returned, and the event routine simply exited. If the CPU is free, it is reserved for the requestor. If the CPU is busy with a lower-priority task, that task is interrupted and queued, and the CPU then reserved for the higher-priority task. Once the CPU has been reserved for the task, the end of its current CPU execution interval (event 3) is scheduled. Note that the mean execution interval is selected according to the task's class.

Two points from our earlier discussion of facility operations bear repeating here. First, note that recording the tour start time and requesting the CPU must be done in separate event routines. A blocked CPU request will be queued and, when the CPU becomes available at some later time, event 2 will be rescheduled for it. If the tour start time were to be recorded in the same event routine in which the CPU request is issued, the start time would be recorded twice: once on the initial CPU request and again on the request's reexecution. Second, even though events 1 and 2 occur at the same simulation time, transfer between the two event routines is done indirectly, via a schedule() call, rather than directly. When cause() returns an event, it records that event as the current event. If a CPU request is blocked, the current event number — event 2 — is saved in the queue entry created for the request and, when the CPU becomes available, event 2 is rescheduled. If control is transferred directly between event routines, smpl loses track of the current event.

Event 3 marks the completion of a task's CPU execution interval. The CPU is released, a disk unit selected at random, and the disk request scheduled. If there are requests queued for the CPU, smpl will dequeue the request at the head of the queue and return it to execution. There are two possibilities. If the request was a blocked CPU request, event 2 is scheduled for it at the current simulation time; reexecution of event 2 will reserve the CPU for the dequeued request. If the request was a preempted request, the CPU is reserved for it by smpl, and event 3 is rescheduled for the request.

Event 4 represents the initiation of a task's disk request. (By now it should be clear why selection of the disk unit and the request for that unit are in separate event routines.) If the selected unit is busy, the request is queued; otherwise, the unit is reserved for the requestor and the end of the disk operation scheduled.

Event 5 is the completion of a task's disk request and of its current tour. The disk unit is released, the time of the current tour is computed and added to the accumulated tour times of the task's class, and the count of completed tours for that class is incremented. The start of the next tour for this task is scheduled, and the count of the number of tours to be simulated is decremented. When this count reaches 0, the mean tour times for class 0 and class 1 are computed and displayed. The values obtained using the random number generator described in Chapter 8 are 99.34 and 69.37 ms., respectively.

Most of the smpl functions described earlier in this chapter are used in this simulation program, so it is important to understand what the program does and why it does it. Also, many models will have the same general form as this one, perhaps with additional facility stages. Similar models are used in other contexts; for example, the central server network of Figure 2.1 might represent a memory bus and memory modules, rather than a CPU and disks. (We'll look at simulation and analytic models of a multiprocessor memory system in Chapter 5.)

To practice using smpl functions, you may want to try extending this model; there are a number of possibilities. The level of detail of disk request processing can be expanded by defining facilities to represent disk controllers and data channels, decomposing the disk service time into seek, latency, and transfer times, and adding event routines to initiate and terminate these activities. The model can be extended to represent transaction processing by adding an event routine to generate transaction arrivals and dynamically allocating and deallocating task attribute array entries as transactions arrive and depart.

A matter of style. The format of this and subsequent programs in this book differs in some respects from common **C** usage. Differences include the use of `then` (defined as empty in *smpl.h*) and the positioning of braces. This reflects only the author's preference in program style and not any advocacy of style. In moving the **smpl** source code in the Appendix to your system, you should feel free to reformat it according to your own preference.

2.8 Debugging Aids

Error messages. Various errors are detected by **smpl**. When an error is detected, **smpl** displays or prints an error message, generates a simulation report (if the current output destination is the printer), and terminates simulation program execution. Error messages give the simulation time at which the error was detected and one of the following diagnostic clauses.

- empty element pool
- empty name space
- facility defined after queue/schedule
- negative event time
- empty event list
- preempted token not in event list

- release of idle/unowned facility
- stream argument error
- uniform argument error: `a>b`
- random argument error: `i>j`
- erlang argument error: `s>x`
- hyperx argument error: `s not >x`

smpl maintains a common pool of elements from which the event list and data structures for facilities and queues are constructed. The size of this pool is fixed when **smpl** is compiled. An empty element pool error occurs when the total number of static and dynamic entities for which pool elements must be allocated exceeds the size of the pool. Sometimes this simply is due to the size of the model, and the only cure is to increase the size of the pool. It frequently is caused by a "runaway" simulation program which generates arrivals but not departures. A second pool is used to hold model and facility names; when this pool is filled, an empty name space error occurs. You can shorten the names or increase the size of this pool.

An error occurs if a facility is defined after an event has been scheduled or a facility request queued (for reasons which have to do with data structure creation). Sequencing model operations in the required order will eliminate this error.

Scheduling an event with a negative inter-event time usually results from some kind of computation problem (but remember that variates from the normal distribution can be negative).

An error occurs when `cause()` finds the event list empty, usually because a scheduling operation was forgotten someplace (and sometimes because we've unwittingly modeled a deadlock situation).

When a token's use of a facility is preempted by a higher-priority token, **smpl** searches the event list to find an entry for the token being preempted. It assumes that this entry represents the end of the token's execution interval on that facility, and suspends the remaining part of the interval until the facility is once again available for that token. An error occurs if the preempted token can't be found in the event list. This usually results from a program bug, but sometimes results from model complexities which exceed the restrictions imposed by **smpl**'s implicit queueing.

When a facility is released, **smpl** verifies that the token specified in a `release()` call is the same as the reserving token: if it is not, an error occurs. This catches a surprising number of program bugs.

The remaining errors in this list result from invalid arguments in random number generator function calls and were described earlier.

The above errors result in calls to the **smpl** function

```
error(n,s);
  int n; char *s;
```

which also can be called from a simulation program. You may want to do this to generate a simulation report on a program-detected error. In this case, n (an error code used by **smpl**) should be 0, and s should point to a string containing the diagnostic clause you want included in the error message. An error message always is displayed on the screen; if the current output destination is the printer, it also is printed, followed by the simulation report. (Output destination control is described later on in this chapter.)

Traces. When the cause of an error isn't obvious from an examination of the program, we can use the **smpl** trace to get additional information. Tracing is controlled by calls to the following function.

```
trace(n);
  int n;
```

n, the trace control flag, should be in the range 0 - 4; any other value is ignored. Values in the range 1 - 3 turn tracing on; a 0 value turns tracing off.

```
time 79.898    --    token 7    -- CAUSE EVENT 5
               --    token 7    -- RELEASE disk
               --    token 7    -- SCHEDULE EVENT 1
               --    token 7    -- CAUSE EVENT 1
               --    token 7    -- SCHEDULE EVENT 2
               --    token 7    -- CAUSE EVENT 2
               --    token 7    -- PREEMPT CPU:   INTERRUPT
               --               --     SUSPEND EVENT 3
               --               --     QUEUE token 4   (inq = 3)
               --               --     RESERVE CPU for token 7
               --    token 7    -- SCHEDULE EVENT 3
time 87.828    --    token 7    -- CAUSE EVENT 3
               --    token 7    -- RELEASE CPU
               --               --     DEQUEUE token 4   (inq = 2)
               --               --     RESERVE CPU for token 4
               --               --     RESUME EVENT 3
               --    token 7    -- SCHEDULE EVENT 4
               --    token 7    -- CAUSE EVENT 4
               --    token 7    -- REQUEST disk:   QUEUED   (inq = 1)
time 96.976    --    token 2    -- CAUSE EVENT 5
               --    token 2    -- RELEASE disk
               --               --     DEQUEUE token 7   (inq = 0)
               --               --     RESCHEDULE EVENT 4
               --    token 2    -- SCHEDULE EVENT 1
               --    token 7    -- CAUSE EVENT 4
```

Figure 2.3. smpl Trace Message Sequence

If n is 1, the trace is free-running; trace message are generated continuously on the screen or printer, depending on the current output destination. If n is 2, trace messages are sent to the screen; execution is paused whenever the screen fills. If n is 3, trace messages also are sent to the screen but with a pause after every message. In both cases, execution is resumed following a pause by pressing any key. User trace messages can be intermingled with **smpl** trace messages. After each user trace message is displayed or printed, a trace(4) call will cause **smpl** to update line counts and issue a page change or screen pause if appropriate.

When the error occurs early in the execution of our simulation program, we can turn tracing on as part of model initialization and step through model execution, screen by screen, until the error occurs. After we get the early (and usually easy) bugs out, and encounter errors later in the simulation, this approach becomes too time-consuming. We can add an event routine to our simulation program which, when the corresponding event occurs, will turn tracing on. During initialization, we schedule that event to occur some time earlier than the error; how much earlier is a matter of guesswork -- the error and its cause may be far apart in time.

When tracing is on, messages are generated whenever a facility is defined, requested, or released, and whenever an event is scheduled or caused. Trace messages give the time at which the operation occurred (if it has changed since the previous trace message) and identify tokens involved in the operation. Messages for schedule and cause operations give the associated event number. Messages for facility request and release operations give the facility name and the current queue length at the facility, and show the queueing and dequeueing of tokens.

Figure 2.3 shows a sequence of trace messages from the execution of the simulation program of Figure 2.2. This sequence traces the execution of a token from the completion of one disk request up to its initiation of its next disk request. This token — token 7 — represents a higher-priority (class 1) task.

The trace sequence begins at the end of a tour for token 7: event 5 occurs, the disk is released, and event 1 scheduled. There is no inter-event delay between event 5 and event 1, so event 1 occurs immediately (event 1 simply records the tour start time), and event 2 is scheduled. Again, there is no delay between events 1 and 2, so event 2 occurs immediately. Event 2 is a CPU request. Since the CPU is reserved by a lower-priority token, token 4, preemption takes place. The event 3 scheduled for token 4 is suspended, token 4 is placed on the CPU queue (whose length now becomes 3), and the CPU is reserved for token 7. Token 7 then schedules its release of the CPU, event 3. Note that all these operations take place at the same point in simulation time.

In this particular sequence, there are no intervening events between events 2 and 3 of token 7. When its event 3 occurs, token 7 releases the CPU. Token 4, which was interrupted earlier, is dequeued (reducing the CPU queue length to 2), the CPU is reserved for it, and its suspended execution interval resumed. Token 7 schedules event 4 and, on its occurrence, issues its disk request. This request finds the disk unit busy and is queued; note that it is the only request queued for this unit.

The next event to occur is the completion of a disk request for token 2. When this token releases the disk, token 7 is dequeued and event 4 rescheduled for it. After token 2 has scheduled the start of its next tour, token 7's disk request (event 4) is reinitiated.

smpl trace messages usually provide enough information to pinpoint problems in simple simulation programs. However, while these messages can show which operations are performed, they can't show why; as program complexity increases, so does the need for user-level debugging aids. If you get involved in developing large simulation models, build in debugging facilities from the start.

SMPL debugging aids. SMPL provides several facilities to help speed debugging. Simulation time is continuously displayed on the screen, and execution can be paused at any time by pressing a key. For more precise control, a breakpoint can be set from the keyboard to pause execution at a specified time or a specified parameter value is reached. Tracing can be turned on and off via function keys. SMPL provides a "dump" capability, which displays the state of the simulated system, including facility status and users, queue entries, and event list contents (an example appears in Section 7.4). The dump display can be generated at any time from the keyboard; it also is generated whenever an error occurs. The ability to control basic debugging aids from the keyboard greatly reduces the amount of time spent modifying and recompiling simulation programs.

2.9 Data Collection and Reporting

smpl collects data on facility utilization and queueing, and uses this data to produce the simulation report. This report gives the utilization, mean busy period, mean queue length, and release, preempt, and queue operation counts for each facility. The reported measures represent operations completed from the start of the current measurement interval up to the time of the report. The measurement interval starts at simulation time 0 unless the reset() function is called. reset() clears facility counters and accumulators, discarding measurement data collected up to the time of its call, and sets the start of the measurement interval to the current simulation time. The simulation report is generated and sent to the current output destination by the following function call.

```
report();
```

This function generates the simulation report and sends it to the current output destination. Figure 2.4 shows the simulation report obtained by adding a report() function call to the simulation program of Figure 2.3. The report heading includes the model name, the current simulation time, and the measurement interval length (which corresponds to the simulation period in this case). Facility names are those specified in facility() function calls. In this model, all facilities have single servers. For a multi-server facility, the number of servers is appended in brackets to the facility name.

```
                    smpl SIMULATION  REPORT


MODEL:  central  server  model                    TIME:   96527.553
                                              INTERVAL:   96527.553


                    MEAN BUSY  MEAN QUEUE      OPERATION  COUNT
FACILITY     UTIL.    PERIOD     LENGTH     RELEASE  PREEMPT   QUEUE
CPU         0.8151     6.202      1.286      12687     2682    7335
disk        0.7712    29.970      0.933       2484        0    1838
disk        0.7561    29.704      0.847       2457        0    1787
disk        0.7804    29.844      0.971       2524        0    1896
disk        0.7886    30.029      1.051       2535        0    1931
```

Figure 2.4. smpl Simulation Report

The utilization of a facility is computed by dividing the accumulated busy time of all servers by the length of the measurement interval; the utilization of a multi-server facility may be greater than 1. Busy times are accumulated when a server is released, so the utilization does not reflect facility execution intervals in progress at the time of the report. This end effect usually is insignificant because of the relative length of the run, but should be kept in mind when using a report covering a small simulation period in debugging.

The mean busy period is computed by dividing the accumulated busy time by the release count. The release count is the sum of release operations effected via a `release()` call and those resulting from facility preemption. For non-preemptable facilities, the reported mean busy period should be approximately equal to the mean facility execution interval specified in the simulation program. Note that the mean disk busy periods in this report are very close to the specified mean disk service time of 30 ms.

For preemptable facilities, the reported mean busy period is not necessarily the same as the mean execution interval, since it reflects interrupted intervals. However, we can compute the mean execution interval from the reported data. The product of the mean busy period and the release count (or the product of the utilization and the measurement interval) gives the total busy time. The preempt count is the number of actual preemptions which occurred, so the difference between the release count and the preempt count is the number of completed execution intervals. Dividing the total busy time by this number gives the measured mean execution interval.

Let's compare the measured mean CPU execution interval with that we'd expect from the values specified in the simulation program. From the report data, the mean interval is $(6.202 \times 12687)/(12687 - 2682) = 7.865$ ms. The two classes of tasks in this model have different mean CPU execution times; to compute an overall mean, we need counts of the number of completed CPU execution intervals for each class. We can obtain values very close to these counts by adding statements to the simulation program to print the class 0 and class 1 tour counts, $n[0]$ and $n[1]$. For this particular implementation, these are 5827 and 4173. The mean CPU times specified for class 0 and class 1 are, respectively, 10 ms. and 5 ms., so we'd expect an overall mean of $(5827 \times 10 + 4173 \times 5)/10000 = 7.914$ ms. The measured mean of 7.865 ms. is very close to this value.

The mean queue length of a facility is the average number of tokens in the facility's queue; it does not include tokens in service. The mean queue length is computed using the method described in Section 1.5. The mean number of tokens in queue and in service at a facility is the sum of the facility utilization and the mean queue length. The sum of utilizations and mean queue lengths for all facilities is the mean number of tokens in the system (for the report of Figure 2.4, the sum is 8.9994).

The release count is the sum of all facility releases, including those resulting from preemption. The preempt count is the number of actual preemptions (not the number of preempt() function calls). The number of complete facility operations is the difference between the release count and the preempt count. This number, divided by the measurement interval length, is the facility's throughput. The average time in queue at a facility can be computed by dividing the mean queue length by the throughput of the facility.

The queue count is the number of dequeue operations performed during the measurement interval. It includes requests queued because the facility was busy and requests queued after preemption. The difference between the queue count and the preempt count is the number of blocked requests.

Sometimes you'll want to develop a report tailored to a particular model. The U(), B(), and Lq() functions described in Section 2.4 (together with the operational relationships discussed in Section 1.4) can help in doing this.

SMPL Reports. SMPL provides additional data collection and reporting tools. These include the table facility, used to collect, tabulate, and plot distributions of model variables, and the time series display, used to plot a variable such as average or instantaneous queue length versus time. With SMPL, any report can be displayed at any time simply by pressing a function key. We'll look at the design of the table facility in Chapter 9.

2.10 Output Control

Error and trace messages, and the simulation report, are sent by **smpl** to the current output destination. This destination is initially set to *stdout*. (Turning tracing on with a trace control flag of 2 or 3 also sets the output destination to *stdout*.) You can redirect output to the printer or a disk file, or find out what the current destination is, via a call to the following function.

```
p=FILE *sendto(dest);
    FILE *dest;
```

If dest is null, sendto() returns the file pointer of the current destination. If it is not null, the associated file becomes the current output destination.

2.11 Summary

This chapter has described the simulation, debugging, and reporting functions of **smpl**, and discussed their use in a queueing network simulation program. We'll look at more **smpl** simulation programs in Chapters 5 and 6. If you have questions about any of these functions, read the appropriate section on implementation in Chapter 8, or check the source code in the Appendix. The simulation functions discussed in this chapter are summarized in Figure 2.5. A few utility functions were not described here; you'll come across these in moving **smpl** to your system. (When this move is accomplished, you can use the program of Figure 2.2 as a test case. If you use the same random number generator, you should be able to reproduce exactly the mean tour values, the trace sequence, and the simulation report.)

If the subject of operational analysis (introduced in Section 1.4) is new to you, it would be a very useful exercise to read Chapters 2 and 3 of Lazowska et al [1984] and apply the relationships discussed in these chapters to the analysis of the output from this model. Go through the arithmetic to compute throughputs, queueing times, and residence times at each facility, and for each class at the CPU. This may seem just a matter of bookkeeping (and in some respects it is), but an understanding of these relationships is very important in model development and testing, and sometimes will eliminate the need to build a model at all.

2.12 Problems

1. Run the M/M/1 queue simulation model of Figure 1.7 and use the data provided by the **smpl** simulation report to compute the system throughput X and mean residence time W. Replace the server in this model by two servers operating at one-half the speed of the original single server (doubling Ts),

INITIALIZATION	
`smpl(0,s)`	initialize simulation subsystem
`reset()`	clear measurement counters & accumulators

FACILITY DEFINITION, OPERATION, AND QUERY	
`f=facility(s,n)`	define facility & return descriptor
`r=request(f,j,p)`	reserve facility: r=1 if queued
`r=preempt(f,j,p)`	preempt facility: r=1 if queued
`release(f,j)`	release facility & dequeue request
`r=status(f)`	get current facility status: r=1 if busy
`n=inq(f)`	get current queue length
`u=U(f)`	get utilization
`b=B(f)`	get mean busy period
`l=Lq(f)`	get queue mean length

EVENT SCHEDULING	
`schedule(e,t,j)`	schedule event
`cause(e,j)`	cause event (e, j are pointers)
`j=cancel(e)`	cancel event & return token
`t=time()`	get current simulation time

DEBUGGING AND REPORTING	
`trace(n)`	set trace mode
`error(0,s)`	display error message & halt
`report()`	generate simulation report
`lns(n)`	count output lines on current page
`endpage()`	advance (pause) on full page (screen)
`newpage()`	initialize page/screen line count
`d=sendto(d)`	get/set output destination

RANDOM VARIATE GENERATION	
`n=stream(n)`	set/get random number stream number
`v=ranf()`	generate uniform [0,1] variate
`v=uniform(a,b)`	generate uniform [a,b] variate
`v=expntl(x)`	generate exponential variate
`v=erlang(x,s)`	generate Erlang variate
`v=hyperx(x,s)`	generate hyperexponential variate
`v=normal(x,s)`	generate normal variate
`k=random(i,j)`	generate random integer

Figure 2.5. smpl Function Summary

run the revised model, compute X and W for this $M/M/2$ queue, and compute the ratio of residence times for the two systems. (Both systems have the same expected throughput $1/\mathrm{Ta}$.) Increase the system load by reducing Ta to 125.0, and repeat the two runs; what happens to the residence time ratio?

2. Extend the $M/M/1$ queue model of Figure 1.7 to provide a preemptive priority queueing discipline. Assume there are two independent customer classes: both have mean inter-arrival times of 400 units and mean service times of 100 units, but class 2 customers have higher priority than class 1 customers. Implement some type of customer descriptor record so that arriving customers can be marked with their class and arrival time; instrument the model to compute and report the mean residence time for each class and for all customers. Run this model using the same simulation period as the model of Figure 1.7, and compare the values of W obtained for the combined classes with that obtained for the $M/M/1$ queue with first-come, first-served queueing.

3. A simple timesharing system model. A timesharing system (problem 4, Chapter 1) has 16 user terminals connected to a computer system with two identical disks. Figure 2.6 shows a queueing diagram of this system. Workload characteristics are the same for all 16 users; user think times have a negative exponential distribution with a mean think time Z of 5 seconds.

Processing of a terminal request requires a mean CPU time of 480 milliseconds (ms.) and an average of 12 disk requests. The mean CPU execution interval per disk request therefore is 40 ms. Inter-disk-request intervals are exponentially distributed. For modeling purposes, it can be assumed that, when a disk request completes, another CPU execution interval is initiated with probability px or terminal request processing is completed (and another think time initiated) with probability $1 - \mathrm{px}$. px is defined as $1 - 1/\mathrm{nio}$, where nio is the average number of disk requests per terminal request. (n io = 12, then, in this case.)

Disk requests are distributed randomly, independently, and uniformly across the two disks. The service time for a disk request is the sum of seek, latency, and transfer times; data is transferred in units of one block (or sector). Disks have a revolution time of 16.7 ms., a minimum seek time of 0 ms., a maximum seek time of 50 ms., and a transfer time of 0.52 ms. per block. While the mean seek time is not known, observation indicates that most seek times are in the vicinity of 16 ms., so it is assumed that the seek time distribution can be modeled by a triangular distribution with range [0, 50] ms. and mode 16 ms. (see problem 3, Chapter 1). Latency times are distributed uniformly in [0, 16.7] ms., and disk requests transfer one block of data.

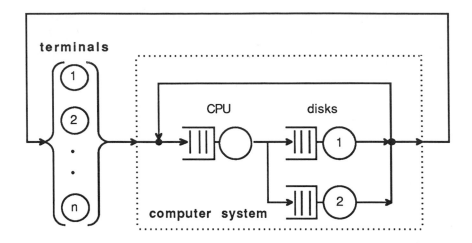

Figure 2.6 Timesharing System Queueing Diagram

Build a **smpl** model of this system, instrumenting the model to collect terminal request response times and to report the mean response time. All queues have first-in, first-out queueing. Make a simulation run of 2000 terminal requests and perform an operational check of the results, using utilizations and queue lengths from the **smpl** simulation report to verify the mean response time. Determine the mean number of terminal requests in the system.

4. Representing memory. The above model has no provision for representing the effect of memory capacity on response time. The simplest way to repre-sent memory is to assume that the system has a multiprogramming level (mpl) of m active users. When a terminal sends a request to the system, that request is accepted by the system and its execution initiated if the number of requests currently being executed is less than m; otherwise, the system queues the request until one of the m executing requests complete. Assume the system has a mpl of 6, and add memory queueing to your model. (One possibility is to represent memory as a facility with 6 servers.) Make a simulation run of 2000 terminal requests and perform an operational analysis of the results. Compute the response time components: memory waiting time, mean cpu residence time per terminal request, and mean disk residence time per terminal request. Compare the mean response time and mean number of requests in the system with those obtained for the model of problem 3.

5. Representing swapping. The work performed by a user at a terminal in this system involves a continuing series of interactions between the user and a program executing in the computer system. Each user interacts with a differ-ent program (or, equivalently,with a different instance of a common pro-gram). To execute, a program requires memory and certain logical resources which, collectively, are called an *address space*. It is assumed that the multiprogramming level, or mpl, specifies the number of address spaces in the computer system.

The program assigned to a given address space is said to be resident. Resident programs have two states: active and dormant. A program is active while executing and dormant when it has completed execution and returned a response to the terminal. When the system receives a terminal request, it determines if the user's program is resident. If it is, the program is scheduled for execution. If it is not, and there is an address space containing a dormant program, the system *swaps out* the dormant program to disk and *swaps in* the requested program to that address space.

Extend the model of problem 4 to represent swapping, based on the following assumptions. The computer system has 6 address spaces. (These can be represented by a facility with 6 servers; a server is reserved when the program in an address space becomes active and released when the program becomes dormant.) When a terminal request arrives for a non-resident program and all address spaces contain active programs, the request is queued until one of these programs becomes dormant and an address space can be assigned to the request. The system then swaps out the dormant program and swaps in the program being activated. If a request for a non-resident program finds several address spaces with dormant programs, it swaps out the program which has been dormant the longest.

The number of disk blocks transferred by a swapout is assumed to be distributed uniformly between 30 and 60. The system chooses a swapout des-tination disk at random; if the chosen disk is busy, the swapout is assigned to the other disk regardless of that disk's status. The number of blocks and source disk for a program's swapin are established when the program is swapped out. The operating system serializes swap operations so that only one swap, in or out, is in progress at any one time by placing swapout and swapin requests on a FIFO queue. (A smpl facility can be used to represent this queue.) If a terminal request arrives to find its program being swapped out to accommodate an earlier arrival, the swapout is allowed to complete. If an address space is available, it is assigned to the newly-arrived request and a swapout initiated for the dormant program in that address space. Since swaps are serialized, the swapin of the program for this request will not be initiated until its swapout completes.

Make a simulation run of 2000 terminal requests. Compute the response time components as before (keep in mind that swap queue delays and disk transfers for swapouts do not contribute to the response time except when a program swapin has to wait on its own swapout).

6. Incorporating CPU scheduling. Suppose terminal requests are classified, more or less arbitrarily, as class 0 or class 1, depending on whether their CPU time requirements are less than or greater than 250 ms. Instrument the model of problem 5 to report response times by class, as well as the overall response time.

a. Some systems use round-robin (RR) CPU scheduling so that a request for a small amount of CPU time will not be disproportionally delayed by execution of a request requiring a large amount of CPU time. With RR scheduling, the CPU is cyclically allocated to the requests in the CPU queue. Each request, in turn, receives CPU service for a fixed *quantum* of time (or for the time remaining in its current execution interval, if smaller than a quantum). Incorporate RR scheduling in the model of problem 5, using a quantum time of 25 ms. Simulate 2000 terminal requests. Compare the results with those obtained in problem 5. What effect did the incorporation of RR scheduling have? Why?

Note that if your version of **smpl** uses 16-bit `ints`, the large number of CPU operations required in simulating this system with RR scheduling will cause some counters associated with the CPU facility to overflow, so that some reported CPU measures will be meaningless. To circumvent this, generate a simulation report and reset **smpl** after every 32767 CPU releases, and merge the reports by hand at the end of the run. Alternatively, use the U( ), B( ), and Lq( ) functions to get facility measures after every 32767 CPU releases, and write a function to merge and report these measures.

b. Suppose the system attempts to favor class 0 requests by computing CPU request priority based on accumulated CPU time as follows:

$$\text{priority} = \max(0, 10 - \lfloor 0.01 * \text{accumulated CPU time} \rfloor)$$

where $\lfloor x \rfloor$ denotes the floor function of x — the largest integer equal to or less than x. Thus, a request is assigned a priority of 10 upon arrival, and its priority is reduced by 1 whenever it accumulates another 100 ms. of CPU time until it has been reduced to 0. Incorporate this scheduling algorithm into the model of problem 5 (no RR scheduling) and simulate 2000 terminal requests. Compare the mean response time of class 0 requests with that obtained without priority scheduling. What can be done to improve the response time of class 0 requests? How would you model the proposed improvement?

3. Model Development and Testing

3.1 The Modeling and Analysis Process

This and the following chapter discuss the steps involved in developing and using a simulation model. The key step in this process is that of abstracting a system design into a model design. No amount of discussion of this task can take the place of experience, and even the experienced modeler finds new challenges in each new system. The sooner you translate your interest in simulation into experience, the better! It is useful to spend some time building simulation models of queueing systems with known analytic solutions to become familiar with **smpl**, to develop simulation programming skills, and to gain experience with the output analysis methods discussed in the next chapter. To develop skills in abstracting from system design to model, though, requires working with an actual system. It is best to begin with an existing system with which you're familiar, and for which data can be obtained for workload characterization and model validation. Start with a simple model: if possible, select a modest subsystem that can be isolated from the rest of the system. Picking a modeling subject in advance of reading this chapter will help establish a context for the discussion which follows.

The modeling and analysis process is outlined in Figure 3.1. (The nice linear flow shown in this figure rarely happens in practice; we'll usually go through several iterations of parts of this process.) The process can be divided into three phases: development, testing, and analysis. This chapter is concerned with the development and testing phases.

The first step in development is describing system operation from a performance viewpoint. This description then is abstracted, in accordance with the objectives of the analysis, into a model description. This specifies the facilities to be represented in the model and their interconnection, the work to be represented and its attributes, and the operations involved in

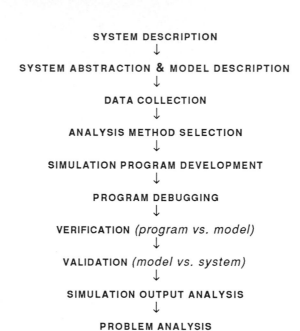

Figure 3.1. The Modeling and Analysis Process

accomplishing this work. The level of the detail of the model determines the data to be collected. Next, the appropriate analysis method is chosen, and a model implementation is developed. We'll assume this takes the form of a simulation program; alternatively, it could involve translating the model design and data to input parameters for a queueing network analysis package.

The testing phase comprises three steps: debugging, verification, and validation. All too often, the simulation program is considered to be de-bugged when it runs to completion without errors and produces "reasonable" results: single-server facility utilizations are between 0 and 1, and so on. Verification insures that the simulation program is indeed an implementa-tion of the model. Validation insures that the model is a reasonable representation of the real system.

3.2 System Description

We've generally assumed that the designer and modeler are the same person. When they are different persons, the modeler's first task is learning how the system works and describing its operation from a performance view-point; this description provides the basis for developing a model. The modeler relies on the designer to provide the knowledge needed. If the two fail to communicate, the analysis effort is, at best, a waste of time; at worst, it can result in bad design decisions. Communication problems can be both technical and inter-personal.

Effective technical communication places responsibilities on both design-er and modeler. The designer has a broad view of the system: the modeler, a narrow one. However, the modeler has to learn enough about the design to determine what aspects are critical to its performance and must be included in the model. The designer and modeler are mutually responsible for the latter's education. The modeler needs to gain both a working knowledge of the overall design and a detailed understanding of the part of the system to be modeled. He has to understand this part in more detail than he plans to model it. The designer has a continuing responsibility for answering questions about design details; because the modeler's view differs from the designer's, these questions may cut across design levels and modules. The modeler needs to explain to the designer what analysis results can be expect-ed, why particular questions are being asked, and how the answers will be used. The design may be incomplete (for reasons motivating the analysis in the first place), and designer and modeler need to work together to develop the assumptions needed to carry out the analysis.

The learning process is difficult enough when designer and modeler have a good working relationship; it becomes almost impossible if there are inter-personal difficulties. Rightly or wrongly, the burden of avoiding usually these falls on the modeler. At the start, he has to show that he has assimilated all available information on the design project and avoid asking questions any dumber (from the designer's viewpoint) than necessary. Notes of answers to questions should be kept, so questions don't get asked twice. The modeler has to work to establish rapport with the designer and demonstrate the ability to contribute to the design. He has to be very clear about what he can and cannot do; otherwise, the first mistake will destroy his credibility. Above all, the modeler has to be sensitive about publicizing results; broadcasting performance problems is certain to harm future communication.

The knowledge the modeler gains in this learning process is an abstrac-tion of the design, a model in its own way, and reflects a number of assump-tions, some explicit, some implicit. The modeler's view of how the system operates should be documented, this system description reviewed by the designer, and any appropriate revisions made. When the designer agrees with the description, it becomes an informal contract between designer and modeler. The designer usually will let the modeler know when design changes affect this description, and will readily accept results from models based on it. The time spent in organizing and writing this description will be more than compensated for by the errors it eliminates. The form of this description depends on the type and scope of the system being modeled; it may be nothing more than a one-page flow diagram.

3.3 System Abstraction and Model Description

A model is an abstraction of a system, and represents a particular view of that system. Models frequently are described in terms of the method used to obtain performance measures: analytic model, simulation model, measurement model. (The last describes taking a certain level of view of actual system operation and collecting data at that level.) At this point in the modeling and analysis process, we want to develop a representation of the system which captures its essential performance-determining characteristics. We should not develop this representation with a particular analysis method in mind; if we do, we can easily and unconsciously introduce invalid assumptions. What we want to do is describe what is to be represented in the model: choosing an analysis method comes later.

A model description of a simple system typically takes the form of a diagram showing system resources (both hardware and software) and their interconnection, annotated to show the flow of work through the system and the operations involved, and accompanied by explanatory notes and descriptions of assumptions. It identifies decisions and timings dependent on attributes of work as well as timings dependent only on the system design. For complex systems, multiple levels of diagrams may be used to show the configuration, and flow charts or psuedo-programs used to describe processing operations. Its style depends on the design background of the modeler (hardware or software) and on his analysis orientation (e.g., queueing networks); the way in which it is developed depends on how the abstraction process is approached.

There are no formal rules for abstracting a system design into a model description. Our simulation texts are no help in this area, and our performance texts don't offer much more. Approaches differ from problem to problem (and person to person), but basically either employ synthesis or decomposition.

Synthesis. Synthesis begins at the level of the design description. To form a higher-level description, elements of the system are combined (or perhaps just ignored), and associated activities are correspondingly combined and simplified. In making each simplification, we need to ask ourselves if and how we've preserved the essential underlying characteristics. Have we adjusted the processing time of the higher-level activity? If we've combined resources, have we properly accounted for delay times? What is the possible impact on the distribution of processing times? Each simplifying assumption should be recorded; those which make us nervous should be marked for later investigation. The synthesis process may take several steps, each creating a higher level of description. When the desired level of detail is reached, we should review all the assumptions made and assess their probable impact on the results of the analysis. If the net effect is likely to be optimistic (or pessimistic), now is the time to make a note of it; it's easy to lose sight of it in later stages.

Decomposition. Decomposition is the reverse of synthesis. The system initially is viewed as a single entity, its work viewed at the highest level (computer system, job; disk subsystem, request; LAN, message). Work is decomposed into its principal activities, the system into the set of resources used by these activities; this process is repeated through increasing levels of detail until the desired level is reached. In decomposition, we start with very general assumptions and refine them in advancing from one level of detail to the next. We may be less at ease with some of these than equivalent assumptions arrived at by synthesis: the step-by-step construction of the latter seems a stronger basis. On the other hand, we may feel that decomposition provides a better overall representation; we can always add detail if we're in doubt. Again, we need to note our assumptions and estimate how they might bias the results. In either approach, the strongest assumptions probably will be very much the same, and will involve describing work.

Which approach should you choose? Sometimes you won't have a choice: it'll be dictated by the design approach. Sometimes a synthesis approach seems obvious because of your knowledge of the system; at other times, the workload data available determines the approach. Large systems are best approached via decomposition. If the choice seems open, use decomposition: it is better to begin at a high level of abstraction and add detail later than to begin with too much detail.

There are several advantages to an iterative decompositional approach in which a series of models, each of increased detail, is developed and analyzed. It is easier to uncover cause-effect relationships in higher-level models than in very detailed ones; this may shorten the analysis effort. A higher-level model is useful in verifying a lower-level model; a high-level analytic model can be the principal means of verifying a lower-level simulation model. Hierarchical development of a model blends nicely with a stepwise refinement approach to simulation program development.

Maintaining a roughly uniform level of detail at any given level of description supports a hierarchical development of the model. However, the final model may reflect several levels of detail, particularly when the analysis focuses on a particular subsystem. This target subsystem is represented at the level of detail needed to satisfy analysis objectives; other subsystems are modeled primarily to establish an operating point for this subsystem, and can be represented in less detail.

One last note. There are two ways we can view a system and its work: we can view work as operating on the system, or we can view the system as operating on the work. In high-level models, we usually take the first view. For example, in a high-level model of a computer system, we think of jobs or tasks as reserving and releasing facilities and allocating and deallocating memory. The system is viewed only in terms of static entities; its dynamic components — operating system processes, in this example — are lumped together with the work, rather than explicitly represented. This is fine at a high level of abstraction, but there is a limit to its decomposition. If we try to carry it too far, we'll end up building one awkward construct after another, and we'll lose similitude between model and design. In developing a highly detailed model, it is better to take, at the very start, the view that the system operates on its work and explicitly represent the dynamic entities, as well as the static entities, of the system.

3.4 Data Collection

When development of the model description is complete, we'll have a good idea of the kind and level of detail of data we need to "drive" the model. The next task is to list the model parameters which have to be specified numerically and determine their values. These parameters can be categorized as workload parameters (such as inter-arrival times, execution times, storage requirements, record types and lengths) and system parameters (usually timings for various operations, such as the memory cycle time). A parameter may have a single fixed value, or it may have to be specified in terms of the distribution of its values.

It's useful to start by determining values of system timing parameters; the requisite analysis of the system may show that some of these are functions of workload parameters and result in additions to our list. When modeling an existing system, it may be possible to measure parameters either directly (via hardware or software instrumentation) or indirectly (via regression analysis). When modeling a design, parameter values will have to be estimated (they are rarely over-estimated).

Determining values of workload parameters and, in particular, specify-ing distributions, is the hardest part of the analysis process. Measurement and characterization of actual system workloads can provide values directly to the analysis of existing system, and can provide a basis for estimating values for use in analyzing new systems. Workload characterization is a subject in its own right and outside the scope of this book; unfortunately, it also seems to be outside the scope of most performance evaluation books. The best single reference on computer system workload characterization (at the job or task level of view) is Ferrari et al [1978]; the methods and consider-ations discussed in this book can be applied in other subject areas. Ferrari's earlier book [Ferrari 1978] also is useful. A review of conference proceedings and technical periodicals in your area of interest may turn up some useful information, although papers on workload characterization are an order of magnitude less frequent than papers on analysis. The subject doesn't lack importance — it just has a high work to glory ratio.

It is difficult to carry out a workload characterization study of a particular environment, and extremely difficult to study a range of environ-ments. The difficulties increase with the level of detail with which the system is viewed. In undertaking a study, we'll often find that existing measurement tools are inadequate, and that collection of the data we need requires adding instrumentation to the system. This may not be possible; even when it is, the added overhead or added risk may limit its use so that studying a range of environments is impossible. The data that we do collect can present a variety of analysis challenges, and it is difficult to sub-stantiate any claims of representativeness. The difficulties in doing a good job of workload characterization aren't an excuse for its circumvention, but rather emphasize the need to allocate adequate resources and time to it in planning performance studies.

While there is no substitute for the insights gained from studying actual system behavior, blind use of measurement data — because it's "real" — can create a false sense of confidence in the analysis and its results. We need to be careful first in extrapolating from the measurement environment to the analysis environment and second in drawing conclusions about results. In working with real systems, it is very hard, and frequently impossible, to demonstrate that a design performs as desired: the universe of work is too large to fully explore. However, it only takes one data point in that universe to demonstrate that a design doesn't perform. If an analysis based on workload measurements indicates a performance problem, we'll probably be very confident that the design doesn't work. However, if the analysis doesn't indicate a problem, we won't be equally confident that the design does work. The confidence we do have will be a direct reflection of our confidence in the workload characterization process.

We'll often have to undertake an analysis even though we have very little data to work with. If we can estimate a "reasonable" set of parameter values, and an analysis based on these values finds a problem, we've earned our keep. However, if it doesn't, we haven't proved anything; we'll have to estimate a range of values for each parameter, and carry out additional analyses. Because of the number of combinations of parameters, we may do sensitivity analyses to identify those which significantly effect results. Other tactics include specifying parameter values to obtain worst-case or best-case results. We may be able to arrive at reasonable assumptions about the means or ranges of parameter values. However, in the absence of insight from measurements, it is difficult to make equally reasonable assumptions about distributions. (Some of the considerations in choosing a distribution are discussed in Section 1.2.) The sensitivity of results to distributional assumptions can be analyzed, but the number of data points involved limits how much of this can be done. Often all we can do is worry -- with justification.

Shortage of data provides added motivation for an iterative approach to the modeling and analysis process. There's not much point in refining model assumptions beyond those we have make about parameters. A higher-level model requires fewer (although broader) assumptions than a more detailed model. If we do find a performance problem using a higher-level model, we've saved development effort. If we don't, a higher-level model, particularly one that can be evaluated analytically, speeds sensitivity analyses.

As we collect data and specify the values of the parameters on our list, we should make careful notes of the assumptions made. Using these assumptions, we may be able to derive an exact analytic result for our model or, if we use simulation, provide a tight confidence interval for a result. In either case, "exactness" of results doesn't compensate for looseness of assumptions — something we need to remember when we print our results to three decimal places!

3.5 Analysis Method Selection

The choice of an analysis method is based in part on the required system and data representations, and in part on our tools and skills. We always should try arithmetic first; if an operational analysis shows that some facility is 110% busy, we don't need to carry the analysis further. In some cases, we can estimate performance bounds; if the lower bound on response time exceeds our design goal, we're done with the analysis for the time being.[1] When further analysis is needed, the model description is translated into an analytic model or a simulation model.

Analytic versus simulation methods. In following the technical literature on performance evaluation, you'll come across this comparison now and again. The phrasing may lead you to believe that, as a simulation modeler, you are lacking in purity and grace. In doing performance analysis in a real-world design environment, what counts is function, not form. The best method is arithmetic: beyond that, the choice depends on your particular skills and how effective you are in applying them. Successful performance analysis uses both methods, and uses them together. Only fools and angels don't check analytic results against simulation. Simulation models are used as submodels of analytic models, and conversely, in hybrid modeling, and analytic models can be used in simulation model verification.

Choosing a method. We'll always choose an analytic model when one exists that fits our model description, even when the next iteration in model development requires simulation, because of its solution speed and because we can use it in verifying the simulation model. We may be able to use a commercial queueing network analysis package. (However, the assumptions and approximations used in these packages may not be documented, and we need to be careful in trying to use them outside their intended application range.) If an appropriate analytic model does not exist, we may develop one if time and skill permit, or perhaps we can adapt a model found in the technical literature.

The choice frequently is one of either making further simplifying assumptions in order to use an analytic model or developing a simulation model. If the analytic approach doesn't require a lot of effort, we'll go ahead with it in any case; it may identify a performance problem, and we can use the results in simulation model verification. Deciding whether or not to develop a simulation model depends on how critical we think these assumptions are and on the effort required. If the effort is modest, we'll develop the simulation model anyway and use it to check the analytic results as well as the effects of the additional assumptions.

---

[1]Lazowska et al [1984] describe computation of performance bounds for batch-, terminal-, and transaction-oriented computer systems; their approach can be adapted to other problem contexts. Stuck and Arthurs [1985] give numerous examples of performance bounds estimation.

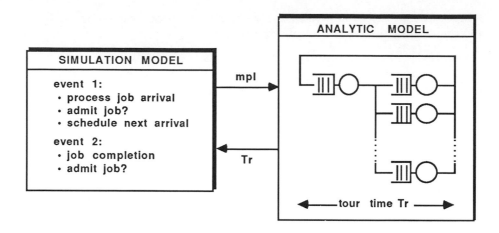

Figure 3.2. Simulation and Analytic Components of the Hybrid Model

3.6 Hybrid Modeling

Hybrid modeling combines analytic and simulation modeling. It is particularly useful when a model represents processes whose execution rates differ by orders of magnitude. A common example is a model of job execution in a computer system, where each job may execute from tens to thousands of IO requests. An analysis of job performance might require simulation of several thousand jobs to achieve the desired level of confidence; this would necessitate simulating hundreds of thousands of disk requests, and the resulting computational cost would be prohibitive. Schwetman [1978] and Chiu and Chow [1978] solve this problem via a hybrid modeling approach. A simulation model is used to generate job arrivals and make job-level scheduling decisions; a queueing network model is used to determine how long each job executes. To examine their approach, we'll look at a simple hybrid model of computer system job scheduling.

The objective of this model is assumed to be the evaluation of a scheduling policy which, on the basis of a job's memory requirements, determines when to admit a job into execution. The simulation and analytic model components of this hybrid model are illustrated in Figure 3.2. The simulation model operates only at the job level, and represents just two events: job arrivals and job completions. The analytic model (in this example, a simple central server model) represents the compute and disk activities of active jobs.

arrival event routine
- generate job attributes:
    - ... memory requirements
    - ... no. of tours (Nt)
- job -> admission queue
- schedule next arrival
- call **job_schedlr**
- cause next event

job_schedlr function
- return if no job satisfies admission rules
- call **update**
- dequeue & activate selected job
- mpl+=1
- cancel currently-scheduled completion
- call **next_completion**
- return

update function
- call **solve** to compute mean tour time (Tr)
- compute mean no. of tours completed since last update (n)
- decrement tour counts (Nt) of all active jobs by n
- return

next_completion function
- find active job (job i) with smallest no. of tours
- call **solve** to compute mean tour time Tr
- schedule job i completion: te = Nt(i)*Tr
- return

completion event routine
- call **update**
- deactivate job, accumulate job performance measures
- mpl-=1
- call **next_completion**
- call **job_schedlr**
- cause next event

Figure 3.3. Hybrid Model Event Routines and Simulation Functions

The simulation model generates arrivals, determines when a job is to be admitted into execution, computes job completion times, schedules job completions, and accumulates performance measurement data when jobs complete. It computes the next job completion time by finding the job with the smallest number of CPU-disk tours remaining, invokes the analytic model to determine the mean tour time, and computes how long that number of tours will take. To compute the mean tour time, the analytic model requires mean CPU and disk service times, disk routing probabilities, and the number of jobs executing (i.e., the multiprogramming level, or mpl). For simplicity, we'll assume that mean service times and routing probabilities are the same for all jobs and are established when the model is initialized. Consequently, the analytic model only needs the current mpl to compute the mean tour time. Note that, if desired, we could change the service times and routing probabilities of the set of active jobs as jobs enter and complete execution.

The event routines and functions of the simulation model component are outlined in Figure 3.3. **arrival** is caused when a job arrival events occurs. It generates the attributes of the job, enters the job in the admission queue, schedules arrival of the next job, and calls the job scheduling function to determine if the job can be admitted to execution. One of the attributes generated for a job is the number of CPU-disk tours to be executed.

The job scheduling function, **job_schedlr**, is called whenever a jobs arrives or leaves the system. It scans the admission queue for a job which satisfies the rules of the admission policy. If such a job is found, **update** is called to update tour counts (since placing another job in execution will change the mean tour time). **update** calls the **solve** function to evaluate the analytic model and compute the mean tour time. The time elapsed since the last update is divided by the mean tour time to determine the mean number of tours completed since then, and the tour counts of the active jobs are decremented by that number. **job_schedlr** then dequeues and activates the selected job and increments the multiprogramming level. Increasing the number of jobs in execution will affect tour times, making the scheduled next job completion event invalid, so it is cancelled (it also is possible that the newly-activated job may complete execution before any other job). The **next_completion** function is called to schedule the next completion. Although not shown in the outline of Figure 3.3, the scheduling function should go on to try to activate additional jobs, since completion of one job might free enough memory space to permit several jobs to enter execution.

The **next_completion** function scans the set of active jobs to find the one with the smallest number of tours remaining. It invokes the analytic model to determine the mean tour time, computes the remaining execution time for that job by multiplying the number of tours by the mean tour time, and schedules completion of that job.

The **completion** event routine is "caused" when a job completion event occurs. It updates tour counts, deactivates the completed job (i.e., deallocates its job descriptor table entry), and accumulates job performance measures, such as the time spent in the system. It calls **next_completion** to schedule the next job completion, and calls the job scheduling function to see if jobs in the admission queue can now be activated.

Job measures such as the mean system residence time and the mean number of jobs in the system are computed using the methods described in Sections 1.4 and 1.5. Performance measures for entities of the analytic model are computed by collecting measures for each inter-update interval and weighting them either by the relative interval length or relative number of operations in the interval. (As a practical exercise in applying operational analysis, try working out the computation of overall throughput, utilization, mean queue length, and mean residence time for the CPU.)

Hybrid modeling can provide substantial savings in computation time. In our example, there are only two events per job (ignoring cancelled events) and only two events in the event list at any time, so the simulation part is very fast. The analytic model has to be evaluated only on job activation and completion. The number of arithmetic operations required for its exact solution is proportional to the product of the multiprogramming level and the number of servers, and this should be small compared with the number required to simulate a job's disk requests. Even faster solutions can be obtained using approximation methods. Schwetman [1978] compared hybrid and simulation models of several systems, and reported CPU time improvement factors ranging from 18 to 200. The improvement for a particular model depends on the relative complexity of the analytic model and the simulation model it replaces.

Hybrid modeling is not applicable in every situation. The analytic model usually requires stronger assumptions than the simulation model it replaces, and this won't always be acceptable. The hybrid model discussed here adds the assumption that the use of mean, rather than actual, tour times does not significantly affect job residence times. This assumption is based on the notion of decomposability in the sense used by Courtois [1977] (alternatively, see Courtois [1975]). However, when the main functions of some parts of a model are to establish an operating point for or provide work to the key part of the model, the assumptions associated with these supporting parts often are less critical. In such cases, it may be possible to replace a set of simulation operations by an analytic function.

Given, for example, an analytic function for the distribution of operation times, we can use the distribution's inverse to generate random operation times. Sometimes a set of operations can be represented by a graph model whose parameters (execution times, branching probabilities) are determined by simulation. Rather than explicitly simulating these operations and scheduling each execution time, it may be possible to obtain the mean overall execution time and variance using analytic reduction methods (see Beizer 1978] or MacDougall [1975]). Depending on model assumptions, this mean can be used as the operation time, or the mean and variance can be used to generate a sample operation time from a distribution. Some before-hand experimentation is needed to determine the distribution's form.

Hybrid modeling is not discussed in any of the referenced simulation texts, and receives only limited notice in most performance evaluation texts. Most of the useful reference material has appeared in the form of technical conference and journal papers. Schwetman's work (cited earlier) provided much of the impetus for current work in this area. Chiu and Chow [1978] describe its application to a complex computer system model. Shanthikumar and Sargent [1983] divide hybrid models into four classes, discuss each class, and give several examples of hybrid modeling.. Blum et al [1984] present experimental comparisons of hybrid, analytic, and simulation models, and discuss advantages of and problems in decomposition. Thomasian and Gargeya [1984] describe a two-phase procedure for modeling a memory-constrained timesharing system with two customer classes. In the first phase, an analytic model is used to compute system throughputs for the possible combinations of customers; these throughputs are input parameters for the second phase, which uses a simulation model to estimate mean response times. O'Reilly and Hammond [1984] describe an approach to local area network modeling in which some stations in the network are represented individually via simulation while the remaining stations are represented collectively by an analytic model. This is not a complete list; other examples can be found by reviewing the technical literature in your area.

3.7 Simulation Program Development

Developing a simulation program is very much like any other program development task, although the quasi-concurrent nature of simulation program execution sometimes gives it an operating system flavor. The main considerations are

- simulation model design
- program organization

- parameter management

- debugging aids

- instrumentation

We'll discuss the first three topics in this section; debugging and instrumentation are discussed in later sections.

Simulation model design. After deciding upon simulation as the analysis method, the next step is to transform the model description into a simulation model design. This is — or at least should be — the first point in the modeling process at which the simulation language's view is imposed on the model. Our language is event-oriented, so the model design defines sequences of activities with their initiating and terminating events. However, if the model is complex, we should try to approximate a process-oriented view by developing separate definitions for different classes of processes (where a process can be a job, a task, or a request). This essentially involves defining a separate event-oriented model for each class and specifying any inter-model coordination required (in addition to that provided by facilities). In designing this model, we should try to maintain as much resemblance between it and the system design as is reasonable at the model's level of abstraction. (This similitude of model and system doesn't guarantee model validity, but is a great help in achieving it.) As we outline activity and event sequences, the data used at each step is identified and data structures developed for each process class. A manual simulation of the final design can help catch errors of omission.

Program organization. The next transformation is from model design to program design. The organization of the program depends on the complexity of the model. For simple models with few activities, the simulation program may look much like those of Figures 1.7 and 2.2 — a single procedure with events identified by number. For somewhat larger models, we'll probably use separate function procedures for each event routine and define events symbolically for easier program modification. For complex model designs, where we've defined separate models for each class of process, the program is organized as a set of submodels, each of which may comprise a set of function procedures. (There is a limit on how complex a model we should attempt using **smpl** or any other event-oriented language.) Some submodels may be combined at this point (perhaps just to reduce code volume) in which case their data structures have to be merged and modified.

Organizing the simulation program as a set of submodels representing different process classes is facilitated by **smpl**'s implicit queueing. Individual submodels can execute independently, performing any necessary coordination via operations on facilities. Explicit queueing would require that submodels operate directly on one another. In modeling process coordination mechanisms, **smpl** facilities can be used to represent such diverse entities as a hardware flip-flop controlling a buffering operation or an operating system semaphore. This representation range is somewhat limited by the inability to dynamically create and destroy facilities (although **smpl** could be extended to provide this).

The events defined in the simulation model design may be split or may be combined into simulation program event routines. An activity initiation event may have to be split into two event routines when it involves facility reservation, since a blocked facility request results in reexecution of the event routine which issued the request. Statements which should not be reexecuted, such as those selecting the facility to be reserved or the token involved in the operation, should be placed in a separate event routine (for the reasons discussed in Section 2.4).

When an event representing the end of one activity and an event representing the initiation of another activity occur at the same instant in simulation time, some code and execution time can be saved by combining both events in one event routine. There are several things to consider before doing this. If the event routine contains a facility request, reexecution of the routine following a blocked request will cause problems. When the two activities belong to logically different classes and the events coincide simply because one activity freed a resource needed by the other, the loss of structure resulting from combining event routines may not be worth the slight gain in efficiency. Even when the activities belong to the same class and are logically connected, debugging and expandability considerations may make separation of event routines worthwhile.

For complex models, a top-down iterative approach to simulation model development and programming is recommended. In this approach, the model is initially defined at a high level of abstraction, comprising a small number of macroscopic activities, perhaps defined only in terms of their execution times. The level of detail of the model and the program are advanced in a series of steps. At each step, (only) one activity of the model is refined into a more detailed representation, and the simulation program is revised, debugged, and verified at this new level of detail. At any point in model development, the simulation program is executable and verifiable; each advance in the level of detail can be checked against the preceding level.

Parameter management. Assigning values to model parameters is one of the more tedious aspects of simulation program development. We have to decide which parameters we want to assign values to from outside the program (i.e., at run time) and which will be assigned values within the program (at compile time). Usually we will considerably under-estimate the number of parameters we'll want to vary at run time.

There is one commandment for specifying parameters within the program: don't "hardwire" numeric values in the code. If we do, we'll inevitably have to change them and, with equal inevitability, we'll miss one. The C macro facilities are very helpful in this regard, not only in defining simple symbolic constants but also in doing things like switching random variate sampling functions.

Simulation program size and use determine how much effort to expend in developing capabilities for run time input of parameter values. A large number of parameters, or program use by other than the developer, justify a certain amount of sophistication in the way of an input language as well as some error checking. The development effort required can be surprising. In some large simulation programs, one-third of the code is input processing, one-third is report generation, and a modest one-third represents the model itself. However, even the smallest model is much more convenient to use if an input processor is provided, and we might as well implement it at the start, rather than waiting until we get tired of recompiling. SMPL provides facilities for defining and labeling input and output parameters, assigning input parameter values either from the simulation program or from a display, and reporting output parameter values (see Chapter 7). These facilities, although simple, have proved to be very useful.

Defining values of compile-time parameters and providing input facilities for specifying values of run-time parameters doesn't completely solve the parameter management problem; we also need to tabulate parameter values as part of model output. If we don't, we'll frequently find ourselves staring at a simulation report and wondering under what conditions the results were obtained.

3.8 Simulation Program Debugging

Debugging is the task of getting the simulation program to the point where we thinks it works -- it runs without errors and the results it produces seem reasonable. Verification is the task of proving, as best we can, that the program is a valid implementation of the model.

The tools used in simulation program debugging are the traditional ones: error diagnostics, traces, dumps, and reports, all blended with a judicious sprinkling of print statements. smpl error messages, traces, and reports were described in Chapter 2. SMPL adds a dump capability which shows the contents of the event list and queues, and the status and users of each facility.

You may want to add a similar capability to your version of smpl (an example appears in Chapter 7).

For small models, the standard smpl debugging aids, perhaps supple-mented by user trace messages and print statements, usually are adequate. Large models should have trace, dump, and other debugging aids designed into the program from the start. These should provide a logical view of model operation. To control the volume of output, they should provide selectable levels of detail for selectable parts of the model. Particular attention should be given to model data structures: errors often occur in the dynamic allocation and deallocation of token attribute records, particularly in the management of associated indexes and pointers.

The procedure outlined below has proven to be efficient in the early stages of program debugging.

1. On the first successful compilation of the program, try executing it. Maybe it will run the first time out; in any event, we need get the notion out of our system!

2. Set up the simulation program to execute a single token, turn tracing on, and trace the execution of this token. Review the trace data and the simulation report to determine if the program executed correctly. It should be straightforward to locate any problems.

3. Now revise the setup to execute two tokens sequentially (so that execution of the second token can't begin until execution of the first token completes), and again trace and review token execution. The objective is to find problems left behind by the first token, such as facilities that didn't get released, data elements that didn't get deallocated, and so on. Printing values of pointers and indexes can help identify problems.

4. Revise the program once again to execute two tokens concurrently, trace token execution, and look for problems in the interaction of the two tokens. It may be necessary to initiate execution of the two tokens at the same time to insure that queueing, preemption, or other resource conflicts occur. Verify the flow of each token from event to event: problems in event routine organization, such as unplanned reexecution of statements, often show up as breaks in this flow.

5. Expand on this controlled execution process if the model is complex. For example, the program can be modified to direct tokens along specific execution paths, or to examine limit conditions such as communication network node blocking on a packet limit. Sometimes

the process can be simplified by isolating submodels (or simply sections of the model) and driving them independently.

6. When selective execution no longer turns up errors, try full execution of a modest number of tokens. Watch the trace awhile to see if queues build up because facilities aren't getting released. If a simulation error occurs, note the time of its occurrence. Add an event routine to the simulation program to turn tracing on, and schedule this event to occur some time earlier than the error. (With **SMPL**, this can be done by setting breakpoints from the keyboard.) How much earlier is a matter of guesswork: cause and effect may be widely separated in time. The errors initially found at this step frequently are caused by "end game" problems: conditions reached for the first time in program execution, such as allocation of the last element in a free element list.

7. When the model runs to completion without errors, review the simulation report. Look at utilizations, queue lengths, and distributions of requests across facilities to see if the values make sense intuitively and if they are consistent in an operational analysis sense. In some cases (e.g., more than one token class), this analysis may require adding instrumentation on the simulation program. If the results are operationally correct but counter-intuitive, find out why: there may be an error in service time computation or an unanticipated (but perhaps valid) delay situation.

In the personal computer arena, several C tools are available which could be used to advantage in simulation program debugging; these include debugging environments and C language interpreters. Another tool which has been occasionally useful in debugging is the **SMPL** time series display (see Chapter 6). This display can be used to plot facility utilization, instantaneous or average queue length, or an specified parameter value, versus time. When things go awry at some point during execution without an error being detected, the effects sometimes can be seen in the queue length display.

3.9 Verification

When the program produces reasonable results, debugging can be considered complete (at least until a parameter change or use of a different random number stream turns up another error), and we can turn our attention to the next problem: verifying that the simulation program is a valid implementation of the model. For small models, this may be obvious from inspection; for larger models, some substantiating analysis is needed.

At a minimum, verification requires a comparative "walkthrough" of the model description and the simulation program. Sometimes this is all that is feasible, and success of the analysis effort depends on how diligently it is done. However, additional verification via comparison with analytic models often is possible. The simulation program is modified to represent a model for which analytic results can be obtained, and the simulation and analytic results are compared. This *analytic verification* does not, of course, guarantee that the program matches the model. However, it does provide a way to eliminate errors in at least part of the modeling process. If analytic verification is successful, then any remaining errors are either in transforming the model description to a model design or extending assumptions from the analytic model to the simulation model.

A careful review is the only means of verifying the transformation of model description to model design; however, since analytic verification involves both simulation and analytic model design, it provides some cross-checking. The extensions from analytic model to simulation model (suppressed for verification) may take various forms, including distributional assumptions, added level of detail, queueing disciplines, and token classes and priorities. Although it may not be possible to analytically verify these extensions in the context of the complete model, it may be possible to isolate parts of the model and verify them independently. Sometimes a subsection of a closed system model can be verified by isolating it and treating it as an open system model, adding the necessary event routines to generate arrivals and handle departures. In any case, extensions should be informally checked as part of the process of returning the simulation program to its original form. We'll often have some idea of what the effect of a changed assumption should be, and can at least check to see that results change as expected. For example, if we changed a distribution from hyperexponential to exponential for purposes of verification, we would usually expect to see queueing increase when the distribution was restored to a hyperexponential one. If we isolated part of the model and verified that part in an open system, we would expect its queueing delays to decrease when it becomes part of a closed system with a finite number of customers.

The work involved in analytic verification can be reduced substantially by planning for it at the start -- providing parameters to control extensions, and developing, debugging, and verifying the model hierarchically. The only hazard in this is a tendency to bias model development toward verification, rather than application.

Where do we find analytic models to use in verification? For a variety of single-queue, single- and multi-server open queueing systems, closed-form expressions for expected values of parameters such as mean queue length and residence time can be found in several of the referenced texts, in particular, Allen [1978] and Kleinrock [1975]. Less extensive coverage appears in Banks and Carson [1984], Kobayashi [1978], and Trivedi [1982]. Both Allen and Kobayashi present results for the simplest closed queueing system, the machine repair model. A simple algorithm for solution of central server queueing systems was devised by Buzen [1973]; these systems are discussed in Kobayashi, Trivedi, and several other texts. Ferrari [1983] provides a comprehensive discussion of Buzen's algorithm, including load-dependent servers, and includes a Fortran implementation of a central server model for computer system analysis. However, the central server model is just a particular form of queueing network; algorithms for the solution of more general network forms are available. Lazowska et al [1984] provide Fortran programs for the solution of single job class and multiple job class networks. These are useful in their own right for the task we're considering here; using the techniques and algorithms described by Lazowska et al, these programs can be tailored and extended as required in a particular application environment, and are useful in analysis as well as verification. Finally, in addition to general analytic models, specific analytic models from the technical literature can be useful in verification, particularly when they have been validated.

The results obtained from simulation rarely, if ever, will agree exactly with those obtained analytically. Simulation is a sampling process; in a simulation experiment, we generate a large number of sample values and use the sample mean as an estimate of the actual mean. Consequently, some difference between simulation and analytic results can result from sampling variation. If this difference is small, we may not worry about it. Alternatively, we can carry the analysis further: collect additional data, compute confidence limits for the simulation estimate, and determine if these limits include the analytic result. (This output analysis process is discussed in the next chapter.) For reasons discussed in the next section, we should not expect to see comparable percentage differences for all measures.

Another possible source of variation between analytic and simulation results is approximations used in the analytic model. If the analytic model is one we've developed ourselves, we are at least aware that approximations are used, and we may be able to "back off" to an exact solution. If we're using a queueing analysis package of some kind, result variations can be hard to interpret. Package solution methods and use of approximations often are considered proprietary and are not documented. (However, problems usually arise only when the package is used differently than intended.)

3.10 Validation

Validation is the task of demonstrating that the simulation model is a reasonable representation of the actual system: it reproduces system behavior with enough fidelity to satisfy analysis objectives. The question of how much is enough can be answered only in terms of these objectives and perhaps the results obtained in the current iteration of the analysis process. For example, demonstrating that a model tracks real-system trends may be sufficient in a comparative analysis in which one alternative significantly outperforms the other. On the other hand, when a critical system parameter must be estimated within a few percent, the simulation model must be demonstrably capable of providing that accuracy. The simulation model usually is developed to analyze a particular problem and may represent different parts of the system at different levels of detail. The model doesn't have to be equally valid for all parts of the system over the full spectrum of system behavior; it just has to meet the requirements of the problem.

The subject of validation gets terse treatment in our simulation texts. Of these, Banks and Carson [1984] provide the best coverage, followed by Law and Kelton [1982]. The discussion and references in Sargent [1984] provide a good starting point for reviewing the literature. Balci and Sargent [1982] provide a bibliography indexed by validation technique and by the statistical technique used to compare measurement data and model results. Schatzoff and Tillman [1975] and Teorey [1975] describe validations of computer system simulation models. Schatzoff and Tillman illustrate the use of experiment design methods and probability plots in simulation model validation; Teorey presents a procedure for validation and illustrates it by application to an IO subsystem model.

For purposes of this discussion, there are two different cases of validation to consider. In the first case, the system being modeled exists and can be measured, the analysis objective is to evaluate a proposed change to the system, and validation is based on comparison of model results with measurements. In the second case, the system being modeled exists only as a design, and the analysis objective is to estimate performance of the design or perhaps to evaluate alternative designs; little or no comparative data exists, and validation mostly is a matter of design-model comparison.

Validation of models of existing systems. In this case, measurements of the existing system are compared with results from a simulation of the existing system; if they agree, it is assumed that a simulation of the modified system will produce valid estimates of the effects of the proposed change. It all sounds so simple! The only problems are measurement, comparison, and extrapolation.

Collecting system performance measures for use in validation ideally is done when collecting workload characterization data. Conceptually, we want to collect workload data over some period of operation, collect system performance measures over that same period, drive the simulation model with the workload data, and compare model results with measurements. Practically, this can be hard to do. Measurement tool limitations can make it difficult to match workload and performance data: for example, work in execution at the beginning and end of the measurement period may not be properly accounted for, and lengthening the measurement period is not always a solution. Available performance measures may be incomplete, inconsistent or overlapping, and not at the desired level of detail.

A number of measurement problems can be avoided or at least identified in advance by developing a *measurement model* of the system. The measurement model is derived from the analysis model description. It defines the measurements and measurement points required for a complete description of system performance, in an operational analysis sense, at the desired level of detail. While it may not be feasible to instrument the system to provide these measures, this model provides a framework to evaluate and apply available measurements. The objective is to try to match these measurements to those defined in the measurement model, adjusting the measurement points defined in the model and the level of detail of parts of the model if necessary but maintaining completeness if at all possible. (The difficulties in doing this emphasize the need for something better than the usual ad hoc approach to the design of system measurement facilities.) The final version of the measurement model itself is validated by comparing aggregated workload data with traffic and utilization measures.

Once the measurement model has been developed, the simulation model's instrumentation should be revised or extended to report the same performance measures as the system. Measures can be reported in the form of means, means and variances, or distributions. While we can instrument the simulation model to provide any form, system measurement facilities often limit the forms in which measurement data can be reported. Because of both reporting limitations and statistical considerations, comparison of measurements and model results generally is based on mean values.

The only test we can apply to a comparison of mean values from *one* measurement period with means from *one* simulation run is a subjective one: how close are the values? Except for trace-driven models, the work performed by the simulated system and by the actual system are the same only in a statistical sense; differences in measurement and model values arise because of sampling variation as well as because of simplifying assumptions made in modeling. In a subjective comparison, we rely on our judgement to determine if the values are "close enough".

In making this comparison, we shouldn't expect the same percentage difference for all measures. To see why, consider an **M/M/1** queueing system. The mean number of customers in this system can be defined in terms of server utilization as follows:

$$L = U/(1 - U) \tag{3.1}$$

The percentage change in L, PL, resulting from a percentage change of Pu in U can be obtained via differentiation:

$$PL = Pu/(1 - U) \tag{3.2}$$

For example, at a base utilization of 0.5, a five percent change in utilization translates into a ten percent change in the mean number in the system. Consequently, a difference in measurement and model facility utilizations can result in a larger difference in measures such as queue length and response time, independent of all other effects. The magnifying factor of (3.2) applies only to the **M/M/1** queueing system. It will be smaller for some systems (e.g., systems with limited population or lower service time variance) and larger for other systems; in most practical cases it won't be explicitly known.

Other subjective validation methods include comparison of distributions. If measurement facilities permit reporting the distribution of values of, for example, system residence time, we can instrument the model to produce a corresponding distribution, and compare — by inspection — the two distributions. (A statistical comparison is not possible because the sample values forming these distributions are not independent.) If the tails seem significantly different, remember that they may represent only a few sample values. The **SMPL** table facility (see Chapter 9) can be used to collect, tabulate, and plot distributions of simulation data; it can also be adapted for use in post-measurement data reduction.

Statistical techniques for comparing measurement and simulation results are discussed in the references cited earlier in this section. In the simplest case, multiple simulation runs are made to obtain the sample mean and sample standard deviation for the simulation value, and a t test used to decide if the results are "close enough". This is easy to do and we often want to compute confidence intervals for simulation results anyway, as we'll discuss in the next chapter. In other cases, multiple sets of measurements are required, and the additional data collection effort can pose problems unless planned in advance.

We'd like to validate the model over a range of operating conditions broad enough to encompass the planned analysis. (Doubling the validation points from one to two will much more than double our confidence!) However, doing this — particularly collecting the required measurement data — can be costly. A formal method for analyzing experimental cost versus the risk of accepting an invalid model has been proposed by Balci and Sargent [1981], [1982]. While the method may be outside the scope of the studies envisioned here, the discussion of validation hypotheses is worth reviewing.

When the difference between measurements and simulation results is more than we're willing to accept (or able to rationalize), we face a chore called (euphemistically) model calibration. At some point in the modeling process, we made a mistake. Most often it will be one of omission and will result in model values being less than measured values. The problem may be an invalid simplifying assumption. This assumption may have been made implicitly, so — in addition to checking explicit model assumptions against the system — we need to review system operation to see if we've left something out. Close comparison of measurement and model data may provide some clues, as when queue lengths agree in one part of the system but not another; this can result in a quest for additional measurement data. Sometimes the problem is in data collection: for example, operating systems often provide inadequate and incomplete measurements of overhead time. In this case, the modeler is faced with the temptation to "calibrate" (diddle) the model by adjusting model input parameters to obtain output values which match the measurement data. (It is hard to throw the first stone here.) Trying to find out why measurements and model results don't agree can be very frustrating. It also can be very rewarding, because it frequently provides new insights into system behavior.

When the model has been accepted as a valid representation, it is revised — very carefully — to represent the proposed change, and a new set of simulation results are obtained and compared with those for the existing system. Typically, the revised model uses the same set of workload parameters as the validated model; we assume that the workload is un-affected by the change. This assumption warrants examination: all systems are closed systems with feedback effects if we look far enough. Although we may have only been able to validate the original model at one or two points, we often want to compare outputs of the original and revised models over a range of input parameter values. Our confidence in the validity of analysis results depends on the extent of the difference between the original and revised systems, and will be higher for results obtained close to the validation points.

Validation of models of designs. When the system being modeled does not exist, validation primarily is done by review; the model is examined in terms of the system design, and each assumption and abstraction scrutinized and justified. This needs the involvement of other design team members as reviewers, critics, and contrarians; satisfying an expert audience is the best test of the validity of model design and of system timing value assumptions. Workload parameter values usually are determined by extrapolation from past systems. The design team's review of these usually is based on judgement and experience, rather than on the factual knowledge used to compare model and system designs: it may be helpful to augment their review with one by knowledgeable system users. Workload representative-ness always is a concern; when the objective of the analysis is an absolute prediction of the performance of the design, it is a key concern. When the objective of the analysis is a relative comparison of design alternatives, we may be able to satisfy it using workload parameters which are "reasonable", although not necessarily representative (see the discussion in Section 3.4).

Similitude between system design and model is a key factor in vali-dation. The more the model resembles the design, the more likely is it to be valid, and the easier it is for the reviewing designer to understand how the model represents the design. Similitude is one aspect of what our simulation texts refer to as "face validity". Correspondence of the simulation model to the system design is guaranteed by a synthesis of design specification and simulation model: "the simulation is the design" (Randell 1968]). Simulation/design synthesis is outside our scope: see MacDougall [1975] for a brief discussion and additional references.

The two cases of validation described here represent ends of a spectrum. A major change to an existing system presents much the same problem as a new system design. Our confidence in a model of a new design is increased if we can at least validate the approach with a similar model of an existing system. In practice, validation often is blended with verification. If com-parison of measurements and model results is successful, then the simulation program is assumed to be both a valid implementation of the model design and a valid representation of the system. In modeling a new design, comparisons of simulation program versus model design and of model design versus system design tend to be done concurrently.

The final step in validation takes place when the system change is made or the system design implemented, and predicted and actual performance can be compared. This, unfortunately, doesn't happen very often in practice. The final implementation may differ from the original design for reasons not related to performance, and, in any case, the modeler is busy with a new project and has little interest in auditing old work. In a system design environment, there seldom is much pressure to carry out validation studies; once the analysis has been done and the design decision made, alternatives are discarded and the system gets built. The model become of historical interest only, so few modelers ever pay for their sins. However, *you* will never *know* how good or bad your analysis was unless you validate its results by comparison with system measurements.

3.11 Problems

1. Estimating performance bounds sometimes eliminates the need for more elaborate analysis and, in any case, provides a way of determining that our simulation results are at least sensical. For a timesharing system such as that of problem 3, Chapter 2, Lazowska et al [1984] give *asymptotic* bounds for throughput and response time.[2] The validity of these bounds depends only on the assumption that the service time of one terminal request does not depend on the number or location of other requests.

Let D_k be the mean service demand (time) of a terminal request at server k. Define $D = \Sigma D_k$ as the sum of the service demands of a request for all K servers in the system, and define $D_{max} = \max(D_1, D_2, ..., D_K)$ as the largest service demand for any server. X, R, and Z denote the throughput, response time, and think time.

Consider throughput first. With a single terminal, there are no delays and the throughput is $1/(D+Z)$. With N terminals, the throughput is at best $N/(D+Z)$, assuming no request ever has to wait for another request. At worst, each request finds N–1 requests ahead of it, and and incurs a delay of $(N–1)D$, and the throughput is $N/(ND+Z)$. Since a (single) server cannot have a utilization of greater than 1, throughput is limited by the server with the largest service demand to $1/D_{max}$. The resulting bounds on X are shown in Figure 3.4(a).

The response time for a system with a single terminal is D. In the best case, no request ever is delayed by another, and the response time continues equal to D as N increases up to the point at which the utilization of the busiest server reaches 1. At this point and beyond, the throughput is limited to $1/D_{max}$ and, by the Response Time Law, the response time from this point on is $ND_{max} - Z$. In the worst case, each request has to wait a time $(N - 1)D$

---

[2]Another method of bounds analysis called *balanced system bounds* was developed by Zahorjan et al [1982], and is discussed by Lazowska et al . Balanced system bounds are "tighter" than asymptotic bounds, and so are more useful for checking simulation results. The discussion of bounds analysis in Chapter 5 of Lazowska et al is recommended reading.

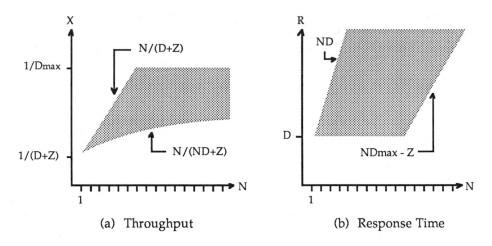

(a) Throughput   (b) Response Time

Figure 3.4 Asymptotic Bounds for a Timesharing System

for other requests and so has a response time of ND. Figure 3.4(b) shows the bounds on R.

Plot the throughput and response time bounds for the timesharing model of problem 3, Chapter 2 for N in the range 1 to 24. Locate the throughput and response time values obtained from simulation on this plot. Assume that the CPU in this system is replaced by a CPU of twice the speed, and plot response time bounds again.

2. The bounds described above can be applied to a "batch" system such as that of Figure 2.1 by setting Z to 0. Assume that, for any N, the proportion of class 0 and class 1 tasks is the same as that in the model of Figure 2.3. The CPU time per tour is the weighted sum of the class 0 and class 1 CPU times. The per tour service demand for a given disk is the product of the visit ratio for that disk and the mean service time of that disk. The *visit ratio* is the number of requests for that disk divided by the number of requests for all disks, measured over an arbitrary interval. In this case, visit ratios and service times are the same for all disks. Compute bounds for the throughput (in tours per unit time) and mean tour time of this system.

3. An important verification technique (Section 3.9) is cross-checking simulation and analytic model results, so queueing network analysis pro-grams are useful tools of the simulation modeler. While the analysis of networks which involve such things as priority scheduling and simultaneous resource possession (Section 5.5) may be relatively complex, some networks can be analyzed using very simple programs. For example, Figure 3.5 shows a

```
#include <stdio.h>

#define real double
#define mxK 9        /* max. no. of service centers + 1    */

real D[mxK],          /* D[k] = service demand at center k */
     R[mxK],          /* R[k] = residence time at center k */
     Q[mxK],          /* Q[k] = no. customers at center k  */
     Z;               /* think time (0 for batch system)   */
int  K,               /* no. of centers (excl. terminals)  */
     N;               /* no. terminals (mpl for batch)     */

main()
  {
    K=3; N=16; Z=5000.0;
    D[1]=12*40.0; D[2]=D[3]=6*(22.0+8.33+0.52);
    mva();
  }

/*-- Exact MVA for Single Class, FIFO Center Networks --*/
mva()
  { /* exact mean value analysis for closed queueing     */
    /* networks with a single customer class and only    */
    /* first-in, first-out service centers.              */
    int k,n; real s,X;
    for (k=1; k<=K; k++) Q[k]=0.0;
    for (n=1; n<=N; n++)
      {
        for (k=1; k<=K; k++) R[k]=D[k]*(1.0+Q[k]);
        s=Z; for (k=1; k<=K; k++) s+=R[k]; X=(real)n/s;
        for (k=1; k<=K; k++) Q[k]=X*R[k];
      }
    printf(" k     Rk       Qk       Uk\n");
    for (k=1; k<=K; k++)
      printf("%2d%9.3f%7.3f%7.3f\n",k,R[k],Q[k],X*D[k];
    printf("\nX = %7.4f, R = %9.3f\n",X,(real)N/X-Z);
  }
```

Figure 3.5 Queueing Network Analysis Program

program which can be used to analyze simple closed queueing networks with a single customer class and in which all facilities — service centers — have single servers with first-in, first-out queueing. The analysis method used by this program is called exact *Mean Value Analysis* (MVA); for details and references, see Chapter 6 in Lazowska et al [1984].

This program can be used to analyze timesharing system models like that of problem 3, Chapter 2, or batch system models like that of Figure 2.2 (although only one job class can be represented). Inputs to the program are the number of service centers K, the number of terminals N, the terminal think time Z, and the demand at each service center D[k]. For a timesharing model, D[k] is the total service demand at center k per terminal request. For a batch model, N is the multiprogramming level, Z is 0, and D[k] is the average service demand at center k per tour or per task completion, depending on what unit we want to use in computing throughput and response time. In Figure 3.5, `main()` sets parameters values for the timesharing model of problem 3, Chapter 2. Note that `main()` specifies only the total service demand per request; the number of CPU and disk operations per request is not needed by `mva()`. The `mva()` function computes and tabulates, for each service center, the mean residence time, mean queue length (which includes the customer in service), and utilization. It also prints the system throughput and response time.

Use this program to compute the throughput and response time of the timesharing system of problem 3, Chapter 2, for from 1 to 24 terminals. Plot these values on the throughput and response time bounds plots of problem 1. Change your simulation model of this system to use negative exponential disk service times (with the same mean service time as the original model), and run the simulation with 2, 4, 8, 16, and 24 terminals, Mark the throughput and response time values from these runs on your plots. Do the results tend to verify your simulation model? For the 16-terminal system, how close are the simulation results produced with exponential disk service times to those of the original simulation?

4. Use the program of Figure 3.5 to analyze the queueing network model of Figure 2.1. Compute the mean CPU queue length (including the task in service) and mean CPU residence time from the simulation report of Figure 2.4. Compute the relative difference in queue length and residence time between the simulation results and the MVA results. How would you revise the simulation model to obtain a "tighter" verification?

5. The program of Figure 3.5 can be used as the analytic component of a hybrid model. Use this program to build a hybrid model of the timesharing system of problem 4, Chapter 2, in which memory is represented simply by a

fixed multiprogramming level. Compare the results from the hybrid model with those produced by the simulation model, and compare the execution times of the two programs. Describe how you would extend this model to represent a system with variable-length memory demands and allocation.

6. Develop a debugging and verification plan for the timesharing system model of problem 6(b), Chapter 2, and carry it out. List the errors you find (if any), and describe how they could be avoided in future models.

4. Output and Problem Analysis

4.1 Introduction

Sooner or later in the simulation process we have to answer the question "How long should the simulation run?". It tends to be posed in this way because we have to explicitly specify the time or activity count at which simulation program execution is to terminate. However, implicit in this question is the qualifying phrase "to achieve a specified accuracy", and it is only with the inclusion of this phrase that the question makes sense. It is not an easy question, and so often is ignored in its entirety. Simulations frequently are run "long enough", as determined by intuition, patience, or budget, and the output values from a single run are assumed to be the "true" solutions to the problem with no idea of their accuracy.

In this chapter, we'll look at considerations in and some approaches to estimating and controlling simulation output accuracy. This subject is called simulation output analysis. Simulation inputs are obtained by generating random samples, or variates, from probability distributions; simulation outputs are functions of these random variates, so output analysis is a statistical problem. There are a number of approaches to this problem, some requiring more statistical sophistication than others. We'll review those best suited for the designer - modeler, and list references for further study. The last part of this chapter outlines certain aspects of problem analysis, such as methods for the comparison of design alternatives.

Types of simulations. Simulation run length is, in some cases, determined by the problem itself; the measure of interest is defined in terms of the time required to accomplish a specific set of activities or perhaps in terms of the number of activities required to reach a specified state, given initial conditions determined by the problem. From an output analysis perspective, this type of simulation is called a *terminating*, or *transient*, simulation. Simulation of a computer system's initial program load ("cold start") process would be a transient simulation. For this type of simulation, the question becomes one of how many times the simulation must be repeated (with different random number streams) to achieve a specified accuracy.

In a *steady-state* simulation, both the initial conditions and the length of the simulation are determined by the modeler, and the measure of interest is defined in terms of a limiting value reached as the length of the simulation run goes to infinity. Suppose we are interested in the mean waiting time in a queueing system; theoretically, as the length of a simulation of this system approaches infinity, the <u>distribution</u> of waiting times becomes unchanging and the mean waiting time converges to a limiting value. Practically. run lengths are finite and simulation provides only a sample set of values from this distribution; one of our problems is to determine how close the mean estimated from these sample values is to the true mean of this underlying distribution. In a steady-state simulation, by definition, output values should be independent of initial conditions (achieving this is a second problem).

Most simulations in a computer system design environment are of the steady-state type, just as most analytic models in this environment are concerned with equilibrium behavior. Except where noted, our discussion deals with output analysis for steady-state simulations.

Types of measures. Most of the time, the performance measure of interest is the mean (average) value of a simulation output variable. This variable may represent a discrete-time or a continuous-time random process (random, because it depends on random values of input variables). For a discrete-time process, the simulation produces a sequence of n sample values $X_1, X_2, ..., X_n$ whose mean (denoted by $\overline{X}$) is

$$\overline{X} = \sum_{i=1}^{n} X_i/n \qquad (4.1)$$

For a continuous-time process, the output variable X has a sample value X_t at any instant t in time and the mean is

$$\overline{X} = \int_{0}^{T} X_t\, dt/T \qquad (4.2)$$

where T is the period of time simulated. $\overline{X}$ is called the *sample mean*. Because it is a function of random variables, it also is a random variable; different sample sequences or periods will produce different values of $\overline{X}$.

However, as n approaches infinity in (4.1), or **T** approaches infinity in (4.2), $\overline{X}$ converges to a limiting value E[**X**], called the expectation of **X**. For con-ciseness, we'll represent E[**X**] by μ. μ can be thought of as the true mean of the distribution of **X**: we'll call it the *distribution mean.*

Mean queueing or mean system residence times are examples of means of discrete-time processes. While the underlying distribution of queueing times or system residence times usually is continuous, simulation produces a set of discrete values. Probability measures also are means of discrete-time (or continuous-time) processes. For example, suppose it is desired to determine the probability that a customer arriving in a queueing system finds the server busy. Define an output variable (called an *indicator variable*) X_i which is set to 1 if arriving customer i finds the server busy and 0 otherwise, and simulate n arrivals; the mean value of **X**, as given by (4.1), is an estimate of the desired probability.

Mean queue lengths and facility utilizations are the most common exam-ples of means of continuous-time processes. If X_t is the number of customers in queue at time t, then the mean number of customers in the queue is given by (4.2). If X_t is the state of a single-server facility at time t, where the state is defined as 1 if the facility is busy and 0 if it is not, then the utilization of the facility is given by (4.2). Other system state measures can be similarly defined. While queue lengths and facility states change at discrete points in time, their values are defined continuously over time. (In **smpl**, the inte-gration of (4.2) is accomplished by summing length-time products in the case of queue lengths and busy periods in the case of facility utilizations; sums are accumulated only on state changes, so reported mean queue lengths and utilizations may not be exact because of edge effects.)

Measures other than the mean sometimes are important. For example, an estimate of the mean response time in a model of an interactive system doesn't tell us all we want to know; we'd also like to know something about the distribution of response times. The *variance* is a measure of the disper-sion of a distribution. The variance of a set of n sample values $X_1, X_2, ..., X_n$ is

$$s^2 = \sum_{i=1}^{n} (X_i - \overline{X})^2 / (n - 1) \tag{4.3}$$

s^2 is called the sample variance. As n approaches infinity, s^2 converges to a limiting value $E[s^2] = E[(X - \mu)^2]$, denoted by σ^2. Thus, $\overline{X}$ and s^2 are the sample mean and variance, and μ and σ^2 are the distribution mean and variance. (In (4.3), $\sum(X_i - \overline{X})^2$ is divided by n-1, not n, so that $E[s^2]$ will indeed be equal to $E[(X - \mu)^2]$: see Kobayashi [1978], p322.) The square root of the variance is the *standard deviation*, and the ratio of the standard deviation to the mean is called the *coefficient of variation*.

Any of these three measures let us assess, in a comparative sense, the dispersion of a distribution. However, at least in the case of response times, what we'd really like to do is estimate quantiles of the distribution. (A *quantile* is equivalent to a percentile: the 0.9 quantile is the same as the 90th percentile.) For example, we'd like to determine a value t for which 90 percent of response times are equal to or less than t, or perhaps estimate the median response time (the value of t at the 50th percentile). Quantile estimation is a difficult task, both computationally (the entire output sequence has to be stored) and statistically. However, it is fairly easy to do the inverse — estimate the proportion of values equal to or less than t — using an indicator variable as described earlier, and this may be an adequate measure of variability in practice.

We'll have our hands full here with output analysis for means, and won't consider variance or quantile estimation. Our simulation texts aren't much help on these topics: see Welch [1983] for discussion and references.

4.2 Confidence Intervals

To reiterate, our problem is to estimate how close the sample mean obtained from a finite-length simulation is to the distribution mean μ or, equivalently, how long run lengths have to be to obtain a sample mean arbitrarily close to μ.

Let's consider a particular problem: estimation of the mean queueing time in an M/M/1 queueing system. (We'll use this system because a great deal is known about it and because we already have a **smpl** model of it (Section 1.7). This model can be instrumented to collect queueing times, or the mean queueing time can be computed from the mean queue length given in the simulation report using equation (1.12).) Assume the mean interarrival time Ta is 125, the mean service time Ts is 100, let Xi represent the queueing time of customer i, and let X be the mean queueing time resulting from a simulation of 5000 customers. How close is X to μ?

Ten simulation runs,using a different **smpl** random number stream for each run, gave the following mean queueing times.

(1)	331.993	(6)	447.532
(2)	366.052	(7)	420.858
(3)	403.524	(8)	355.959
(4)	464.856	(9)	492.144
(5)	393.393	(10)	389.200

Run (and stream) numbers are in parentheses. The means range from about 332 to about 492, illustrating the kind of the error we can make by using the mean from a single run as the "true" solution to an analysis problem. The mean for the ten runs is 406.554; how close is this to μ?

We can answer this question by computing a measure called a confidence interval. Suppose we have a set of N sample values $Y_1, Y_2, ..., Y_N$ from a distribution with true (but unknown) mean μ. The sample mean is

$$\overline{Y} = \sum_{i=1}^{N} Y_i/N \tag{4.4}$$

Define $1 - \alpha$ as the probability that the absolute value of the difference between the sample mean and μ is equal to or less than H:

$$P[\,|\overline{Y} - \mu| \leq H] = 1 - \alpha \tag{4.5}$$

Then a confidence interval for the mean is defined as[1]

$$P[\overline{Y} - H \leq \mu \leq \overline{Y} + H] = 1 - \alpha \tag{4.6}$$

The interval $\overline{Y} - H$ to $\overline{Y} + H$ is called the *confidence interval*, H is called the confidence interval *half-width*, and $1 - \alpha$ is called the *confidence level* or *confidence coefficient*, typical values of which are 0.90 or 0.95. The confidence level $1 - \alpha$ is specified by the analyst; H then is determined by the sample values, number of samples, and the value of α.

H is a function of random variables and so is a random variable itself; consequently, the interval $\overline{Y} \pm H$ is a random interval. Different experiments, producing different sets of values of Y, will have different confidence intervals. (4.6) states that if we perform a large number of such experiments and compute a confidence interval for each experiment, the proportion of intervals containing μ is $1 - \alpha$. A confidence interval containing the distribution mean μ is said to *cover* the mean, and $1 - \alpha$ is called the nominal coverage probability or, simply, the nominal coverage.

When $Y_1, Y_2, ..., Y_N$ are <u>independent</u> random variables from a normal distribution with mean μ, H is given by

---

[1] A measure such as the mean, which is a single number, often is called a <u>point estimator</u>; the confidence interval is called an <u>interval estimator</u>.

$$H = t_{\alpha/2;N-1}\, s/N^{1/2} \qquad\qquad\qquad (4.7)$$

where $t_{\alpha/2;N-1}$ is the upper $\alpha/2$ quantile of the t distribution with N-1 degrees of freedom and s^2 is the sample variance:

$$s^2 = \sum_{i=1}^{N} (Y_i - \overline{Y})^2/(N-1) \qquad\qquad (4.8)$$

s^2 is the estimated variance of the distribution of the sample values Y_i. s^2/N is the estimated variance of the distribution of the sample mean $\overline{Y}$, and $s/N^{1/2}$ is the standard deviation of the distribution of the sample mean; the last sometimes is called the *standard error* of the mean.

Under the assumptions of independence and normality, the sample mean is distributed in accordance with a t distribution. The standard t distribution is defined to have a mean of 0 and a standard deviation of 1; $100(\alpha/2)$ percent of sample values from this distribution are more than $+t_{\alpha/2;N-1}$ standard deviations from the mean, and an equal percentage are more than $-t_{\alpha/2;N-1}$ standard deviations from the mean. Therefore, $100(1-\alpha)$ percent are *within* $\pm\, t_{\alpha/2;N-1}$ unit standard deviations of the mean. In (4.7), then, H is computed by multiplying the number of unit standard deviations specified by α and N-1 by the standard deviation of the sample mean. N-1 is called the *number of degrees of freedom* ; the shape of the t distribution and the quantile associated with a given standard deviation change as N-1 changes.

Table 4.1 is an abbreviated tabulation of values of $t_{\alpha/2;N-1}$. More extensive tabulations are provided in Law and Kelton [1982], Banks and Carson [1984], and in most statistics texts. Fishman [1978] provides Fortran subroutines to compute quantiles of the t and normal distributions. C functions based on these subroutines are included in the appendix; these were used to generate Table 4.1. As N increases, the t distribution approaches the normal distribution, quantiles of which (denoted by $z_{\alpha/2}$) often are used when N is greater than 25 or 30. The values of $z_{.05}$ and $z_{.025}$ are, respectively, 1.65 and 1.96.

If we define Y_i as the mean queueing time from run i, we can use (4.4) - (4.8) to compute a confidence interval for the mean queueing time from the ten simulation runs. The independence assumption is satisfied because each simulation run used a different random number stream. The assumption of normality is based on the Central Limit Theorem which (loosely) states that means of random samples of size n from any distribution with finite variance are approximately normally distributed for large n. (We'll revisit this in Section 4.4.)

N−1	$\alpha/2=.05$ t	$\alpha/2=025$ t	N−1	$\alpha/2=.05$ t	$\alpha/2=.025$ t
4	2.13	2.78	15	1.75	2.13
5	2.02	2.57	16	1.75	2.12
6	1.94	2.45	17	1.74	2.11
7	1.90	2.37	18	1.73	2.10
8	1.86	2.31	19	1.73	2.09
9	1.83	2.26	20	1.73	2.09
10	1.81	2.23	21	1.72	2.08
11	1.80	2.20	22	1.72	2.07
12	1.78	2.18	23	1.71	2.07
13	1.77	2.16	24	1.71	2.06
14	1.76	2.15	∞	1.65	1.96

Table 4.1. Selected Values of $t_{\alpha/2;N-1}$

The computation of a 95 percent confidence interval for the mean queueing time from the **M/M/1** queueing system simulations is outlined below.

$1 - \alpha = 0.95$, so $\alpha = 0.05$

sample mean $\overline{Y} = 406.55$

sample variance $s^2 = 2540.08$

standard deviation of the sample mean $s/N^{1/2} = 15.94$

$t_{.05/2;9} = 2.26$ (from Table 4.1)

confidence interval half-width $H = 2.26 \times 15.94 = 36.02$

confidence interval $= 406.55 \pm 36.02$

Thus, we are 95 percent confident that the true mean queueing time is between 370.53 and 442.47. (The theoretical mean is 400.) Remember the interpretation of this: if we repeat this experiment many times, computing a confidence interval each time, 95 percent of these confidence intervals will contain the true mean. This confidence is based on results from a set of ten simulation runs: note that only four of these ten runs produced a mean contained in the confidence interval.

Sometimes the confidence interval is described in relative terms as a percentage of the mean. In this example, the relative confidence interval half-width is about 8.86 percent of the sample mean. Subject to the interpretation emphasized above, we can view this as a measure of the accuracy of our estimate of the mean queueing time; since we are 95 percent confident that this interval contains μ, we are equally confident that $\overline{Y}$ is within 8.86 percent of μ.

In our analysis of the **M/M/1** queue, simulation of 50,000 customer completions (10 runs of 5000 completions) provided a relative half-width of 8.86 percent. What would it take to cut that in half? Let's look back at (4.7). H is the product of three terms: $t_{\alpha/2;N-1}$, s, and $N^{-1/2}$. The first term is a function of N, but decreases by only fifteen percent or so as N becomes infinite. For fixed s, then, we would have to increase N by a factor of almost four to reduce H by a factor of 2 — make 40 runs of 5000 completions. We also could reduce s by increasing n, the length of each run; it can be shown that s decreases with the square root of n. Thus, a 2X increase in accuracy requires a 4X increase in total simulation run length; a total of about 200,000 customer service completions would be needed to cut H in half.

Estimation of a confidence interval is what simulation output analysis is all about. The foregoing discussion should be supplemented by further reading. A good introductory statistics text, such as Mendenhall and Scheaffer [1973], will provide a conceptual introduction to confidence interval estimation and its relation to hypothesis testing. A succinct introduction to the subject is provided by Kobayashi [1978]. Simulation-related references are given later in this chapter.

4.3 The Effect of Correlation

The method of confidence interval estimation described in the preceding section can't be applied directly to a sequence of simulation output variables because these are correlated and the requisite assumption of independence does not hold. The correlated behavior of queueing times in our M/M/1 queue simulation (with Ta = 125 and Ts = 100) is illustrated in Figure 4.1, which plots customer queueing time versus customer number for the first 1000 service completions of simulation run 1.[2] Note how the queueing times tend to cluster into sequences of very long and very short times (the mean queueing time for these 1000 customers was 253.1). Since service times are exponentially distributed, the majority of service times are short, less than the mean, but a few are very much longer. When one of these long service times occurs, customers back up at the server and incur long delays. Eventually a long inter-arrival time occurs, the server catches up, and delays diminish. Thus, delays tend to be positively correlated; a long delay is more likely to be

---

[2]This figure was generated using **SMPL**'s time series display, described in Chapter 7.

queueing time

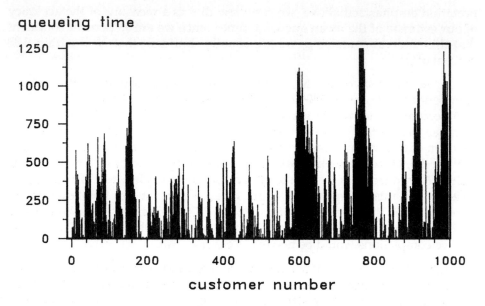

Figure 4.1. A Queueing Time Sequence in an M/M/1 Queue

followed by another long delay than by a short delay, and conversely. Many computer systems and subsystems behave in a similar way. As a result of this correlation, s^2/N underestimates the variance of the sample mean, and so (4.7) underestimates the confidence interval half-width.

We can intuitively see why the estimated variance of the sample mean is affected. With independent samples, two sample values X_i and X_{i+1} provide two different pieces of information for constructing this estimate. However, if X_i and X_{i+1} are correlated, the two values together may provide only a little more information than a single value provides, so N correlated samples provide less information than N independent samples. How much less depends on the degree of correlation.

For an analytic perspective, suppose X_1, X_2, ..., X_n are a sequence of sample values from a discrete-time random process with mean μ and variance σ^2. Under certain conditions, the *autocovariance function* of the process is defined as

$$R_j = E[(X_i - \mu)(X_{i+j} - \mu)] \tag{4.9}$$

R_j is the expectation of the product of deviations from the mean of values spaced j samples, or lags, apart. Note that $R_0 = E[(X_i - \mu)^2] = \sigma^2$, and

$|R_j| < R_0$. We'll assume that R_j is a function only of j, the difference between positions in the sequence, and not of the positions themselves: the sequence then is said to be *covariance stationary*. (For simulation output, this is true only if "warmup" effects either are eliminated from the output sequence or are insignificant.)

The *autocorrelation function* is defined as

$$\rho_j = R_j / R_0 \qquad (4.10)$$

The value of ρ_j for a given j is called the jth lag *autocorrelation* (or *serial correlation*) coefficient. Note that $-1 \le \rho_j \le +1$, and $\rho_0 = 1$. If X_{i+j} tends to be large when X_i is large and small when X_i is small, ρ_j will be positive. If X_{i+j} tends to be small when X_i is large and conversely, ρ_j will be negative. If neither tendency exists, ρ_j will be 0 (for $j > 0$).

Whether or not the sample values are correlated, the best estimate of μ is, as before, the sample mean

$$\bar{X} = \sum_{i=1}^{n} X_i/n \qquad (4.11)$$

The variance of the sample mean, $\text{Var}(\bar{X})$, can be shown to be[3]

$$\text{Var}(\bar{X}) = \left[1 + 2\sum_{j=1}^{n-1} (1 - j/n)\,\rho_j\right] \sigma^2/n \qquad (4.12)$$

For n large enough so that ρ_j becomes 0 as j approaches n,

$$\text{Var}(\bar{X}) \approx \xi\,\sigma^2/n \qquad (4.13)$$

where

$$\xi = 1 + 2\sum_{j=1}^{\infty} \rho_j \qquad (4.14)$$

If the sample values are independent (uncorrelated), $\xi = 1$ and $\text{Var}(\bar{X}) = \sigma^2/n$. In this case, the variance of the sample mean can be estimated from the

---

[3]Our discussion here follows Kobabayshi [1978]. Welch [1983] provides a derivation; Welch's (6.150) is equivalent to (4.12) above.

sample variance s^2/n, as we did in the previous section. If the sample values are positively correlated, which usually is true for computer system simulation model output values, $\xi > 1$ and $\text{Var}(\overline{X}) > \sigma^2/n$. In this case, a confidence interval based on estimating the variance of the sample mean as s^2/n would underestimate the width of the confidence interval and give a false idea of the accuracy of the simulation results.

ξ can be viewed as the number of correlated samples equivalent to one independent sample; n/ξ sometimes is called the effective sample size. ξ rarely is known, and the various simulation output analysis methods proposed in the literature either try to estimate it or make it approximately 1 (i.e., obtain independent samples).

Queueing times in an **M/M/1** queueing system represent one of the few processes for which ξ can be analytically determined. For this process, Daley [1968] shows

$$\xi = \frac{1+r}{1-r} + \frac{2r(3-r)}{(2-r)(1-r)^2} \tag{4.15}$$

where r is the traffic intensity — the mean service time divided by the mean inter-arrival time. For the **M/M/1** queue, the server utilization is equal to the traffic intensity. (The traffic intensity traditionally is represented by the symbol ρ, but that symbol is used in this chapter to represent the serial correlation coefficient — also by tradition.)

It is instructive to use (4.15) to determine the simulation run length required to achieve a specified accuracy for the mean queueing time in an **M/M/1** queueing system. Let's assume that the sample size n is large enough so that we can use the normal, rather than the t, distribution, in forming the confidence interval. The confidence interval half-width then is

$$H = z_{\alpha/2} [\sigma^2/n]^{1/2} \tag{4.16}$$

where $z_{\alpha/2}$ is the upper $\alpha/2$ quantile of the normal distribution and σ^2 is the variance of the queueing time distribution (since σ^2 is known for the **M/M/1** queue, we use it here rather than an estimator).

Suppose we want to obtain a 5 percent relative confidence interval half-width at a 95 percent confidence level for the mean queueing time. Then, $H = .05\mu$, $\alpha = 0.05$, $z_{\alpha/2} = 1.96$, and

$$.05\mu = 1.96 \, [\xi\sigma^2/n]^{1/2} \tag{4.17}$$

r traffic intensity	ξ sum of correlation coefficients	σ/μ coefficient of variation	n required sample size
.05	1.273	6.245	76290
.10	1.599	4.359	46685
.20	2.472	3.000	34187
.30	3.802	2.381	33126
.40	5.944	2.000	36535
.50	9.667	1.732	44564
.60	16.857	1.526	60354
.70	33.188	1.363	94703
.80	82.333	1.225	189774
.90	362.636	1.105	680948

Table 4.2. Required Sample Sizes for 5% Accuracy in M/M/1 Queueing Time Estimation

which, after some rearrangement, gives

$$n = \xi \, [39.2\sigma/\mu]^2 \tag{4.18}$$

Note that σ/μ is the coefficient of variation. For the **M/M/1** queue, the mean and variance of the queueing time distribution are (see, for example, Allen [1978])

$$\mu = r\mathrm{Ts}/(1 - r) \tag{4.19}$$

$$\sigma^2 = r(2 - r)[\mathrm{Ts}/(1 - r)]^2 \tag{4.20}$$

where Ts is the mean service time. The ratio σ/μ is

$$\sigma/\mu = [(2 - r)/r]^{1/2} \tag{4.21}$$

For a given traffic intensity r, we can use (4.15) to compute ξ, (4.21) to compute σ/μ, and then compute n from (4.18).

Values of $r, \xi, \sigma/\mu$, and n are tabulated in Table 4.2. This table is interesting in several respects. First, note that correlation, as represented by ξ, increases as the traffic intensity increases. This makes intuitive sense:

higher traffic means that more customers are likely to arrive during a long service time and incur long — and correlated — delays, as discussed at the start of this section. The coefficient of variation, on the other hand, decreases as the traffic increases: while both μ and σ increase, μ increases faster. As the traffic increases, more and more customers incur delays, reducing the variability of delays. Note that, as a result of the interaction between ξ and σ/μ, required sample sizes increase as r becomes very small as well as when r becomes large.

Values of n in Table 4.2 are relevant only to queueing times in the M/M/1 queue: the important point is their magnitude. Sample sizes often have to be on the order of tens of thousands, rather than thousands, to achieve the accuracy we desire. The required size will depend on the structure of the system being modeled, the output variable being estimated, and the values of model input parameters for any particular run.[4] We can't determine the sample size required for one experiment and expect it to apply to other experiments involving model structure or parameter changes. The sample size required to achieve a given accuracy cannot be determined in advance (except in a few cases, such as the M/M/1 queue, where the expected results are known anyway), but has to be determined from the experimental data. Thus, with a pre-determined sample size, we can estimate the accuracy but not control it.

In the two output analysis methods of interest to us here, we collect N independent estimates of the mean value of the output parameter of interest and use (4.4) - (4.8) to compute a confidence interval estimate. To achieve independence, we use independent runs, as we'll discuss in Section 4.6, or we use subruns of a single long run, making the subruns long enough so that means of consecutive subruns are approximately independent (discussed in Section 4.7). In addition to independence, our confidence interval estimation procedure is based on the assumption that the means of individual runs or subruns are normally distributed.

4.4 The Question of Normality

The Central Limit Theorem assures us that the mean of n independent and identically distributed random variables is approximately normally distributed for large n: the distribution of the sample mean is said to be *asymptotically normal*. Output variables from an individual run or subrun

---

[4]For specified accuracy in estimation of similar parameters, open systems (Section 2.7) tend to require longer runs than closed systems -- but each experiment is unique.

may be identically distributed (in the absence of warmup effects) but, as we've just seen, are unlikely to be independent. We might ask, then, how lack of independence affects this assumption, and how n, approximate normality, and confidence interval accuracy are related.

With regard to the first question, asymptotic normality is assumed to hold even though the output process is correlated. This has been demonstrated in a general way for certain types of processes (see Law [1983] for references) and has been shown to be true for output parameters of certain queueing systems. With regard to the second question, the consensus seems to be that warmup effects, in the case of individual runs, and correlation effects, in the case of subruns are the most serious concerns; when n is made large enough to overcome these, it also will be large enough to provide approximate normality. The normality of the means from individual runs or subruns can be examined analytically using the Shapiro-Wilk test (see Fishman [1978] or Bratley et al [1983]), or graphically (see Kobayashi [1978]). Finally, interval estimates for μ based on the normality of the sample mean are known to be *robust* — insensitive to moderate departures from normality.

4.5 Output Analysis Methods

A number of methods for estimating a confidence interval for the mean of a simulation output variable have been described in the literature. These include methods called (1) replication, (2) batch means, (3) regeneration, (4) autoregression, (5) spectral analysis, and (6) standardized time series. Methods (1) - (3) try to eliminate the effects of correlation, while methods (4) and (5) try to estimate them. Method (6), which is relatively new, estimates a confidence interval based on properties of a transformation of the simulation output sequence. The easiest methods for the beginning modeler to deal with from a conceptual standpoint are those of replication, batch means, and regeneration.

The regenerative method exploits the fact that, at a random point in simulation time called a *regeneration point*, a model returns to the same state it was in at a previous regeneration point and, in a probabilistic sense, restarts or regenerates its behavior from that point. The interval between successive regeneration points is called a *regeneration cycle*. Since these points represent identical model states, the behavior of one cycle is independent of that of other cycles. Output variables, such as means, of different cycles are independent and identically distributed random variables, which provides a basis for confidence interval estimation. Because cycle lengths are random, the procedure for confidence interval estimation differs from that described earlier.

The fact that cycles are clearly independent and identically distributed gives the regenerative method a stronger theoretical basis than most other methods. It can be hard to define a regeneration point in a complex model — at least one which occurs frequently enough to result in a reasonable number of cycles — and this problem has to be solved every time a new model is developed. Consequently, we'll concentrate here on the replication and batch means methods. However, if you have occasion to develop a model that will receive extensive use, you should consider the regenerative method. Brief introductions are given by Bratley et al [1983], Kobayashi [1978], Law and Kelton [1982], and Welch [1983]. For a more extensive introduction, see Crane and Lemoine [1977] or Iglehart [1978].

Law [1983] surveys all six methods listed above and provides extensive references supplemented by a bibliography.

Approaches to confidence interval estimation can be classified as *fixed sample size* procedures or as *sequential* procedures. Most output analysis methods can be adapted to either procedure. In a fixed sample size proced-ure, a simulation experiment of fixed total length is performed and the confidence interval estimated from the results of the experiment upon its completion. As noted earlier, a fixed sample size procedure lets us estimate the accuracy of the result, but not control it: what we see upon computing the confidence interval is what we get. In a sequential procedure, the desired accuracy is specified, confidence interval estimates are computed at selected intervals, and the experiment continued until the desired accuracy is obtained. Sequential procedures can be manual or can be automated. We'll consider both procedures in our discussion of the replication and batch means methods of output analysis.

4.6 Replication

Replication is, at least conceptually, the easiest method of output anal-ysis. Suppose we make k runs (replications), each generating m sample values of an output variable y, using a different random number stream for each run.[5] Let $Y_1, Y_2, .., Y_k$ be the means of the k runs. The means are independent, since a different random number stream was used for each run and, for sufficiently large m, will be approximately normally distributed. A

---

[5]For simplicity, our discussion assumes a discrete-time process and describes run or subrun lengths in terms of the number of sample values generated (number of observations). Analysis methods for a continuous-time process are essentially the same, except that lengths are measured in time, not counts.

confidence interval for the mean then can be constructed as described in Section 4.2.

$$\text{sample mean:} \quad \overline{Y} = \sum_{i=1}^{k} Y_i / k \tag{4.22}$$

$$\text{sample variance:} \quad s^2 = \sum_{i=1}^{k} (Y_i - \overline{Y})^2 / (k-1) \tag{4.23}$$

$$s^2 = [(\sum_{i=1}^{k} Y_i^2) - k\overline{Y}^2]/(k-1) \tag{4.24}$$

$$\text{half-width:} \quad H = t_{\alpha/2; k-1}\, s / k^{1/2} \tag{4.25}$$

$$\text{confidence interval:} \quad \overline{Y} \pm H \tag{4.26}$$

Remember that the Y_i here represents the means of individual runs, and $\overline{Y}$ is the mean of the means of these runs. $\overline{Y}$ sometimes is called the *grand mean*. It usually is easier to compute the sample variance with (4.24) than with (4.23).

In a fixed sample size procedure based on replication, the total number of observations n = mk is determined in advance. This commonly is done by constructing the simulation program with the model proper as a subprogram which executes a run of length m and returns a mean Y_i, calling this subprogram k times with the random number stream incremented on each call, and computing the confidence interval as shown above. In deciding how to divide n between m and k, it is best to keep k relatively small, on the order of 5 or 10, and m relatively large. The trade is between confidence interval width and coverage probability. As we can see from (4.24), smaller values of k tend to increase H; however, they permit a larger value of m for a given n. Larger values of m tend to reduce s^2 and consequently H, and so compensate to some degree for the effect of a small number of replications of H. Also, larger values of m reduce warmup effects and improve normality, both of which improve confidence interval coverage (i.e., increase the probability that $\overline{Y} \pm H$ contains μ to a value closer to the theoretical coverage of $1 - \alpha$).

Replication also can be employed in a sequential procedure, increasing either m or k until the desired value of H is obtained. The recommended way of doing this is to make k runs of initial length m = m0, saving the state of the simulation at the end of each run, compute H and, if H is larger than desired, increase m, restart each run, and compute H again. This keeps k small, but has the practical disadvantage of requiring a save/restart capability. It also is possible to keep adding replications until the desired value of H is obtained. If this approach is used, results should be interpreted conservatively, since the actual coverage generally will be less than $1 - \alpha$. This decrease is inherent in the sequential sampling process, and may be compounded by warmup effects if the run length is too small. For a discussion of the sequential sampling problem, see section V.A.4 in Kleijnen [1975]; also see the recommendations of section 2.9 in Fishman [1978].

The warmup problem. As a matter of programming convenience, it is customary to initialize a simulation with the simulated system in an "empty-idle" state. For example, the queueing network model of Section 2.7 is initialized with all facilities idle and all tokens scheduled for event 1, so that all tokens are queued for (or using) the CPU at simulation time 0. This (probably) is an uncommon state for this system, and it takes some time for the model to "warm up" — for tokens to be distributed among facilities in a more representative way. Values of output variables collected during this warmup period may not be representative of steady-state behavior and, if the run length is not sufficiently large, may bias Y_i. Instead of Y_i being an estimator of μ, it is an estimator of $\mu(m,0)$: the expected value of Y for the first m customers given an empty system at time 0. This problem is called the *warmup* problem, the *initial transient* problem, or the *initialization bias* problem.

In replication analysis, there are three approaches to overcoming this problem:

- prevent it by establishing initial conditions representative of steady state behavior,

- eliminate its effect by deleting the first l initial (and presumably biased) sample values of a run, or

- reduce its effect on Y_i to an insignificant level by making m sufficiently large.

There are two difficulties in establishing representative initial conditions. First, it isn't clear how they should be defined. For example, let p_n be the proportion of time during which a single-server queueing system contains n customers, and let $\bar{n}$ be the average number of customers in the system. Suppose we make a pilot run and obtain $p_0 = .4$, $p_0 > p_n$ for $n>0$, and $\bar{n} = 1.5$. To establish representative initial conditions, should we start with 0, 1, or 2 customers in the queue? 0 represents the most probable state, while 1 or 2 (depending on how we round) represents the average length. There is no

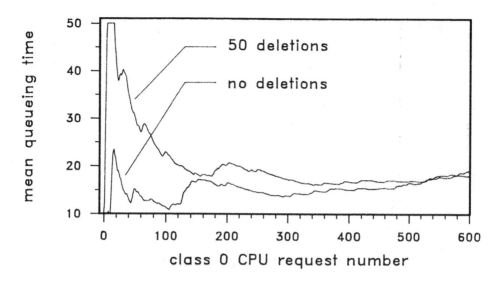

Figure 4.2. Mean Queueing Time in a Queueing Network Simulation

established procedure. Law [1983] shows, for an **M/M/1** queue, how the expected queueing time after i completions is affected by the number in the system at time 0: the most rapid convergence resulted with an initial number much greater than the mean. The problem becomes much harder for systems with multiple queues, since their joint behavior has to be considered.

The second difficulty is that, even if we have a satisfactory definition of representative initial conditions and a means of estimating their values, creating these conditions might require considerable programming effort. For example, consider a computer system model representing a CPU, memory, channels, and disks, and what would have to be done to distribute tasks across these resources and their queues in a predetermined way. The easiest way to deal with both difficulties is to run the model long enough to reach steady state. This suggests the second approach: delete the values collected during this initialization period and continue execution.

The effect of deletion on the initial transient is illustrated in Figure 4.2. This figure plots the mean CPU queueing time versus the number of CPU requests for class 0 (low priority) tokens in our queueing network model. Results are shown for two simulation runs, one without deletion and one with values for the first 50 CPU requests deleted. Note the initial bias in the mean caused by starting the simulation with all tokens scheduled for the CPU, and the reduction in this bias resulting from deletion. (The expected mean CPU queueing time is 20.) Also, note that the effect of this bias

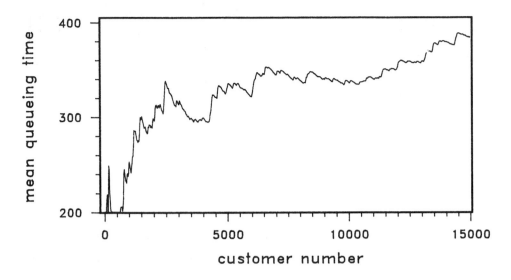

Figure 4.3. Mean Queueing Time in an **M/M/1** Queue Simulation (Single Run)

becomes insignificant as the run length increases, illustrating the third approach to the warmup problem.

As such things go, our queueing network model is relatively well behaved: convergence of the mean queueing time towards its expected value occurs fairly quickly. 10 runs of 1000 requests each produce a relative half-width of about 10 percent at a 95 percent confidence level. Our **M/M/1** queueing system model is a different story. Figure 4.3 plots mean queueing time versus customer number for this model with Ta = 125 and Ts = 100 (a traffic intensity of 0.8). The run represented in this figure began with the system empty, and no values were deleted. Here we see very slow convergence of the mean towards its expected value (of 400), due in large part to the correlation of queueing times. For the first several thousand customers, the mean is far below its expected value (again illustrating the danger of using the result from a single run).

Figure 4.4 is more encouraging. This figure again plots mean queueing time versus customer number, this time with the mean queueing time after n customer completions averaged over a set of 10 simulation runs. Two sets of runs are represented: one without deletion and one with deletion of the first 150 queueing times. (For the runs with deletion, the total run length was 4150 queueing times). Without deletion, the effect of initialization bias is evident in the slow upward climb of the mean toward its expected value.

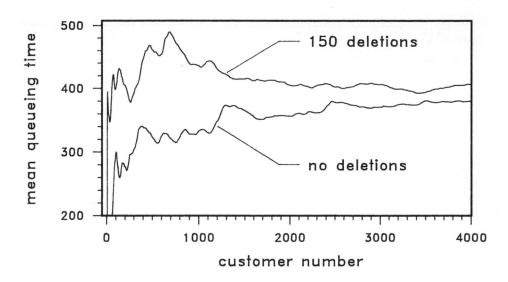

Figure 4.4. Mean Queueing Time in an **M/M/1** Queue Simulation (10 Runs)

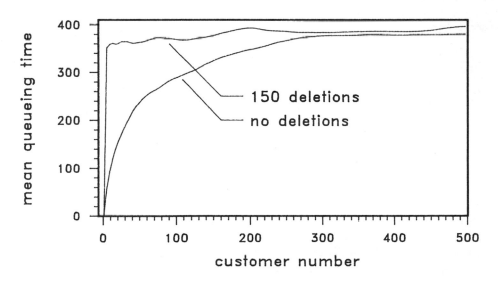

Figure 4.5. Mean Queueing Time in an **M/M/1** Queue Simulation (200 Runs)

However, with deletion, the mean becomes close to the expected value after about 2000 sample values.

Figure 4.5 plots the mean queueing time after n customer completions averaged over 200 runs, with and without deletion. With sample variations largely smoothed out, the effects of initialization bias are very clear. Note, though, that even with 150 deletions there appears to be some bias in the mean.

The difficulty in the deletion approach is in determining the number of values to delete or, equivalently, when steady state is reached. For an overall run length of m and a deletion amount l, m–l sample values are collected in a run. If l is too small, coverage will be reduced because the sample mean is biased, as we've seen, and so a confidence interval around it has less likelihood of containing μ. If l is larger than necessary, the sample variance is increased, increasing the width of the confidence interval; this, while clearly undesirable, is less risky than reduced coverage. In the absence of a reliable means of identifying steady state, our best tactic is to be generous with both l and m. Considerable research has been done on deletion and on recognition of steady-state behavior: an excellent summary and references are given by Law [1983].

The trade between run length m and number of replications k was mentioned earlier in this section: for a given n = mk, smaller values of k improve coverage at the expense of increased confidence interval width. This is illustrated by the data of Tables 4.3 and 4.4. These tables summarize the results of 3000 simulation runs for the M/M/1 queueing system with a traffic intensity of 0.8. Runs were made without deletion. For each run, the mean queue time was recorded at 500, 1000, 2000, and 4000 customer completions. The runs were grouped into 600 sets of 5 replications, 300 sets of 10 replications, and 150 sets of 20 replications. For each set, a 95 percent confidence interval was computed. The average relative half-widths ($H/\overline{Y}$) of these intervals are shown in Table 4.3, and the proportions of intervals which actually contained μ are shown in Table 4.4. Diagonal entries in these tables represent equal values of mk.

Table 4.3 shows that doubling the number of replications results in a greater reduction in the width of the confidence interval than doubling the run length. Note, though, that for a given mk, increasing k from 5 to 10 reduces the relative half-width by about 20 percent, while increasing k from 10 to 20 reduces it by only about 10 percent. Also note that large values of mk are required to obtain accuracies in the vicinity of 10 percent.

Now look at Table 4.4, which shows measured coverages — the proportions of confidence intervals actually containing μ — for this experiment;

m	number of replications - k		
run length	5	10	20
500	.475	.294	.204
1000	.363	.224	.153
2000	.270	.165	.111
4000	.194	.118	.079

Table 4.3. Relative Half-Widths for M/M/1 Queue Simulations

remember that the nominal coverage was 0.95. Note that, for a given mk, making the run length large results in better coverage than does making the number of replications large. In fact, if the run length is too small, making a large number of replications can even reduce coverage because it results in a smaller interval around a biased mean. We can see this in the coverages for run lengths of 500. Consequently, this model requires run lengths of several thousand sample values, independent of the number of replications, to obtain coverage near the nominal value. This again indicates that we need to be generous in specifying run lengths. Also, with a sequential approach based on replication, it is crucial to make the run length sufficiently large.

m	number of replications - k		
run length	5	10	20
500	.883	.853	.853
1000	.893	.897	.913
2000	.937	.940	.960
4000	.952	.947	.953

Table 4.4. Measured Coverages for M/M/1 Queue Simulations

Table 4.3 suggests that something more than 40,000 sample values are needed to obtain an accuracy of 10 percent. It is interesting to compare this with the required sample size predicted in the analysis of Section 4.3. For $H = .10\mu$ and $\alpha = 0.05$, equation (4.18) becomes

$$n = \xi[19.6\sigma/\mu]^2$$

substituting the values of ξ and σ/μ corresponding to a traffic intensity of 0.8 in Table 4.2 gives n = 47463. (While we're looking at Table 4.2, note the required sample size for 5 percent accuracy at this traffic intensity!)

Recommendations for replication. To achieve comparable accuracy, our **M/M/1** queue simulation requires run lengths some four times greater than those of our queueing network model.   An infinite-population, high-utilization queueing system, such as the **M/M/1** queue, presents one of the more difficult problems in simulation estimation (which, in addition to its potential for analytic confirmation, is why the **M/M/1** queue invariably is used in studies of output analysis methods). Fortunately, most **smpl** computer system models will be better behaved than our **M/M/1** model because of controls and limits inherent in the systems themselves. Unfortunately, it isn't safe to conclude this in advance: each model and each set of input parameter values present unique run length requirements.

The wide spectrum of simulation model behavior makes it tempting to equivocate on specific run length recommendations. However, the beginning modeler needs numbers, not caveats, so the following recommendations are offered for a sequential procedure using replication. These assume a desired accuracy (relative half width) of 10 percent at a 95 percent confidence level for an output variable **y**.

1. Use a basic run length of 2500 sample values. If the input variables which are major contributors to the value of **y** have coefficients of variation greater than 1, increase this to 4000. For open systems with high utilizations (traffic inten-sities in the 0.6 - 0.9 range), increase the run length to 5000.

2. Make 5 replications and compute the confidence interval half width H_5.

3. If $H_5 < .10\overline{Y}$, the desired accuracy has been obtained. Otherwise, make k* – 5 additional replications, where[6]

$$k^* = \lceil 5(H_5/.10\overline{Y})^2 \rceil \qquad (4.27)$$

---

[6] $\lceil x \rceil$ denotes the ceiling function of x — the smallest integer equal to or greater than x.

and compute a new confidence interval half width; this should provide the required accuracy. If $k^* > 20$, it is advisable to start again with the run length (at least) doubled.

4. For a continuous-time process in which the run length is specified in terms of time, as in estimation of mean queue length, set the run time long enough to encompass a number of activities comparable to the counts recommended above. In the case of mean queue length, for example, use a run time which will result in 2500 - 5000 requests for the facility of interest.

The basis for the run length recommendations largely is empirical; the suggested increases try to compensate for effects of high variability and high correlation. Total sample sizes based on these recommendations will be larger than necessary for some models, but it is always better to err in the direction of improved coverage.

The basis for (4.27) is as follows. Suppose $\overline{Y}_5$, s_5, and H_5 are the mean, standard deviation, and half width obtained from 5 replications, k is the number of replications which will produce the desired half width, and $\overline{Y}_k$, s_k, and H_k are the mean, standard deviation, and half width obtained from k replications. Then, from (4.25),

$$H_5 = t_{.025;4}\, s_5/5^{1/2}$$

$$H_k = t_{.025;k-1}\, s_k/k^{1/2} = .01\overline{Y}_k$$

Assume $t_{.025;4} \approx t_{.025;k-1}$, $s_5 \approx s_k$, and $\overline{Y}_5 \approx \overline{Y}_k \approx \overline{Y}$. Then,

$$H_5/H_k \approx H_5/.01\overline{Y} = [k/5]^{1/2}$$

which, rearranged, gives (4.27). Since $t_{.025;k-1} < t_{.025;4}$, the estimated number of additional replications should be conservative.

A recommendation for deletion is not given because the suggested run lengths should be long enough to eliminate warmup effects. However, deletion amounts on the order of 5 percent of the run length may help and certainly won't hurt.

Replication with SMPL. SMPL's graphics display facility, **dis**, described in Chapter 7, can help make a rough estimate of required run length. (This facility was used to generate most of the figures in this chapter.) With **dis**, we can watch the behavior of the mean and decide when steady-state has been reached — a task which is somewhat easier when the mean behaves as in Figure 4.2 than when its behavior resembles that shown in Figure 4.3 — and set the run length at some conservatively longer value. SMPL also permits replication to be controlled from the keyboard without simulation program modification. At the start of each instance of model execution, we can select a new random number stream and set a breakpoint for a count or time via the SMPL run-time interface. When the breakpoint pause occurs, we can delete accumulated sums and counts, set another breakpoint for run termination, and, at the end of the run, report the appropriate measures, all from the keyboard.

4.7 Batch Means

The batch means method circumvents the warmup problem by dividing one long run into a set of k subruns of length m, called batches, computing a separate sample mean for each batch, and using these batch means to compute the grand mean and the confidence interval. Assuming deletion is used to achieve steady state initial conditions for the first batch, each sub-sequent batch begins with the system in steady state. If the batch size m is sufficiently large, the batch means will be approximately independent and normally distributed; a confidence interval then can be computed just as in replication, with batch means taking the place of run means. Since warmup effects have to be dealt with only once, rather than k times as in the case of replication, the batch means method is potentially more efficient: fewer sample values may be needed to achieve a given accuracy.

The behavior of a batch means analysis for our **M/M/1** simulation model is illustrated in Figure 4.6. The data represented in this figure is from a simulation with the first 200 sample values deleted and a batch size of 2000 (using a random number stream different from that used to produce Figure 4.3). Batch means are shown as •'s, the upper and lower limits of the confidence interval are represented by the dotted lines, and the grand sample mean is represented by the the solid line. Note the slow convergence of the confidence interval toward the mean.

Implementation of a sequential procedure for batch means analysis is straightforward. Figure 4.7 shows a simple batch means analysis module which can be linked with a simulation model to analyze any discrete-time output variable. The *stat.c* file included in this module provides the T() function to compute quantiles of the *t* distribution (see Appendix).

At the start of the simulation, the init_bm() function is called to specify the number of values to be deleted m0 (actually, in this case, the number to be ignored before starting data collection) and the batch size mb. The obs() function is called each time the model generates a new value of

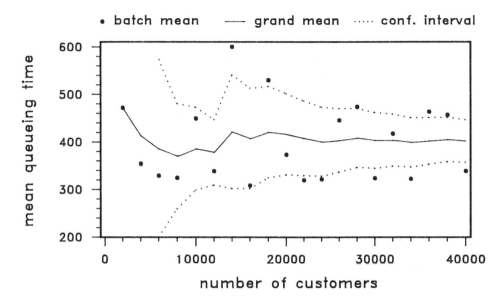

Figure 4.6. Batch Means Analysis Output for an **M/M/1** Queue Simulation

the output variable. If the deletion count is non-zero, `obs()` decrements it and returns. Once the deletion count has been reduced to zero, values of the variable are summed until a full batch is accumulated. The batch mean is computed, added to the batch mean sum, and its square added to the mean squared sum. If ten or more batches have been collected, the grand sample mean and the confidence interval half width are computed. If the relative half width is 0.10 or less, the function return value r is set to 1 to advise the model that the desired accuracy has been obtained. The model can obtain values of the mean, half width, and number of batches by a call to the `civals()` function.

Collection of a minimum of ten batches is based on recommendations made by Schmeiser [1982] whose analysis showed that, for a fixed total sample size n = mk, 10 to 30 batches provides a reasonable compromise between confidence interval coverage and width. The module of Figure 4.7 is "hardwired" for an accuracy of 10 percent at a confidence level of 95 percent, but can easily be modified to permit specifying the desired accuracy and confidence level as initialization parameters. One caution: the number of sample values generated in a batch means analysis may be large, so `int` overflow in **smpl** may be a concern.

```
#include <smpl.h>
#include <stat.c>

static int d,k,m,n;
static real smy,smY,smY2,Y,h;

init_bm(m0,mb)
  int m0,mb;
    { /* set deletion amount & batch size */
      d=m0; m=mb; smy=smY=smY2=0.0; k=n=0;
    }


obs(y)
  real y;
    {
      int r=0; real var;
      if (d) then {d--; return(r);}
      smy+=y; n++;
      if (n==m) then
        { /* batch complete: update sums & counts */
          smy/=n; smY+=smy; smY2+=smy*smy; k++;
          smy=0.0; n=0;
          if (k>=10) then
            { /* compute grand mean & half width */
              Y=smY/k; var=(smY2-k*Y*Y)/(k-1);
              h=T(0.025,k-1)*sqrt(var/k);
              if (h/Y<=0.1) then r=1;
            }
        }
      return(r);
    }

civals(mean,hw,nb)
  real *mean,*hw; int *nb;
    { /* return batch means analysis results */
      *mean=Y; *hw=h; *nb=k;
    }
```

Figure 4.7. Batch Means Analysis Module

You'll find it useful to develop a similar module (or extend this module) for analysis of continuous-time process means, such as mean queue length or mean number in system. For a continuous-time process, the batch "size" is specified as a time interval t, so it is convenient to schedule an event for execution every t time units to compute the current batch mean and confidence interval, and update accumulators. With regard to the last, some care is needed in updating the length-time product sum at batch end time. To see what needs to be done, look at Figure 1.5 and imagine the time axis to be divided into fixed intervals. Try using this module with the M/M/1 simu - lation program of Figure 1.7 to estimate the mean queue length.

One modest extension is worth considering. A trace option to display the batch number, batch mean, and current half-width at the end of each batch will help keep track of the progress of the simulation (and will keep you from worrying about whether or not your model is stuck in a loop).

Recommendations for batch means analysis. The batch means method can be used in a fixed sample size procedure or in a sequential procedure; we'll generally use the latter. Since we don't have to worry about warmup effects (except for the first batch), we can use a batch size which is shorter than the run length we'd use in replication and use a starting number of batches larger than the starting number of replications. This may provide quicker convergence of the half width to the desired value for some process - es. However, in specifying the batch size, we also need to be concerned about independence and normality. Since successive values of output variables usually will be correlated, successive batch means also will be correlated if the batch size is too small, resulting in under-estimation of the half-width. Also, means produced using a small batch size are less likely to satisfy the assumption of approximate normality, resulting in reduced coverage.

These considerations lead to the following recommendations for a sequential procedure using batch means analysis. These recommendations assume a desired accuracy of 10 percent at a 95 percent confidence level.

1. Use a batch size m equal to one-half the run length for replication recommended in the preceding section.

2. Delete $l = 0.1m$ initial observations.

3. Collect k = 10 batches and compute the confidence interval half-width H.

4. If the desired accuracy has not been obtained, collect another batch and compute H again. Repeat as necessary.

These recommendations will result in a total run length larger than needed for some models, but it is best to be conservative.

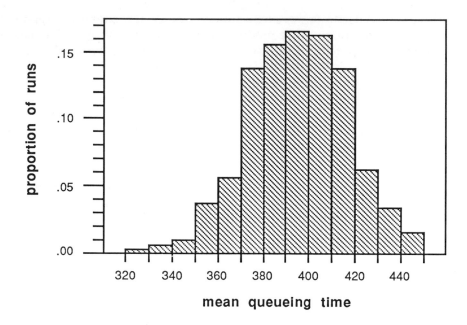

Figure 4.8. Distribution of Means for 300 M/M/1 Queue Simulations

Effect of a sequential procedure on coverage. The previous section noted that use of a sequential procedure will result in a reduction in coverage. Results quoted in Section 2.9 of Fishman [1978] indicate that the reduction is not severe; under certain specific conditions, a sequential procedure based on a confidence level of 0.95 can be shown to result in a coverage of 0.928. In an empirical examination of the effect on coverage, 300 simulations of the M/M/1 queue with Ta = 125, Ts = 100, were performed using the batch means analysis algorithm of Figure 4.7 to estimate the mean queueing time. The specified accuracy was 10 percent, the specified confidence level was 95 percent, and the batch size was 2000 with 200 sample values deleted.

The distribution of the means obtained in these 300 runs is plotted in Figure 4.8. The true mean queueing time u is 400, so estimated means in the range 360 - 440 represent an accuracy of 10 percent. The proportion of runs with means in this range was 0.927, very close to the 0.928 coverage mentioned above. Interestingly, the majority (78 percent) of means outside this range were low, suggesting the possibility that some initialization bias remains. The number of batches per run varied from 10 to 45; the average was 22. Thus, some 44200 sample values are required to obtain 10 percent accuracy in this case, about the same number as required for replication.

Independence-seeking algorithms. The major problem in batch means analysis is determining a batch size large enough to insure that batch means are independent. Algorithms to deal with this problem have been developed by several researchers, including Law and Carson [1979] (also described in Law and Kelton [1982]), and Adam [1983]. Typically, these algorithms start with a small batch size, collect a relatively large number of batches, compute the batch means, and compute an estimate of the correlations of the means. If these correlations are not significant, the batch size is assumed to satisfy the independence requirement; the biased nature of correlation estimators makes this decision the key part of the algorithm. If the correlations are significant, the batch size is doubled and additional sample values are collected. (Increasing the batch size by doubling simplifies things by requiring that only batch sums have to be saved.) When a batch size is reached which provides independence of the means, a sequential procedure is used to obtain the desired accuracy.

Batch means analysis with SMPL. The **bma** module of **SMPL** uses the independence-seeking algorithm proposed by Adam, followed by a sequential procedure which varies slightly from Adam's. This module is described in Chapter 6.

4.8 Improving Simulation Efficiency

The efficiency of a simulation is a measure of the number of sample values needed to achieve a given accuracy, and this number depends on the sample variance. We can see this clearly by rewriting (4.25) as

$$k = [t_{\alpha/2;k-1}/H]^2 \, s^2 \qquad\qquad (4.28)$$

where k is the number of replications or batches, each of which comprises m sample values. For a given accuracy and confidence level (and ignoring the variation of t with k)

$$n = mk \approx cs^2 \qquad\qquad (4.29)$$

where c is a constant. Thus, the sample size required for given accuracy is proportional to the sample variance; we can improve the efficiency of a simulation if we can find some means of reducing the variance.

A number of variance reduction techniques have been developed; if you find yourself working with very long run lengths, you should explore these. Of our simulation texts, Law and Kelton [1982] and Bratley et al [1983] provide the best coverage of this subject. Chapter III of Kleijnen [1975] provides a comprehensive discussion of the subject and of related statistical issues. The basic notions underlying some commonly-cited variance reduction techniques are described below.

Indirect estimation. When a problem requires estimation of a mean value V_1, it may be more efficient to estimate a related value V_2 by simulation and compute V_1 from V_2 using an operational law (Section 1.4), rather than estimate V_1 directly by simulation. Carson and Law [1980] show that, for **GI/G/s** queueing systems (which encompass a wide range of single queue open systems), it is more efficient to compute the mean system residence time and mean number in system from the estimated mean queueing time than it is to estimate them directly. They reported variance reductions ranging from 0 to 99 percent with, unfortunately, the reduction falling off as traffic intensity increases. However, their results do suggest that, when a problem analysis requires many runs, some initial exploration of alternative estimators may be worthwhile. A brief discussion of this approach is given by Law and Kelton [1982].

Antithetic variates. Suppose **y** is an output variable of a particular simulation model, Y_1 is the mean of **y** obtained from one replication of the model and Y_2 is the mean of **y** for a second replication. The mean value of **y**, averaged over the two runs, is $\overline{Y} = (Y_1 + Y_2)/2$. Y_1 and Y_2 are random variables; from the basic law for the sum of two random variables, the variance of $\overline{Y}$ is[7]

$$\mathrm{Var}(\overline{Y}) = [\mathrm{Var}(Y_1) + \mathrm{Var}(Y_2) + 2\mathrm{Cov}(Y_1, Y_2)]/4 \qquad (4.30)$$

Usually we make independent replications, so that the covariance of Y_1 and Y_2 is 0. However, if we can make the covariance negative, the variance of $\overline{Y}$ will be less than that would result from two independent replications and, by pooling the Y's from a number of pairs of replications, we should be able to achieve a given accuracy with fewer total replications than would otherwise be needed. To make the covariance negative, we try to create a negative correlation between corresponding output values in the two runs.

Suppose $y_1{}^i$ and $y_2{}^i$ represent the system residence times of the ith customer in replications 1 and 2 of an **M/M/1** queue simulation. If, when customer i has a long service time in replication 1, we insure that it has a short service time in replication 2, and conversely, the system residence times should be negatively correlated. $y_j{}^i$ is a random variate from a

---

[7]The variance and covariance referred to here are not quantities estimated in the simulation, but rather describe the intrinsic variation of the estimated means.

negative exponential distribution which, as shown in Section 1.2, can be generated by the function $-T \ln r_i$, where T is the mean service time and r_i is a uniform random variate. We can create the desired negative correlation by making sure the same sequence of random numbers is used to generate sample service times on both replications, using r_i to generate y_1^i, and using $1 - r_i$ — the *antithetic* of r_i — to generate y_2^i.

The antithetic variate method is difficult to use in complex models. Also, it doesn't work in all cases and can even increase variance, so it can't be used blindly (see the discussions in the references cited above).

Common random numbers. Suppose we want to analyze the effect of two alternative designs on a model output variable y, and two simulation runs, one using alternative 1 and the second using alternative 2, produce means Y_1 and Y_2. We are interested in estimating the difference $D = Y_1 - Y_2$, whose variance is

$$\text{Var}(D) = \text{Var}(Y_1) + \text{Var}(Y_2) - 2\text{Cov}(Y_1, Y_2) \tag{4.31}$$

Here, we can reduce the variance of the estimate if we can make the covariance positive. We should be able to accomplish this in many cases by using identical input parameter values for corresponding customers in the two runs. One way to do this is to create a file of input parameter values, with the ith record in the file providing attribute values for the ith customer in both runs (thus mimicking a trace-driven simulation). Another way is to use a *common random number* sequence to generate values of a particular parameter for both runs, so that the ith customer has the same value of this parameter on both runs. As with antithetic variates, we use a number of pairs of runs to achieve the desired accuracy. (We'll discuss estimation of a confidence interval for the difference between two means in the next section.)

This method has the intuitive appeal of providing a "controlled" environment for the comparison; D is less affected by run-to-run parameter sample value variations than would be the case in independent runs, and so should better reflect actual design differences. While we can't be sure in advance that this method will provide a worthwhile (or any) increase in efficiency, it should definitely be considered when the need for variance reduction arises.

Both antithetic variates and common random numbers require that different random number streams be used to generate sample values of different model input parameters. We'll discuss **smpl** extensions to accomplish this in Chapter 9.

Control variables. Again, suppose that the objective of a simulation experiment is to produce an estimate of the mean of an output variable y. A *control variable* is a random variable which is correlated with y and whose expectation is known. For example, y might be a system residence time (whose expectation we presumably don't know); however, system residence times should be correlated with service times (whose expectation is a model input parameter). We know that some of the variance of y is due to service time variation; the method of control variables exploits this knowledge to obtain an estimate of y which has lower variance than the usual estimate. Details of the method are provided in the references cited earlier.

The control variable method involves some statistical complexity, and isn't recommended for the beginning modeler. Implementation of this method is very much model-specific, so it is best suited for high-use general-purpose simulation models such as queueing network simulators. Lavenberg et al [1977], [1982] describe its application and performance in this context.

There are other techniques for variance reduction: some of these were developed for other forms of simulation (e.g., integral evaluation), and may or may not have application in our area of interest. Kleijnen [1975] provides an extensive discussion. The best choice for the beginning modeler is the common random number method.

4.9 Problem Analysis

Up to now we've primarily been concerned with estimating a single measure for a single simulation experiment. However, in practice, we often want to estimate several different performance measures for a particular design and compare performance measures for different designs. This brings us to a new subject area: the statistical analysis of experiments. We can only touch on a couple of points here, and give some references for further reading.

Multiple measures. Suppose we collect r different performance measures in a simulation experiment and compute a $100(1 - \alpha)$ percent confidence interval for each measure. The probability that all r intervals simultaneously contain the true mean μ of each measure is

$$\text{Pr(all intervals contains)} \geq 1 - \sum_{i=1}^{r} \alpha_i \qquad (4.32)$$

Thus, if 95 percent confidence intervals were computed for three different measures, the probability that all three intervals contain the true means of those measures may be as low as $1 - 3 \times 0.05 = 0.85$.

(4.32) is called the *Bonferroni inequality*. It implies that if we want an overall confidence level of $100(1 - \alpha)$ percent, we should choose values of α_i for the individual measures so that $\sum \alpha_i = \alpha$. The values of the α_i don't have to be the same; we can assign higher values to the more important measures. However, in any case, multiple measures impose either longer run lengths or wider confidence intervals.

Comparing two designs. In modeling computer and communication systems, we'll often be asked to evaluate two alternative designs. There are many ways to do this; we'll look at just one, a paired comparison method for estimating a confidence interval for the difference between two means.

Suppose **y** is the output variable on which the comparison is to be based. For each design, we obtain estimates of the mean **Y** for each of k replications or for each of k batches. If we're using a sequential procedure to achieve a specified accuracy for **Y**, the number of replications or batches may be larger for one design than for the other; if this happens, the extra means are discarded. Let Y_{1i} and Y_{2i} be the means obtained on the ith replication or batch for designs 1 and 2, and D_i be the difference between these means: $D_i = Y_{1i} - Y_{2i}$. A confidence interval half-width HD for the overall mean difference $\overline{D}$ can be computed in the same way as a confidence interval for the mean.

$$\overline{D} = \sum_{i=1}^{k} D_i/k \qquad (4.33)$$

$$s^2 = \sum_{i=1}^{k} (D_i - \overline{D})^2/(k-1) \qquad (4.34)$$

$$HD = t_{\alpha/2;k-1}\, s/k^{1/2} \qquad (4.35)$$

Y_{1i} and Y_{2i} do not have to be independent (nor do their variances have to be equal, which is required by some methods). Consequently, this method accommodates the use of common random numbers to reduce the variance of $\overline{D}$ and thus obtain a "tighter" confidence interval.

Some methods of computing a confidence interval for $\overline{D}$ do not pair means for the two designs and do not require that the number of means be the same for both designs. For a discussion of these and other methods, see Law and Kelton [1982], Kleijnen [1975], or an experimental statistics text such as Box et al [1978].

Multiple comparisons and experimental design. Things get more complicated when we want to compare more than two design alternatives; Law and Kelton [1982] describe methods for selecting the best of n designs and for selecting a subset of given size containing the best of n designs; the latter can be used in a pilot study to select the best candidates for further analysis. Some studies potentially require a very large number of experiments. For example, consider an operating system design study which involves three different processor scheduling algorithms and two different paging algorithms, each combination of which is to be evaluated for a range of values of several workload parameters. A direct approach to this problem requires a very large number of simulation runs; however, through the use of the appropriate experimental design methodology, this number can be substantially reduced. Law and Kelton [1982] and Banks and Carson [1984] provide an introduction to experimental design in simulation, and an extensive discussion is given by Kleijnen [1975]. There are a number of good texts on the statistical design of experiments, such as Box et al [1978].

4.10 Summary

This chapter has presented basic methods for estimating simulation accuracy and for achieving a desired accuracy. We've seen that the one-run, one-number approach to simulation can produce results that are substantially in error. There is no excuse, other than ignorance, for this approach. Computing cost seldom is an issue today, but even if cost is a problem, the production of cheap but wrong results hardly is the solution. Compared to model development and programming costs, the cost of output analysis usually is small and certainly is insignificant compared to the cost of making a bad design decision. The batch means analysis module of Section 4.7 easily can be (and, routinely, should be) incorporated into your simulation models.

While the importance of proper output analysis cannot be over-emphasized, it is equally important not to succumb to the siren song of x percent accuracy at a y percent confidence level. Output analysis methods help us obtain an accurate estimate of a performance measure for a model; how accurately that measure represents system performance depends on the validity of the assumptions used to construct the model and characterize its workload.

4.11 Problems

note. Confidence interval estimates in the following problems are to be computed using a 95 percent confidence level.

1. Make 5 simulation runs of the timesharing system simulation model of problem 5, Chapter 2, using a different random number stream for each run. Record the throughput and response time from each run. Compute a relative confidence interval half-width for each estimate, using equations (4.22) - (4.26). Which estimate has the larger relative half-width? Suppose a relative confidence interval half-width also had been computed for the mean number in the system; how would you expect it to compare with those for throughput and response time?

2. Design and implement a simulation run control function you can use with any **smpl** model based on the sequential replication procedure of Section 4.6. This function should compute and display the current mean and relative half-width of a selected output variable at the end of each run (after the first). At the end of the fifth run, it should compute k*, and display a warning message and pause if k* is greater than 15 (the number of **smpl** random number streams). The function should terminate the simulation when an accuracy of 10% is reached, even if the number of runs is less than k*; however, a minimum of 5 runs should be executed.

Use this function to control execution of the **M/M/2** queue simulation model of problem 1, Chapter 2 (with Ta = 125.0), in estimating the mean system residence time W. To determine what run length to use, compute the expected mean utilization per server. Make three sets of runs, terminating each set after the fifth run. Use streams 1-5 for the first set, streams 6-10 for the second set, and streams 11-15 for the third set. (Make an explicit stream() call after each smpl() call in a run to set the desired stream number, since **smpl** will otherwise use its own stream number.) Record the mean, relative half-width, and k* values displayed at the end of each set of runs. Note the differences in the relative half-widths obtained in five runs (and the consequences of using a fixed sample size procedure).[8]

For comparison with your estimated means, the theoretical mean residence time in the **M/M/2** queue is Ts/(1 - ρ^2), where ρ = Ts/2Ta.

3. Modify your simulation model of the timesharing system of problem 3, Chapter 2, to use exponential disk service times with the same mean service time as the original model. Run the simulation with N = 4, 8, 12, 16, 20 and 24 terminals, using the batch means analysis module of Figure 4.7 to obtain a

---

[8]Your results will depend on the random number generator used; relative half-widths of 0.199, 0.096, and 0.110 were obtained on the three sets of runs using the version of ranf() given in the Appendix.

relative half-width H/R of 10% or less for the mean reponse time R of this system. (If time is a constraint, limit your runs to N = 8, 16, and 20.) Use the recommendations of Section 4.7 to determine the batch size and initial deletion amount. Plot the values of R+H and R–H, together with the mean response time computed using the MVA function of Figure 3.5, versus N. Since this function uses a minimum of 10 batches, the accuracy obtained in a given run may be better than the specified 10%. How does the actual accuracy vary with N?

If your confidence intervals for these runs cover the mean response times computed using the MVA function, and you obtain similar coverage for throughput, you can assume that your simulation model has been satisfactorily verified by comparison with an analytic model. What would you do if the confidence interval for one of the runs did not contain the mean computed using MVA?

4. Design and implement a batch means analysis module to provide a sequential procedure for estimating means of continuous-time processes, such as mean queue length. (See the discussion in Section 4.7.) This can be a companion module to that of Figure 4.7; however, you'll end up with a more useful tool if you integrate the two modules. Instrument the module to display each batch mean as it is computed. Test the module by using it to estimate the mean number in queue and service, L, in the **M/M/2** queue whose mean system residence time was studied in problem 2. Make three runs, each with a different stream; for each run, use the displayed batch means to compute the grand mean and its relative half-width. For verification purposes, the theoretical value of L can be computed from the theoretical value of W using Little's Law.

5. Describe how you would obtain a 10% confidence interval for the probability that a binary search of the table described in problem 7, Chapter 1, requires 4 or more comparisons.

6. Describe how you would obtain a 10% confidence interval for the probability that two or more customers are in queue and service in the **M/M/2** queue of problem 4.

5. A Multiprocessor System Model

5.1 Introduction

In earlier chapters, we discussed two **smpl** simulation models: a simple single-server queueing system model and a two-class queueing network model. In this chapter, we'll look at another example: a model of memory and bus contention in a multiprocessor system. This example presents some new modeling problems and further illustrates the use of **smpl**. We'll begin by developing an analytic model of the system, and then develop a simulation model to check the analytic results. After cross-verifying analytic and simulation results, we'll consider ways of extending the simulation model to eliminate some of the assumptions used in the analytic approach.

5.2 The Multiprocessor System

The system we'll be studying is diagrammed in Figure 5.1. It comprises **N** processors and **M** global memory modules (or, simply, memories) interconnected by **B** buses so that every processor can access every memory. Transfers between processors and memories take place in fixed-size units equal to the bus width, so that each transfer requires one bus cycle. The system is synchronous: all memory requests are initiated at the same point in a cycle.

We'll assume — at least for now — that the **N** processors are physically and functionally identical. Each processor has its own local memory, which may be a cache or may take the form of data registers and an instruction buffer. When executing, a processor issues an instruction fetch or an operand fetch or store request in every machine cycle. This request is satisfied in the processor's local memory with probability **h** and requires access to (global) memory with probability $p = 1 - h$. **h** is called the *hit ratio* and **p** is called the *miss ratio*. Memory request processing takes place as follows.

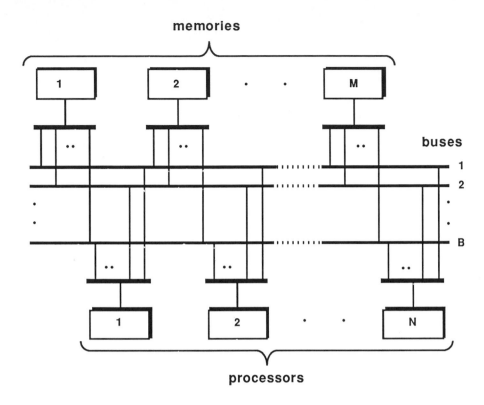

Figure 5.1. Multiprocessor System Elements

1. A processor initiates a memory request at the start of a machine cycle and simultaneously suspends execution. Multiple requests for the same module are resolved by an arbitration mechanism. We'll assume that this mechanism tries to provide fair service via a cyclical scan of processors for requests, with the scan starting point being advanced on each new scan.

2. If a request is successful, the module is reserved for the processor; otherwise, the request is reissued at the start of the next cycle. From the set of up to **M** successful requests, a second arbitration mechanism selects up to **B** requests and reserves buses for these requests. We'll assume this is done in the same order in which modules were reserved. If a request is unsuccessful in obtaining a bus, the module is released and the request reissued at the start of the next cycle.

3. Next, for a successful request, the address and data, if the request is a store, are transmitted over the bus to memory; if the request is a fetch, data is returned over the bus at the end of the cycle.

4. When the bus cycle ends, processors whose requests were successfully completed are returned to execution, and the buses and modules reserved by these requests are released. Unsuccessful requests are reissued, together with new requests, at the start of the next cycle.

Our objective is to determine how processor performance is affected by contention for memory modules and buses.

This system, in various forms, has received a great deal of attention over the years. When the number of buses is equal to the number of memories (**B = M**), the interconnection between processors and memories is equivalent to a *crossbar* network, and performance is affected only by memory contention. Most of the early analysis work focused on this problem; most recent work encompasses systems with **B < M** and considers both bus and memory contention.

5.3 An Approximate Analytic Model

The analytic model we'll develop in this section is based on that described by Mudge et al [1984]: the references in that paper provide a good starting point for surveying work done in this area. There are several measures of performance of interest to us; the one we'll look at first is the system bandwidth, **BW**. This is the overall transfer rate between processors and memory, expressed in terms of transfers per unit time. Since the transfer time is 1 cycle, the overall bus utilization is (numerically but not dimensionally) equal to **BW**, and **BW** sometimes is defined as the average number of busy buses.

The miss ratio **p** was defined as the probability that a processor issues a (global) memory request in a given cycle. If we assume that the probability of issuing a request in any one cycle is the same as, and independent of, the probability of issuing a request in any other cycle, then a processor's execution interval corresponds to a sequence of Bernoulli trials. Execution intervals therefore have a geometric distribution with mean $x = (1 - p)/p$ and variance $\sigma^2 = (1 - p)/p^2$ (see, for example, Allen [1978] or Trivedi [1982]). The geometric distribution is the discrete counterpart of the negative exponential distribution. We'll also assume that memory requests are independently and uniformly distributed across memories (since memory module selection typically is based on the low-order address bits).

Consider the long-term behavior of the system, looking first at those cycles which have no reissued requests from the preceding cycle. Based on the assumptions of the preceding paragraph, the probability that processor i requests memory j is p/M for all i and j. The probability that processor i does not request memory j is $1 - p/M$, and the probability that none of the N processors requests memory j is $(1 - p/M)^N$. Therefore, the probability q that there is at least one request for memory j is

$$q = 1 - (1 - p/M)^N \tag{5.1}$$

Assuming memory request probabilities are identical and independent, the probability f_i that exactly i of M memories have requests is binomial:[1]

$$f_i = \binom{M}{i} q^i (1 - q)^{M-i} \tag{5.2}$$

The expected number of distinct memories requested in the cycle is qM.

While qM requests may be presented to the bus arbitration mechanism in a cycle, no more than B requests can be granted. The expected number of bus requests granted in a cycle — equal numerically to the bandwidth — is

$$BW = B \sum_{i=B}^{M} f_i + \sum_{i=1}^{B-1} i f_i \tag{5.3}$$

The bandwidth estimated from (5.1) - (5.3) applies only to cycles in which no requests are reissued; in this case, the average request rate per processor is the same as the miss rate p, and the overall request rate is Np. In the general case, considering all cycles, the per processor request rate r is greater than the miss rate (since it comprises both initial and reissued requests). An exact analysis is difficult; however, if we can estimate r, we can use it in place of p in (5.1) and obtain an improved estimate of BW.

Now look at the processor inter-request interval — the interval between two successful memory request completions — shown in Figure 5.2. The mean overall length of this interval is T. We can divide T into three parts: an execution interval of mean length $x = (1 - p)/p$, a delay interval whose mean

---

[1]This is an approximation: note, for example, that f_0 should be 0 for $p = 1$, while (5.1) and (5.2) give $f_0 > 0$. However, the error is small, even for M as small as 4.

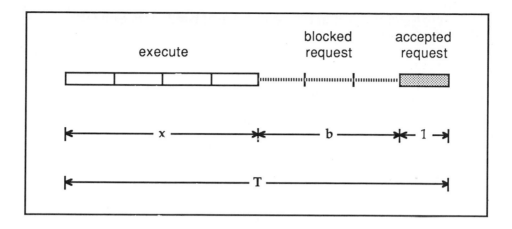

Figure 5.2. Processor Inter-Request Interval Timing

length is defined as **b**, and a 1-cycle transfer time for the accepted request. **b** represents the delay incurred when a request is blocked and reissued in the succeeding cycle. The single processor request rate (counting both blocked and accepted requests) is

$$r = (b + 1)/T = (b + 1)/(x + b + 1) \tag{5.4}$$

dividing numerator and denominator by b+1,

$$r = [1 + x/(b + 1)]^{-1} \tag{5.5}$$

Since **r** represents both blocked and accepted requests, **b + 1 = rT** is the total number of requests issued in **T**. The per processor request completion rate is **BW/N**: the reciprocal of this rate is the mean interval between completed requests **T**, so **T = N/BW** and **b + 1 = Nr/BW**. Substituting the last for **b + 1** in (5.5),

$$r = [1 + xBW/Nr]^{-1} \tag{5.6}$$

(5.6) defines **r** as a function of **r** (both directly and indirectly, since **BW** is a function of **r**), and can be used in a simple fixed-point iterative algorithm (see, for example, Rice [1983]) to estimate **BW**. This algorithm works as follows.

1. Use (5.1) - (5.3) to compute an initial bandwidth estimate BW_0. Define $r_0 = p$.

2. Compute an improved estimate of r from

$$r_i = [1 + xBW_{i-1}/Nr_{i-1}]^{-1} \qquad (5.7)$$

3. Compute

$$q = 1 - (1 - r_i/M)^N \qquad (5.8)$$

and use (5.2) and (5.3) to compute a new estimate BW_i.

4. If $|BW_i - BW_{i-1}| < \varepsilon$, where ε depends on the desired accuracy, terminate; otherwise, return to step 2.

A C implementation of this algorithm, with $\varepsilon = 0.005$, is given in Figure 5.3. You'll need to provide a main program to call BW() with values of p, B, M, N, and to report results. Timing diagram relationships, together with the operational laws discussed in Section 1.4, can be used to obtain other measures: let's look at some of these.

Utilizations and waiting time. The average utilizations of a single bus, single memory module, and single processor are, respectively, $UB = BW/B$, $UM = BW/M$, and $UP = xBW/N$ (from the Utilization Law). The average waiting (blocked) time per request is b: from Figure 5.2, $b = T - x - 1$. Since $T = N/BW$ and $x + 1 = 1/p$,

$$b = (N/BW) - (1/p) \qquad (5.9)$$

We could also obtain this result via the Response Time Law (Section 1.4). This law typically is presented in the context of a time-sharing system, where it has the form

$$R = (N/X) - Z \qquad (5.10)$$

Here, R is the mean response time at a terminal, N is the number of terminals, X is the computer system throughput, and Z is the mean think time at a terminal (mean time between successive system requests). The correspondence between this system and our multiprocessor system is

$$
\begin{array}{rcl}
\text{computer system} & - & \text{memory/bus subsystem} \\
\text{N terminals} & - & \text{N processors} \\
\text{mean think time Z} & - & \text{mean execution interval } x \\
\text{system throughput X} & - & \text{bandwidth } BW \\
\text{mean response time R} & - & \text{mean request processing time } b + 1
\end{array}
$$

```
real BW(p,B,M,N)
   real p; int B,M,N;
      {
        real bw0,bw1=p*N,r=p,x=1.0/p-1.0,BWi();
        do
           {
             bw0=bw1; r=1.0/(1.0+x*bw0/(N*r));
             bw1=BWi(r,B,M,N);
           }
        while (fabs(bw1-bw0)>0.005);
        return(bw1);
      }

real BWi(r,B,M,N)
   real r; int B,M,N;
      { /* compute bandwidth for request rate r */
        int i; real q,bw=0.0,f();
        q=1.0-pow(1.0-r/M,(real)N);
        for (i=1; i<B; i++)  bw+=i*f(i,M,q);
        for (i=B; i<=M; i++) bw+=B*f(i,M,q);
        return(bw);
      }

real Fact(n)
   int n;
      { /* compute n factorial */
        real z=1.0;
        while (n) {z*=n; n--;}
        return(z);
      }

real C(n,k)
   int n,k;
      { /* compute binomial coefficient */
        return(Fact(n)/(Fact(k)*Fact(n-k)));
      }

real f(i,M,q)
   int i,M; real q;
      { /* compute binomial probability */
        real z;
        z=C(M,i)*pow(q,(real)i)*pow(1.0-q,(real)(M-i));
        return(z);
      }
```

Figure 5.3. Bandwidth Computation Algorithm

Making the appropriate substitutions in (5.10) results in (5.9).

Mean queue length. Let L_b be the average number of blocked requests outstanding per processor. From Little's Law,

$$L_b = bBW/N \tag{5.11}$$

from which

$$L_b = 1 - BW/Np \tag{5.12}$$

(5.12) also can be obtained as follows. In any given period of time, a processor spends, on the average, proportions UP executing, L_b waiting, and BW/N transferring: thus, $UP + BW/N + L_b = 1$. Substituting for UP and subsequently for x, and rearranging terms gives (5.12).

System throughput. While the bandwidth provides a direct measure of memory-bus subsystem performance, it is only an indirect measure of system performance. For a given configuration (B, M, N), a processor design change which increases the miss rate will result in an increase in BW but reduced system throughput. Suppose the unit of work in this system is a task, and each task requires an average of n execution intervals: the average service time per task, then, is nx. From the Utilization Law, the system throughput is $N[UP/nx]$ tasks per unit time. For design comparisons, it may be useful to work with the *normalized* system throughput η, obtained by taking $nx = 1$:

$$\eta = NUP = N[xBW/N] = BW[(1/p) - 1] \tag{5.13}$$

Note that if there are no contention delays, $BW = Np$ and $\eta = N(1 - p)$, and if the miss rate p is zero, $\eta = N$.

Our bandwidth analysis is approximate because, among other things, it assumes that memory request probabilities are independent in (5.1) and (5.2). This is equivalent to assuming that a request blocked on access to module j is assigned at random to one of the M modules when reissued. In the actual system, a blocked request for module j is reissued to module j, so the probability that module j is referenced in cycle n is not independent of whether or not it was referenced in cycle n–1. In the next section, we'll look at a simulation model which can be used to verify the approximate analytic model and also evaluate the effect of this independence assumption.

5.4 Verifying the Analytic Model

The kind of simulation model we develop for analytic model verification depends on our objectives. In the case of the multiprocessor system, our objective is to verify that the analytic model adequately represents the behavior of the system, so the simulation model reflects the structure of the system. Sometimes, though, our objective may be to check the assumptions and mathematics of the analysis itself, and our model may be much more abstract in form. As a simple example of this case, suppose we need to deter- mine the average seek distance on a disk. We assume disk requests are independently and uniformly distributed across the C cylinders of a disk,[2] and our derivation results in an average seek distance of approximately C/3. We can verify this result via a simple simulation in which we generate a sequence of random numbers $X_1, X_2, \ldots$, each of which is uniformly distributed in [1, C], and compute the average absolute difference $|X_i - X_{i-1}|$. This type of checking is a great help in catching mistakes in analytic models; we may not be able to apply it to a model as a whole, but often can use it to check individual steps.

A **smpl** simulation model developed to validate our analytic model is shown in Figure 5.4; for reference purposes, we'll call this model *bws1*. This model defines memory modules and buses as **smpl** facilities, while processors are represented as tokens. Global declarations define the miss rate p, the number of processors N, the number of memory modules M, and the number of buses nB (remember that B is a **smpl** function name), together with the facility descriptors module[] and bus. treq[n] is used to record the next memory request issue time for processor n, and req[n] to record the module number of a request; tn, the earliest-occurring request time, is initialized to a large value.

Model initialization is straightforward. smpl() is called to initialize the simulation subsystem, facilities are declared, next_access() is called to determine the initial access time for each processor and to compute tn, and the first event is scheduled at time tn. Each memory module is defined as a single-server facility, while the set of buses is defined as a multiserver facility; since any bus can be used for a transfer, buses need not be distin- guishable.

The next_access() function generates a processor execution interval by generating a random variate from a geometric distribution with mean $(1 - p)/p$; it then adds this interval to the current simulation time to obtain the simulation time at which the processor's next memory request is to be issued. (Note that treq[n] is an event occurrence time, not an inter-event time.) If the request issue time t computed for processor n is less than the

---

[2]This assumption frequently has been shown to be invalid in practice: see, for example, McNutt [1984].

```
#include <smpl.h>
#define busy 1

real
  p=0.250,          /* local memory miss rate          */
  treq[17],         /* next request time for processor */
  tn=1.0E6;         /* earliest-occurring request time */
int
  N=8,M=4,nB=2,     /* no. processors, memories, & buses */
  module[17],bus,   /* memory & bus facility descriptors */
  nbs=0,            /* no. busy buses in current cycle   */
  req[17],          /* currently-requested memory module */
  next=1;           /* arbitration scan starting point   */

/*------------ MEMORY-BUS BANDWIDTH MODEL ------------*/
main()
  {
    int event,i,n;
    smpl(0,"Bandwidth Model");
    bus=facility("bus",nB);
    for (i=1; i<=M; i++) module[i]=facility("module",1);
    for (n=1; n<=N; n++) {req[n]=0; next_access(n);}
    schedule(1,tn,0);
    while (time()<10000.0)
      {
        cause(&event,&n);
        switch(event)
          {
            case 1:  begin_cycle(); break;
            case 2:  req_module(n); break;
            case 3:  end_cycle(n);  break;
          }
      }
    printf("BW = %.3f\n",U(bus));
  }

/*------------ COMPUTE NEXT ACCESS TIME ------------*/
next_access(n)
  int n;
    {
      real t;
      t=floor(log(ranf())/log(1.0-p))+time();
      treq[n]=t; if (t<tn) then tn=t;
    }
```

Figure 5.4. Multiprocessor Simulation Model *bws1*

```
/*------------- EVENT 1:   BEGIN CYCLE   --------------*/
begin_cycle()
  {
    int i,n=next; real t,tmin=1.0E6;
    for (i=0; i<N; i++)
      {
        if (!req[n]) then
          { /* in this version, req[n] always is 0 here */
            if ((t=treq[n])==tn)
              then
                {req[n]=random(1,M); schedule(2,0.0,n);}
              else if (t<tmin) then tmin=t;
          }
        n=(n%N)+1;
      }
    next=(next%N)+1; tn=tmin;
  }

/*--------- EVENT 2:   REQUEST MEMORY AND BUS  ---------*/
req_module(n)
  int n;
    {
      if (status(module[req[n]]!=busy&&status(bus)!=busy)
        then
          {
            request(module[req[n]],n,0); request(bus,n,0);
            nbs++; schedule(3,1.0,n);
          }
        else
          {req[n]=0; if (++treq[n]<tn) then tn=treq[n];}
    }

/*-------------- EVENT 3:   END CYCLE   ---------------*/
end_cycle(n)
  int n;
    {
      release(bus,n); release(module[req[n]],n);
      req[n]=0: next_access(n);
      if (--nbs==0) then schedule(1,tn-time(),0);
    }
```

Figure 5.4. Multiprocessor Simulation Model *bws1* (continued)

current earliest-occurring request time `tn`, `tn` is set to `t`. A geometric variate is generated by the expression

```
floor(log(ranf())/log(1-p))
```

This is obtained from the inverse distribution function of the geometric distribution (see problem 2(c), Chapter 1). Because of the use of the `floor()` function, simulation times will be non-fractional.

The major difference between this model and the simulation models of Chapters 1 and 2 is its synchronous operation. In this model, the unit of time is the bus cycle; time advances in integer multiples of this unit, and events occur either at the beginning or at the end of a cycle. Since the end of one cycle corresponds to the beginning of the next and so are the same instant in simulation time, we can't rely on the event list to insure that events occur in the proper order. In this model, order is maintained by "batching" memory request initiations and completions. There are a variety of other ways to accomplish this. For example, in the actual system, a bus cycle divides into some number of clock cycles. Using the clock cycle as the unit of time would solve the problem, since the beginning of bus cycle *n* would occur at a later clock cycle than the end of bus cycle *n*–1. Another possibility is to extend the event list mechanism to provide **T-** and **T+** scheduling (i.e., to recognize the beginning and end of a time unit).

The model proper comprises three event routines: `begin_cycle()`, `req_module()`, and `end_cycle()`. At any point during the simulation, `treq[n]` is the next request issue time for processor n, and `tn` is the earliest-occurring request issue time. Event 1 is scheduled to occur at time `tn` as part of model initialization and, subsequently, by `end_cycle()`. `begin_cycle()` scans the set of N processors for those issuing requests at time `tn` and, for each such processor, assigns a random memory module as the request destination and schedules the memory (and bus) request, event 2. This check is made only for processors for which `req[n]` is zero: this always is true for model *bws1* (but not for the variant we'll look at in the next section). Each scan of the processor set begins with processor `next`, which is advanced at the end of each scan. This represents the arbitration mechanism of the system more closely than it does the assumed random processor selection of our analytic model. However, it is more efficient to simulate than random processing, introduces less bias than a 1→N scan, and has little effect on the results. As `begin_cycle()` does its scan, it keeps track of the earliest-occurring request issue time following `tn` and, at the end of the scan, updates `tn` to this time.

`begin_cycle()` schedules event 2 for each processor it finds with a request issue time of `tn`: this event, like event 1, occurs at the beginning of a cycle. The event 2 routine, `req_module()`, checks to see if the requested memory module is free and if a bus is free. If these conditions are met, the module and a bus are reserved, the number of buses busy in this cycle, `nbs`, is incremented, and completion of the request is scheduled to occur at the end of the cycle. (Note that the inter-event time is 1.) If the requested module is busy or if a bus cannot be obtained, the request is blocked for reissue at the start of the next cycle: `req[n]` is set to zero and the request issue time `treq[n]` is incremented. If this new request issue time is less than `tn`, `tn` is adjusted accordingly. When the request is reissued, a memory module will selected at random for it, thus satisfying the independence assumption of our analytic model.

Event 3 marks the completion of a request at the end of a bus cycle. The bus and memory module are released, `req[n]` is set to zero, and `next_access()` is called to compute the next request issue time for the processor. `nbs` is decremented and, if end-of-cycle processing is complete for all bus transfers initiated in the current cycle (`nbs = 0`), event 1 is scheduled at time `tn`. The `nbs` count provides the basic mechanism for the request "batching" mentioned earlier. Note that, since `tn` is an event occurrence time, the current simulation time has to be subtracted from it in making the `schedule()` call.

At the end of the simulation interval specified in the `while` statement in `main()`, the utilization of the bus is printed as the bandwidth and model execution then is terminated. Remember that bus utilization and bandwidth are numerically the same only because the bus service time is 1.

The simulation model in Figure 5.4 was coded for compactness and can be improved in several ways. Its performance can be improved by the use of pointers, and by precomputing the factor `1.0/(1.0-p)` in geometric variate generation. Its usefulness can be improved by providing a procedure to read values of the input parameters `nB`, `M`, `N`, and `p` (with **SMPL**, they can be defined as **SMPL** parameters and their values then specified via the parameter display). Finally, procedures for specifying the desired accuracy and determining the requisite run length are needed.

Output analysis. Methods of determining the run length required to achieve a specified simulation accuracy were discussed in Chapter 4. A sequential procedure using the batch means method was recommended, and a set of procedures implementing this method for a discrete-time output variable was presented in Figure 4.7. In our present problem, the simulation output variable — the bandwidth — is a continuous-time variable, so the procedures of Figure 4.7 can't be used directly. However, a similar approach can be used, and the code will be even simpler, since collection of values for and computation of individual batch means doesn't have to be done. For a continuous-time variable, the batch size is defined as a fixed-length simulation interval t. The model schedules an event every t cycles and, when the event occurs, calls `U(bus)` to get the bandwidth — the current batch mean — for the interval, and then calls `reset()` to reinitialize **smpl's** counters and accumulators. Given that at least two batch means have been collected, a confidence interval can be computed and the relative half-width compared with the required accuracy to determine whether to terminate the run or to go on and collect another batch. You'll find extending the batch means analysis module of Figure 4.7 to handle continuous-time as well as discrete-time output variables is not only a good exercise but also a worthwhile enhancement to your set of simulation tools. (See problem 4, Chapter 4.)

When using simulation to verify analytic results, we'll frequently want to use tighter confidence intervals and higher confidence levels than we would in problem analysis so that differences in results due to inherent differences in the two models won't be attributed to sampling variation. (This desire is tempered by the run lengths which may result.) The author's simulations of this system were performed using the sequential batch means procedure discussed above with a specified confidence level and relative half-width of, respectively, 99 percent and 1 percent, a batch "size" of 1000 cycles, and a minimum number of batches equal to 10. Over the range of parameters studied ($2 \leq N \leq 16$, $N/2 \leq M \leq N$, $1 \leq B \leq M$, $0.1 \leq p \leq 1$), the desired accuracy was obtained with the minimum number of batches. Long runs were not required because the coefficient of variation of bus utilization is low: the system is closed, the population (in the study range) is low, and the service time is constant.

Comparison of results. Our multiprocessor model has four parameters: three are discrete-valued and one (p) is continuous-valued. If we limit verification to the parameters mentioned in the preceding paragraph, using an increment of 0.1 for p, checking each parameter value combination will require an extremely large number of runs: 30 runs would be required just for $N = 2$. (How many would be required at $N = 16$?) An exhaustive comparison of analytic and simulation results, then, probably is not feasible; we need to find a more selective approach.[3]

One thing we can do is plot the analytic results to see how **BW** changes with changes in parameter values, and concentrate our verification efforts on the more "interesting" points. What are these? Consider Figure 5.5, which

---

[3]While in this case we want to verify an analytic model (the test model) against a simulation model (the base model), the same problem arises when their roles are reversed so that the simulation model is the test model and the analytic model is the base model.

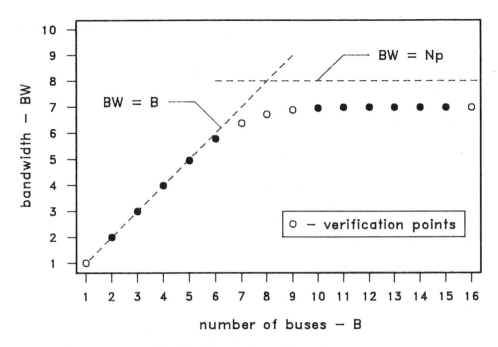

Figure 5.5. Bandwidth Versus No. of Buses for $N = M = 8$, $p = 0.5$

plots bandwidth versus the number of buses, **B**, for **M=N=8** and **p=0.5**. When the number of buses is small, the bandwidth is bus-limited (the buses are said to be saturated), and **BW=B**. The test model probably will yield this result for small values of **B** even if it's not a very good model. In the case at hand, we can verify this by inspection: we don't need to run a simulation. As the number of buses becomes large, bus delays become small and **BW** approaches a limit determined by memory delays: this limit is parallel to the contention-free bandwidth **Np**. Since the rate of change in this range is very small, we can limit our comparison to the endpoint **B=16**. The interesting points are those for **B = 7, 8** and **9**: the points which fall between the region in which **BW** is bus-limited and the region in which it is memory-limited. If the test and base model results at these points and at endpoints are in close agreement, further verification effort probably should be directed elsewhere in the parameter space.

In this approach, each plot usually is generated as a set of curves (e.g., **BW** versus **B** for **p** = 0.1, 0.2, ..., 1.0), and so gives us a kind of two-dimensional view of what, in this case, is a four-dimensional response surface. (If you have actual three-dimensional plotting capability, so much the better!)

While a number of plots are needed, practice brings proficiency in selecting the parameter combinations which provide the most revealing views.

When working blind (without plots), a common approach is to choose verification points at logarithmic increments in parameter values. For example, in the case of the parameters represented in Figure 5.5, we might compare **BW** values at **B** values of 1, 2, 4, 8, and 16. The risk in doing this is the possibility of missing a point of inflection in the response curve when the separation between comparison points is large; this shouldn't be a problem if we have a general idea of what this curve should look like.

In a later section, we'll compare some of the results from *bws1* with those of the analytic model. For now, let's assume that the analytic model has been verified to our satisfaction and consider changing some of the assumptions made in the analytic model and incorporated in *bws1*.

5.5 A Synchronous Queueing Model

Our analytic model effectively assumes that a request blocked on access to module j is reassigned at random to any one of the **M** modules when reissued, and this assumption was reflected in simulation model *bws1*. This assumption easily is removed from *bws1*: delete the statement `req[n]=0` in `req_module()` and, in `begin_cycle()`, delete the `if(!req[n])` statement and add an `if` statement to select a module for the processor's request only if `req[n]` is zero. The resulting model provides more or less random selection of requests for queues and buses, while the actual system may provide some type of request queueing. To see how much effect this has on performance, let's look at a model of the system in which module and bus requests are queued on a first-in, first-out basis.

Model diagram. A queueing model for the system is diagrammed in Figure 5.6. While this is a closed queueing network like that of Figure 2.1, the symbols are new. In Figure 2.1, each symbol represents a simple single-server queue at which requests arrive, queue for service, reserve the server, receive service, release the server, and depart. In Figure 5.6, processors are represented by a *delay server*, whose symbol is a set of circles enclosed in braces. (This sometimes is called an *infinite server*.) A delay server always has enough servers to accommodate requests and so has no queueing: requests arrive, receive service, and depart. The terminals of a timesharing system model can be viewed as a delay server, with the service corresponding to think times. In the multiprocessor system model, this service corresponds to processor execution intervals. Generally, we won't use a **smpl** facility to represent a delay server unless we need to directly determine its utilization; in this case, we can represent it by a facility set whose size is sufficient to

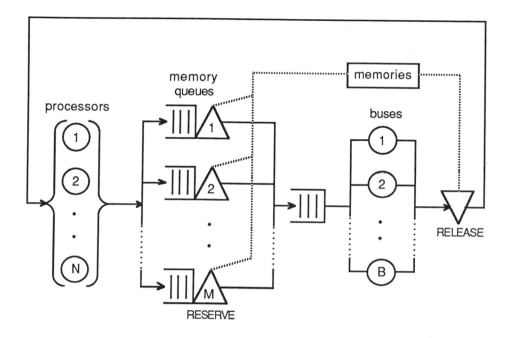

Figure 5.6. Multiprocessor System Queueing Model Diagram

prevent queueing. (This, however, increases simulation overhead. It usually is more efficient to measure the throughput and mean service time, and compute the utilization via the Utilization Law.)

When a processor issues a memory request, the request queues for the selected memory module, reserves it, queues for the bus, and reserves the bus. The bus transfer is performed, the bus is released, and the memory module then released. The memory module and the bus must be simultaneously reserved to perform the transfer. This *simultaneous resource possession* frequently occurs in computer systems (and complicates the analytic solution of queueing network models of these systems: for a discussion in the context of a memory-bus contention model, see Jacobson and Lazowska [1981]). Other examples of simultaneous resource possession include the simultaneous reservation of a disk, control unit, and channel required for data transfer in an IO operation, and the simultaneous reservation of memory space and processor in executing a task. The symbols representing memory operations in Figure 5.6 indicate that queueing and reservation operations are disjoint from release. The interpretation of the symbols is as follows. Upon creation, the box (labeled "memories" here) has m tokens, each corresponding to an allocatable resource unit. In this model, there is one token for each memory module; in a communication system model, there might be one token for each message buffer at a node. A request arrives and queues until a token can be reserved for it: this reservation is represented by the upright triangle. When the request no longer requires the resource, it releases it: the release is represented by the inverted triangle.

Buses are represented as a multiple server: the symbol is an extension of the single server symbol. A request arriving at a multiple server queues for services, reserves any available server and, after receiving service, releases the server and departs.

Symbols used in queueing diagrams in this book are, with variations, in common use. There is, however, no accepted standard.

Simulation model. In building a multiprocessor system simulation model with memory and bus queueing, we can reuse several parts of *bws1*, including the global declarations, the model initialization section in `main()`, and the `begin_cycle()` event routine. The main change required is replacement of the `req_module()` and `end_cycle()` functions in Figure 5.4 with the `req_module()`, `req_bus()`, and `end_cycle()` functions of Figure 5.7. Also, the `switch` statement in `main()` must be changed so that `req_bus()` is called on event 3 and `end_cycle()` is called on event 4. Finally, replacing the `printf` statement in `main()` with a call to `report()` will provide mean memory and bus queue lengths, in addition to utilizations. We'll call the model resulting from these modifications *bws2*.

bws2, like *bws1*, is a synchronous model. Time advances in units of a bus cycle, memory requests are initiated at the beginning of a cycle, and transfers complete at the end of a cycle. `begin_cycle()` scans processors for requests just as it did in *bws1*; in *bws2*, however, processors which have requests queued for a memory module or a bus will have `req[n]` non-zero, and so will be skipped in this scan. For each processor which has a request to be issued at the current time, a memory module is selected and event 2 scheduled.

In `req_module()`, the event routine for event 2, the request is queued if its memory module is busy; otherwise, the module is reserved and event 3 scheduled. In the event routine for this event, `req_bus()`, a bus is requested. If no bus is available, the request is queued. If a bus is available, it is reserved, the count `nbs` of the number of busy buses in this cycle is incremented, and the transfer completion, event 4, is scheduled.

The event 4 routine, `end_cycle()`, is called as each bus request issued in the current cycle completes. It changes `req[n]` to a negative value to indicate that processor n's request is complete, and decrements `nbs`. When nbs reaches 0 (all current bus requests complete), `end_cycle()` scans the set of processors for those with completed requests and, for each such processor,

```
/*-------------- EVENT 2:   REQUEST MEMORY  --------------*/
req_module(n)
  int n;
    {
      if (request(module[req[n]],n,0)==0) then
        schedule(3,0.0,n);
    }

/*-------------- EVENT 3:   REQUEST BUS  ----------------*/
req_bus(n)
  int n;
    {
      if (request(bus,n)==0) then
        {nbs++; schedule(4,1.0,n);}
    }

/*-------------- EVENT 4:   END CYCLE  ----------------*/
end_cycle(n)
  int n;
    {
      req[n]=-req[n];   nbs--;
      if (nbs==0) then
        {
          for (n=1; n<=N; n++)
            if (req[n]<0) then
              {
                release(bus,n);
                release(module[-req[n]],n);
                req[n]=0; next_access(n);
              }
          schedule(1,tn-time(),0);
        }
    }
```

Figure 5.7. Changes to *bws1* for Memory and Bus Queueing

releases the bus and the memory module, sets `req[n]` to zero, and calls `next_access()` to compute the next request time for the processor. When this scan is complete, event 1 is scheduled to issue the next batch of requests.

A key difference between *bws1* and *bws2* is that, in the latter, release operations are deferred until all bus requests issued in the current cycle have completed. If this was not done, then releasing a bus, for example, might cause a queued request to be dequeued and rescheduled for event 3, where it would increment `nbs` and make this count invalid. As implemented in Figure 5.7, all requests issued in the current cycle are allowed to complete, and release operations then performed. This — conceptually — marks the end of the current cycle. The release operations may cause queued requests to be dequeued and rescheduled which — again, conceptually — occurs at the beginning of the next cycle, and `begin_cycle()` may schedule additional requests at this time.

Bandwidths from *bws1* and *bws2* agree closely over a wide range of parameter values (although not the entire range): we'll look at some results later. One advantage of *bws2* is that the mean delay per request, **b**, can be decomposed into memory delays and bus delays.

5.6 An Asynchronous Queueing Model

bws1 and *bws2* were constructed to represent the synchronous operation of a real system: both models used fixed-unit time advancement and carefully aligned request initiation and completion on cycle endpoints. This construction also seemed to be a natural counterpart of the analytic model developed in Section 5.3, which focused on the probability distributions of the number of memory and bus requests made in a cycle. However, queueing network models have been used with some success to model multiprocessor systems, and these have not been constrained to represent synchronous behavior.[4] It is interesting, then, to see how results from an asynchronous queueing model compare with those of our synchronous models.

An asynchronous simulation model of a multiprocessor system is shown in Figure 5.8: we'll call it *bws3*. It is another possible realization of the queueing model diagram of Figure 5.6. *bws3* is derived from, and is a simplification of, *bws2*. The code involved with batching request initiation and completion operations has been discarded: since this left only a handful of statements, the event routines were integrated into `main()`. The distribution used to generate processor execution intervals has been changed from geometric to exponential, since we're not concerned about producing integer-valued execution times. x represents the mean execution interval; note that its value is computed when it is declared.

5.7 Model Results

We now have an analytic model and three simulation models of this system: let's look at some of the model results.

---

[4]See, for example, Jacobson and Lazowska [1981], Smilauer [1985], and Towsley [1986].

```
#include <smpl.h>
#define queued 1

real p=0.250;        /* local memory miss rate           */
int  N=8,M=4,nB=2,   /* no. processors, memories, & buses */
     module[17],     /* facility descriptors for modules  */
     bus,            /* facility descriptor for buses     */
     req[17];        /* currently-requested memory module */

/*------------  MEMORY-BUS BANDWIDTH MODEL  ------------*/
main()
  {
    int event,i,n; real x=1.0/p-1.0;
    smpl(0,"Bandwidth Model");
    bus=facility("bus",nB);
    for (i=1; i<=M; i++) module[i]=facility("module",1);
    for (n=1; n<=N; n++)
      {req[n]=random(1,M); schedule(1,expntl(x),n;}
    while (time()<10000.0)
      {
        cause(&event,&n);
        switch(event);
          {
              if (request(module[req[n]],n,0)!=queued)
                then schedule(2,0.0,n);
            break;
          case 2: /* reserve bus & initiate transfer  */
            if (request(bus,n,0)!=queued) then
              schedule(3,1.0,n);
            break;
          case 3: /* complete:  schedule next request */
            release(bus,n);
            release(module[req[n]],n);
            req[n]=random(1,M);
            schedule(1,expntl(x),n);
            break;
          }
      }
    report();
  }
```

Figure 5.8. Multiprocessor Simulation Model *bws3*

parameters				bandwidth			
N	M	B	p	*bwa*	*bws1*	*bws2*	*bws3*
4	4	4	1.000	2.734	2.739	2.619	2.613
4	4	2	.500	1.583	1.668	1.664	1.665
4	4	1	.250	.807	.827	.927	.839
4	2	1	.250	.818	.827	.927	.839
4	2	1	.125	.481	.487	.737	.484
8	8	8	1.000	5.251	5.253	4.948	4.934
8	8	4	.500	3.273	3.379	3.334	3.352
8	8	2	.250	1.706	1.744	1.751	1.739
8	4	2	.250	1.690	1.711	1.718	1.709
8	4	1	.125	.860	.866	.993	.861
16	16	16	1.000	10.303	10.305	9.614	9.586
16	16	8	.500	6.713	6.847	6.744	6.736
16	16	4	.250	3.553	3.598	3.601	3.596
16	8	4	.250	3.483	3.524	3.510	3.490
16	8	2	.125	1.794	1.794	1.810	1.871

Table 5.1. Analytic and Simulation Model Results

Results for selected sets of parameter values are shown in Table 5.1. The *bwa* column shows bandwidths from the analytic model of Section 5.3; the *bws1*, *bws2*, and *bws3* columns show bandwidths from those simulation models. In constructing this table, values of **M**, **N**, and **p** were selected first, and **B** then was chosen equal to **Np**. This should place bandwidth values in the "interesting" region discussed in Section 5.4.

For the parameters represented in this table, *bwa* and *bws1* bandwidths different at most by about 5 percent (over a wider parameter range, the maximum difference was about 6 percent); thus, we can consider the analytic model to be satisfactorily verified — at least in terms of its derivation. The analytic model assumes random selection of memory and bus requests, with random reselection of memory modules for blocked requests; *bws1*'s selection is quasi-random (for lack of a better name) because of its its processor scan mechanism, and it also has random reselection. On the other hand, *bws2* and *bws3* both provide first-in, first-out queueing of memory and bus requests, and retain the original selection for blocked memory requests. The operation of the actual system probably falls somewhere between these two representations, so it is reassuring that the results from all four models generally are close. At a miss rate of $p = 1.0$, the bandwidths produced by *bma* and *bws1* are noticeably greater than those produced by *bws2* and *bws3*; however, the difference is not large at $p = 1.0$, and decreases as p decreases, except as noted below.

Results for the synchronous queueing model *bws2* and the asynchronous queueing model *bws3* agree closely except for the single bus (B=1) configurations. At N=4, M=2, B=1, and p=0.125, the bandwidth of 0.737 from *bws2* is about 50 percent greater than the 0.484 value produced by *bws3*. Note, though, that the latter value agrees closely with the bandwidth values of *bwa* and *bws1*. We won't explore the difference here, but you may want to implement the two models and examine it more closely. Look at the queueing delays in both cases and also keep in mind the different execution interval distributions.

The simulation results in Table 5.1 all were obtained using a simulation interval of 10,000 cycles; as noted in Section 5.4, this is a consequence of using a batch size of 1000 cycles and a minimum of 10 batches as batch means analysis parameters. Therefore, the models of Figures 5.4 and 5.8 are shown with this simulation interval (determined by the `while` statement in `main()`). If these models are used "as is", **smpl** implementations using 16-bit `ints` may incur `int` overflow, since the average facility release rate can approach **Np** releases per cycle. The batch means analysis extensions to these models included a call to `reset()` at the end of each batch, so the problem did not arise in these cases.

5.8 Extending the Multiprocessor System Model

We now have an analytic model and three simulation models whose results generally are in close agreement, and we can proceed with some confidence to extend any one of these models. Extensions we might consider include the following.

> • **non-identical request rates.** We assumed that processors were identical, each with a request (miss) rate of p. We might want to model a system composed of different processor types with different request rates, such as a mix of central and IO processors. (Also, we may want to incorporate different execution interval distributions for the different types of processors.)

> • **non-random and non-uniform memory addressing.** We assumed that requests were independently, randomly, and

uniformly distributed across memory modules. We may want to represent "bursting" of requests to a particular module (e.g., because of software lock accesses), or the patterns of references to sequential memory addresses generated by block transfers.

- **variable transfer lengths.** We assumed a transfer of one unit (e.g., one word) per request; we may want to extend this to permit multiple units to be transferred per request (requiring multiple cycles).

- **different bus and memory service times.** We assumed that a transfer kept the both memory module and the bus busy for one cycle; we may want to model memory subsystems in which the memory module busy time is longer than the data transfer time.

Analytic models incorporating some of these extensions have been developed. For example, the model of Mudge and Al-Sadoun [1985] provides variable transfer lengths and an arbitrary execution interval distribution. Also, any or all of these extensions easily can be included in a simulation model: once the data structures for processor and request attributes are specified, implementation of the model should be straightforward.

5.9 A CPU Modeling Project

The objective of this project is to develop a model of a pipelined CPU and use this model to evaluate design alternatives for the pipeline's instruction fetch mechanism. This CPU might be the processor element of the multiprocessor system studied earlier in this chapter. This pipeline model, like the multiprocessor model, will be synchronous, with fixed-unit time advancement and events occurring on cycle boundaries. From the viewpoint of this project, the major elements of the CPU are a four-stage instruction pipeline, a single cache for both instructions and data, an instruction fetch (Ifetch) buffer, and a data fetch (Dfetch) buffer, as shown in Figure 5.9. Other CPU elements include a set of general-purpose registers and an arithmetic and logical operation unit (ALU).

The CPU has a simple, register-oriented instruction set in which all memory accesses for data are performed by register load word and store word instructions. All instruction are one word in length, and the paths between the cache and the pipeline are one word wide. The pipeline permits up to four different instructions to be executing (in different stages) simultaneously. All instructions spend at least one cycle in each stage of the pipeline, so the

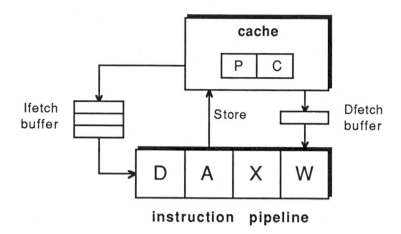

Figure 5.9. Major CPU Elements

minimum instruction execution time is four cycles. However, because of pipe-lining, the CPU has a maximum execution rate of one instruction per cycle.

The pipeline is divided into instruction fetch/decode (D), address generate (A), execute (X), and write register (W) stages. (The pipeline is a static entity; execution of an instruction is a dynamic entity. An instruction may spend several machine cycles in a pipeline stage, either because of its own requirements or because it is blocked by instructions ahead of it. Thus, we distinguish between the X *stage* of the pipeline and the X *cycle(s)* of an instruction.) Instructions flow through the pipeline as follows.

The pipeline attempts to issue an instruction every machine cycle. Unless inhibited, the D stage fetches the next word from the Ifetch buffer and decodes the instruction. This fetch/decode operation is inhibited if the Ifetch buffer is empty, if there already is an instruction in the D stage, or if a taken branch is pending. An instruction can spend more than one cycle in the D stage because the pipeline stage ahead of it is blocked. Also, in every machine cycle, the pipeline issues a cache request, called a sequential Ifetch, to fetch another word into the Ifetch buffer (unless the buffer is full or a taken branch is pending).

A stage actions depend on the type of instruction. In the first A cycle of a fetch or a branch instruction, the memory address is generated and a cache request (data fetch or target fetch) is initiated; the data or instruction word being fetched will be available when the instruction reaches the W stage. Also, the pipeline determines late in the A cycle whether or not the branch will be taken and, if so, discards the instructions in the D stage and Ifetch buffer, cancels the sequential Ifetch, and sets a branch pending flag to inhibit further instruction fetches. Similarly, in the first A cycle of a store instruction, the memory address is generated and a cache request initiated: the word to be stored is sent to the cache as part of the request. For all other instructions, register operands are gated to ALU input registers in the final A cycle of the instruction.

ALU operations are performed in the X stage; some instructions (e.g., multiply) require multiple X cycles.

In the W cycle of an instruction, the result of an ALU operation or a data word fetched from the cache is stored in a register (the word fetched for a non-taken branch instruction simply is discarded). For a taken branch , the word fetched is sent to the Ifetch buffer and the branch pending flag cleared. Pipeline timing is such that the W cycle of the branch and the D cycle of its target effectively overlap, and occur in the same machine cycle.

At the end of each cycle, instructions advance to the next pipeline stage unless that stage ahead is blocked or unless the instruction is in the X stage and requires additional ALU cycles.

The cache has an access time of two cycles; however, it also is pipelined, and can accept a request every cycle. The instruction pipeline issues cache requests for both instruction and data. If both a sequential Ifetch request and a data fetch or store request are attempted in the same cycle, the data request is given priority. The P and C stages of the cache pipeline can be viewed as corresponding to the A and X stages of the instruction pipeline.

Various kinds of delays perturb the flow of instructions through the pipeline, creating "holes" in the stream of instructions observed completing in the W stage. Instructions which require multiple ALU cycles stay in the X stage until complete, blocking the progress of subsequent instructions but providing an opportunity for the instruction fetch mechanism to fill the instruction buffer. (When a fetch instruction follows an instruction with multiple X cycles, the cache delivers the word being fetched before the fetch instruction arrives at the W stage; the word is held in the Dfetch buffer until it can be stored in a register in the W cycle of the fetch instruction.)

Two other delays are sequential instruction fetch (Ifetch) holes and taken branch holes. A sequential instruction fetch request is delayed if an A stage cache request is issued in the same cycle; this can result in the instruction buffer being empty in a later cycle, so that no instruction can be delivered to the D stage. A taken branch causes a multi-cycle hole in the instruction stream, since its target is not available until the start of its W cycle.

loc.	instruction	1	2	3	4	5	6	7	8	9	10	11	12	13	14	15	16
n	ALU	P	C	D	A	X	W	●	●	●							
n+1	ALU		P	C	D	A	X	X	X	X	W						
n+2	ALU			P	C	D	A	A	A	A	X	W					
n+3	ALU				P	C	D	D	D	D	A	X	W				
n+4	any				P	C					D	A	X	...	...		

(a)

loc.	instruction	1	2	3	4	5	6	7	8	9	10	11	12	13	14	15	16
n	FS	P	C	D	A^P	X^C	W										
n+1	ALU		P	C	D	A	X	W									
n+2	ALU			P	C	D	A	X	W								
—				○	○	○	○	○	●								
n+3	any						P	C	D	A	X	W					

(b)

loc.	instruction	1	2	3	4	5	6	7	8	9	10	11	12	13	14	15	16
n	BR	P	C	D	A^P	X^C	W										
n+1	any		P	C	D	○	○	●									
n+2	any			P	C	○	○	○	●								
m	ALU							D	A	X	W						
—									○	○	○	●					
m+1	ALU							P	C	D	A	X	W				

(c)

loc.	instruction	1	2	3	4	5	6	7	8	9	10	11	12	13	14	15	16
n	ALU	P	C	D	A	X	X	X	X	X	X	W					
n+1	BR		P	C	D	A^P	A^C	A	A	A	A	X	W				
m	ALU							D	D	D	D	A	X	W			
m+1	ALU							P	C			D	A	X	W		

(d)

loc.	instruction	1	2	3	4	5	6	7	8	9	10	11	12	13	14	15	16
n	BR	P	C	D	A^P	X^C	W	●	●								
m	BR							D	A^P	X^C	W	●	●				
l	ALU									D	A	X	W	●			
l+1	ALU									P	C	D	A	X	W		

(e)

Figure 5.10. Pipeline Sequence Examples

Figure 5.10 shows various pipeline delay sequences. For purposes of this model, instructions can be grouped into three operation types: FS, BR, and ALU. FS instruction are load, store, and non-taken branch instructions,which issue cache requests in their first A cycle. (An instruction can have multiple A cycles because it is blocked by an instruction with multiple X cycles.) BR instructions are taken branch instructions, which also issue cache requests in their first A cycle. ALU instructions do not issue A-cycle cache requests, but may have multiple X cycles; FS and BR instructions have single X cycles.

In the sequences of Figure 5.10, each instruction occupies a single row, with its pipeline cycles shown in columns of that row. It is assumed that the Ifetch buffer has a capacity of 3 or more instructions and is empty at the start of each sequence. The cache cycles used to fetch a sequential instruction are shown as part of the pipeline cycle sequence for that instruction: e.g., P C D A X W. Cache cycles for data requests are shown as superscripts of the corresponding pipeline cycle: e.g., A^P. The symbol O represents holes propagating through the pipeline, and the symbol ● marks a delay cycle — a cycle in which an instruction does not complete. Not all holes cause delays. Each sequence begins execution at machine cycle 1.

Figure 5.10(a) shows a sequence of 4 ALU instructions; the first, third, and fourth instructions have single-cycle ALU operations, while the second has a four-cycle ALU operation. An observer positioned at the W stage of the pipeline would count three delay cycles. Note how instructions follow-ing the multi-X-cycle instruction are blocked, or *interlocked*, until the next stage becomes free.

Figure 5.10(b) shows the delay caused by cache access contention. The FS instruction at location n initiates a cache request in its A cycle (cycle 4). The sequential Ifetch request which would otherwise be initiated in cycle 4 is delayed until cycle 5, creating a hole in the pipeline flow and a one-cycle delay in instruction execution. Note that if either of the ALU instructions preceding the instruction at n+3 had been multi-X-cycle instructions, this hole would have been masked by the additional X cycles.

A delay caused by a taken branch is shown in Figure 5.10(c). The BR instruction initiates a cache request to fetch the target instruction in its A cycle and, at the same time, cancels execution of the sequential instructions which follow it at locations n+1 and n+2. The target instruction, here a single-X-cycle ALU instruction, begins execution in cycle 6. Sequential instruction fetching also is resumed in cycle 6 but, since two cycles are needed to fetch an instruction, a pipeline hole occurs between instructions m and m+1. A taken branch, then, can result in a delay of three cycles.

The holes created by a taken branch can be partly or fully masked by other delays. In Figure 5.10(d), a taken branch follows a multi-X-cycle ALU instruction; the X cycles completely mask the branch holes. Figure 5.10(e) shows an instruction sequence in which a taken branch has another taken branch as its target; the sequential Ifetch delay usually caused by a taken branch does not occur for the first branch, since execution of its target is not followed by execution of a sequential instruction. (For compactness, Figures 5.10(d) and (e) do not show the hole sequences for the sequential instructions cancelled by a taken branch.)

There are various other cases in which holes are masked by other delays. Try diagramming the pipeline sequences for FS-BR-ALU and FS-ANY-BR-ALU instructions sequences.

Workload description. Design evaluations are to be based on the follow-ing instruction mix.

instruction type	proportion of instructions
BR	0.1437
FS	0.4002
ALU	0.4561
	1.0000

FS instructions are 49.5 percent fetches, 17.5 percent stores, and 33.0 percent non-taken branches.

A BR or a FS instruction always has a single X cycle. An ALU instruction, depending on the ALU operation it performs, can have multiple X cycles. The distribution of ALU operation times is as follows.

ALU (X) cycles	proportion of ALU instructions
1	0.40
2	0.40
4	0.10
8	0.07
16	0.03
	1.00

The distribution of inter-branch headways — the number of instructions executed between taken branches — is tabulated in problem 1, Chapter 1; the function of problem 1.2(c), Chapter 1, can be used to generate sample headways. BR instructions are, by definition, the last instructions of a headway; other instructions in a headway divide randomly and independently into FS and ALU instructions in accordance with the proportions tabulated earlier.

Building and validating the model. A smpl model of the pipeline need not be very large: the author's version comprises less than 100 lines of C code, exclusive of debugging instrumentation. The key is to work backward through the pipeline (W stage → A stage), rather than forward, to determine what happens in each machine cycle.

Since neither measurement data nor analytic results are available to check simulation results, model debugging and validation will rely heavily on examination of traces. The simplest trace to implement produces a line for each machine cycle, with columns showing the contents of each pipeline stage at the end of the cycle, and resembles the following.

cycle	-D-	-A-	-X-	-W-	counters and flags
25	BR	inv	FS	inv	... ...
26	inv	BR	inv	FS	... ...
27	inv	inv	BR	inv	... ...
28	ALU	inv	inv	BR	... ...
29	inv	ALU	inv	inv	... ...

In this example, "inv" marks stages which do not contain a valid instruction. The "counters and flags" part of the trace line includes such things as the number of instructions remaining in the Ifetch buffer and whether or not a sequential Ifetch request was issued.

Traces are useful in checking short runs. Long runs can be checked by analyzing delays produced with constrained instruction mixes and with the Ifetch buffer capacity set to one instruction. For example, suppose all ALU instructions are limited to single ALU cycles and no FS instructions are generated. All delays, then, will be caused by BR instructions; these will cause 2-cycle delays when the target is another BR and 3-cycle delays otherwise. When instruction, total cycle, and delay counts balance, FS instruction generation can be restored and the reconcilation of counts repeated. (Try specifying the delays which can occur in this case.)

Pipeline design analyses. The performance measure of interest in pipeline analysis is the mean instruction execution time in cycle, **I**, which can be obtained by dividing the simulation run time in cycles by the number of instruction completed in the run. Note that $(IC)^{-1}$, where **C** is the cycle time in microseconds, gives the mean instruction execution rate in millions of instructions per second (MIPS). It also is useful to obtain the average X stage execution time (X cycles) per instruction, **E**. (Compare the measured value of **E** with that estimated from instruction mix parameters.) The average number of delay cycles per instruction due to branch and Ifetch holes, **D**, then is given by **I**–**E**.

The mean instruction execution time obtained with an Ifetch buffer capacity of one instruction is to be considered as the "base case". The following design alternatives are to be evaluated in terms of their perform- ance relative to this case. (In specifying confidence intervals for your simu- lations, note that the differences in **I** for some of these cases may be small.)

(a) An increase in Ifetch buffer capacity to 2, 3, or 4 instructions.

(b) An increase in the width of the path between the cache and the Ifetch buffer so that a sequential Ifetch or a target fetch can fetch two instructions in a single cache access. (Assume that the compiler will force target align- ment to a double-word boundary at the cost of reduced code density; what would be the effect on perfomance of not forcing alignment?)

(c) An architectural change which specifies that the sequential instruction following a branch always is executed, regardless of whether or not the branch is taken. (This *delayed branch* instruction is common in current reduc- ed instruction set computers, or RISCs. Patterson and Séquin [1981] trace it back to the MANIAC I, circa 1951.) In evaluating the performance of this alternative, assume that the sequential instruction following a branch (taken or not taken) performs useful work 70% of the time and is a NOP (no operation) 30% of the time, and adjust your relative performance estimate accordingly.

(d) Assume that a future implementation of this CPU will take advantage of new technology to reduce the execution time of multi-cycle ALU operations by 50 percent. Determine how the above alternatives will perform in this new implementation.

6. An Ethernet Model

6.1 Introduction

This chapter presents a macroscopic simulation model of an Ethernet[1] local area network. This model, which we'll call *ether*, can be used to see how network load characteristics, such as message rates and message length distributions, affect performance, and to experiment with protocols and load-adaptive algorithms. We'll use analytic and measurement results from the literature to verify and validate *ether*. An Ethernet simulation presents some new modeling problems. In the synchronous multiprocessor simulation model of the preceding chapter, the key problem was to order events that occurred at the same instant in time. This contrasts with *ether*'s problem: occurrence of an event is recognized at different instants in different parts of the network because of propagation delays. Other problems we'll examine include efficient representation of a large number of request sources and generation of variates from a truncated distribution.

6.2 The Ethernet Network

The network modeled by *ether* comprises N stations connected by a coaxial cable called the channel (Figure 1). A station connects at the cable with a cable tap and transceiver, which in turn are connected via a transceiver cable to the station's controller. Ethernet communication functions are implemented by a combination of controller hardware (and microcode) and station software; the division of function between the two depends on the details of a particular implementation. In the general case, stations may be a combination of various types of computers, workstations, file servers, printers, and other devices (in our case, stations are assumed to be identical). Ethernet can support a maximum of 1024 stations with a total cable length of 2.5 kilometers (connected in a non-rooted tree configuration);

---

[1]"Ethernet" is a trademark of the Xerox Corporation

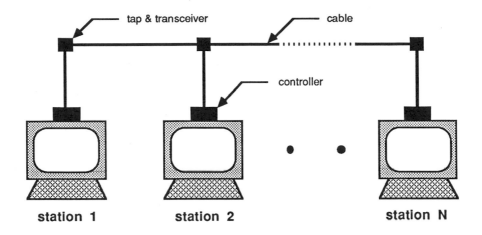

Figure 6.1. A Simple Ethernet Network

cable segments greater than 500 meters are connected by signal repeaters. Data transmission is bit-serial at a rate of 10 Mbps (million bits per second). A detailed specification of Ethernet is given in [DEC et al 1982]; an overview of the Ethernet specification is given by Shoch et al [1982]. The ANSI/IEEE local area network standard 802.3 [IEEE 1985a] is very close to the Ethernet specification.

Data format. In Ethernet, data is transmitted in packages called *frames* (Figure 6.2). A frame comprises header, data, and CRC fields. The data field must be at least 46 bytes in length (for reasons which we'll see later on); if a message of less than this minimum length is to be transmitted, the data field must be padded to meet the minimum length requirement.[2] The maximum length of the data field is 1500 bytes; this limit helps to provide timely channel access to all stations, and also reflects practical buffer length considerations. The header contains the address of the destination station(s), the address of the sending station, and the data length (excluding pad bytes). The data field is followed by a CRC (cyclic redundancy check) code. This code is generated by the transmitting station and used by the receiving station to check for transmission errors. When a station is ready to transmit a frame, it first transmits a preamble of 64 bits: this is a predetermined bit pattern which receiving stations use for synchronization. Depending on the architectural layer at which the system is examined, the

---

[2]*bytes* here describes 8-bit elements without regard to the type of data represented: the Ethernet specification emphasizes this by referring to these elements as *octets*.

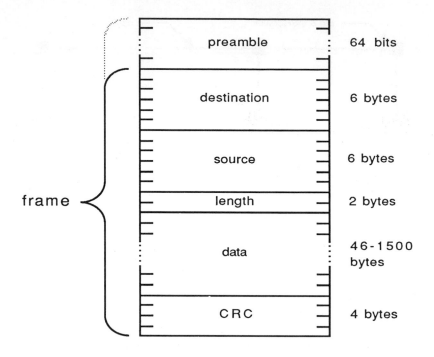

Figure 6.2. Ethernet Frame Format

preamble may be viewed as part of the frame; except as noted, we'll take this view in the rest of this chapter.

The preamble, header, and CRC code total 26 bytes, or 208 bits. If L is the length of the data field in bytes, then the nominal frame transmission time tf is

$$tf = 20.8 + 0.8L \text{ microseconds} \tag{6.1}$$

Note that the minimum frame transmission time (for $L = 46$) is 57.6 microseconds.

Channel access protocol. Ethernet uses a distributed access protocol called *Carrier Sense Multiple Access with Collision Detection*, or CSMA/CD. A station with a message to transmit listens to the channel (senses to see if a carrier is present) and, if the channel is free, initiates its transmission. There is a delay between the time at which a station recognizes that the channel is free and the time at which it initiates transmission: this *inter-frame gap* delay insures that a receiving station

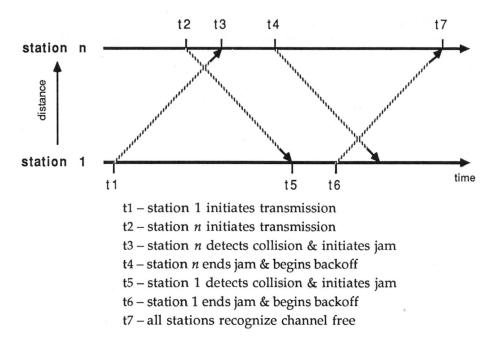

t1 – station 1 initiates transmission
t2 – station *n* initiates transmission
t3 – station *n* detects collision & initiates jam
t4 – station *n* ends jam & begins backoff
t5 – station 1 detects collision & initiates jam
t6 – station 1 ends jam & begins backoff
t7 – all stations recognize channel free

Figure 6.3 Colliding Transmissions in Ethernet

has time to prepare for a new transmission. This delay, denoted here as T_{if}, is specified to be 9.6 microseconds. During transmission, the station continues to listen to the channel; if another station initiates transmission while the first station is transmitting, a collision occurs. When a station recognizes that a collision has occurred, it immediately abandons its transmission of data, transmits a *jam* message to insure that all other stations will recognize the collision (whose duration could be as small as one bit time), and schedules its retransmission attempt after a random delay called a *backoff* delay.

A collision can occur only when one station initiates transmission in a very short interval after another; this interval sometimes is called the *collision window*. Figure 6.3 shows the events involved in a collision. In this figure, the X axis represents time and the Y axis represents the physical separation between stations 1 and *n*. Suppose the channel initially is free and, at time t1, station 1 initiates transmission. Because of propagation delay, this transmission will not reach station *n* until time t3; meanwhile, station *n* has initiated its transmission at time t2. When the carrier signal from station 1 reaches station *n*, station n recognizes that a collision has occurred, initiates transmission of a jam message, and, at time t4, begins its backoff delay. Station n's transmission reaches station 1 at t5: station 1 then recognizes occurrence of a collision, sends its jam message, and begins its backoff.[3] The end of the jam message from station 1 reaches station n at time t7, at which time all stations recognize that the channel is free.

The transmissions of stations 1 and n will collide only if the interval t2 − t1 is less than the propagation time between the two stations: otherwise, station n will recognize that the channel is busy and defer its transmission. Define τ as the end-to-end propagation delay of the channel and T_{jam} as the jam message transmission time. The worst-case collision situation arises when station 1 is at one end of the cable, station n is at the other end, and station n initiates its transmission just before the carrier signal from station 1 arrives: i.e., the interval between transmission initiations is (almost) τ. (This would be equivalent to t2 and t3 coinciding in the timing diagram of Figure 6.3.) In this case, both of the stations involved in the collision transmit for a period of $2\tau + T_{jam}$ before ending their transmission and initiating their backoff delay. Note that station n will sense channel busy for a time 2τ after it ends its jam. Also, note that if station 1 transmits for a period 2τ without detecting a collision, it has "acquired" the channel: it is assured of successfully completing its transmission.

Regardless of the positions of the stations involved in a collision, all stations will not recognize channel free until the frame fragment resulting from the collision has propagated through and disappeared from the network. Ethernet specifies a maximum round-trip propagation time of 450 bit times or 45 microseconds, so the maximum value of τ is 22.5 microseconds. The jam is specified to be from 32 to 48 bit times in length: assuming the max - imum, T_{jam} = 4.8 microseconds. The frame fragment created by a collision, then, may be up to 498 bits in length, corresponding to a transmission time of 49.8 microseconds. The minimum length of a valid frame (excluding the preamble) is 64 bytes or 512 bit times. Thus, a receiving station, after synchronizing on the preamble, can determine from the length of the received data whether it represents a collision fragment or a valid frame.

Slot time. An important parameter in collision recovery is the slot time, T_{slot}, which is specified to be 512 bit times, or 51.2 microseconds. The slot time is the rescheduling quantum used by stations in backing off after a collision. The choice of the slot time value reflects several considerations. To avoid unnecessary collisions, it should be larger than the time required for channel acquisition and also larger than the maximum frame fragment created by a collision; once these requirements are met, it should be small to minimize network response times.

---

[3]Collision recognition time is very small, and is ignored here.

Backoff algorithm. To reduce the chances of repeatedly colliding, the stations involved in a collision randomly delay their retransmiision attempts. The algorithm used in determining this delay is called *truncated binary exponential backoff*. It computes a backoff delay as follows.

1. increment retransmission attempt counter n.

2. if $n > 16$, report transmission error

3. compute $k = \text{minimum}(n, 10)$

4. generate random integer r in the range $[0, 2^k -1]$

5. set backoff delay $= r$ slot times

Thus, the first retransmission attempt is initiated after a backoff delay of 0 or 1 slot times, the second after a delay of from 0 to 3 slot times, up to a delay of from 0 to 1023 slot times for attempts 10-16. After 16 unsuccessful attempts, an error is reported to the user.

The backoff algorithm stabilizes the channel if it tends to become overloaded. As the load on the channel increases, collisions — and stations' retransmission attempts — increase: this increases the average backoff delay, reducing the load on the channel. Extreme delays are avoided by limiting the maximum backoff delay to 1023 slot times.

6.3 Performance Parameters and Measures

Our Ethernet analysis will focus on estimating network throughput and mean frame delay as a function of network load, with the load characterized in terms of the number of stations on the network, the inter-transmission intervals of these stations, and the mean frame length of transmissions.

Throughput may be described in terms of frames per unit time or bytes or bits per unit time; also, the technical literature frequently defines through-put as that part of the channel utilization used for successful data trans-misssion. (Part of the overall channel utilization represents transmissions abandoned because of collisions.) This last definition requires some dimen-sional imagination to be viewed as a true throughput measure; however, because of its widespread use in the literature, we'll use it here: S is defined as the part of channel utilization used for successful data transmission, and is referred to as the *network throughput*. When other measures of throughput are used, explicit dimensions will be given. While this definition of throughput is common in the literature, careful reading is required: successful data transmission sometimes is based on the total frame length, sometimes on the total frame length excluding preamble, and sometimes only on data field length. We'll use the total frame length except where noted.

The mean frame delay time T_d is measured from the time at which a station first attempts to transmit a frame to the time at which transmission of the frame is successfully completed, and so includes channel waiting time, collision recovery time, backoff time, and frame transmission time. It usually is reported in terms of the normalized mean delay, D. Let T_f be the mean transmission time of a frame in the absence of contention: T_f is the product of the frame length in bits and the channel transfer rate of 10 Mbps. The normalized mean delay then is defined as

$$D = T_d/T_f \qquad (6.2)$$

The load on the network commonly is described in terms of the offered load, G — the load excluding contention effects. Define T_i as the mean interval between the time at which a station completes transmission of one frame and the time at which it initiates transmission of its next frame. The N stations in the network are assume to be identical. If the network is viewed as a closed system, the offered load is defined as

$$G = \frac{N T_f}{T_i + T_f} \qquad (6.3)$$

If the network is viewed as an open system, the offered load is defined as

$$G = \lambda T_f \qquad (6.4)$$

where λ is the arrival rate of new requests at the channel. (6.4) derives from (6.3) by defining $\lambda = N/T_i$ and keeping the ratio N/T_i constant as $N \rightarrow \infty$.

A key parameter in portraying the performance of Ethernet and other CSMA/CD networks is α, the ratio of the end--to-end propagation time of the channel to the mean frame transmission time:

$$\alpha = \tau/T_f \qquad (6.5)$$

Since the minimum frame transmission time is 57.6 microseconds (see equation 6.1) and the maximum propagation time is 22.5 microseconds, the maximum value of α is 0.39.

A collision can occur only if one station attempts to transmit within τ microseconds after another; if a station transmits for τ microseconds without a collision, it is guaranteed to complete successfully. For a given offered load, then, a network with short frame transmission times (large α) will spend more time in collision recovery, and so have lower throughput, than a network with long frame transmission times (small α). As we'll see shortly, throughput bounds for CSMA/CD networks can be expressed in terms of α.

6.4 Lam's Model

Lam [1980] developed an analytic model of CSMA/CD networks which provides a simple upper bound on channel throughput and a not-so-simple closed-form expression for the mean frame delay time T_d. We won't discuss the details of Lam's analysis here: the main results are presented for use in verifying the output of *ether*.

Lam's bound on throughput can be expressed as

$$S_{max} = [1 + \alpha(1 + 2e)]^{-1} \tag{6.6}$$

where S_{max} is the maximum throughput for a propagation time/mean frame transmission time ratio of α.

Figure 6.4 plots S_{max} versus α; note how maximum throughput falls off rapidly as mean frame transmission time decreases. It may be easier to view this in terms of mean frame length: the maximum Ethernet propagation time is 22.5 us. or 225 bit times, so α values of .001, .01, and .1 correspond to mean frame lengths of approximately 28000, 2800, and 280 bytes, respectively.

Lam's formula for the mean frame delay time can be expressed as

$$T_d = T_f + \tau(4e + 1)/2$$

$$+ \frac{\lambda\{T_{f2} + \tau T_f(4e + 2) + \tau^2[5 + 4e(2e - 1)]\}}{2\{1 - \lambda[T_f + \tau(2e + 1)]\}}$$

$$- \frac{(1 - e^{-2\lambda\tau})(e + \lambda\tau - 3\lambda\tau e)}{\lambda e[B^*(\lambda)e^{-(1 + \lambda\tau)} + e^{-2\lambda\tau} - 1]} \tag{6.7}$$

where τ is the end-to-end propagation delay, λ is the mean arrival rate, and T_f, T_{f2}, and $B^*(\ )$ are, respectively, the first and second moments and Laplace transform of the frame transmission time distribution. For constant frame lengths,

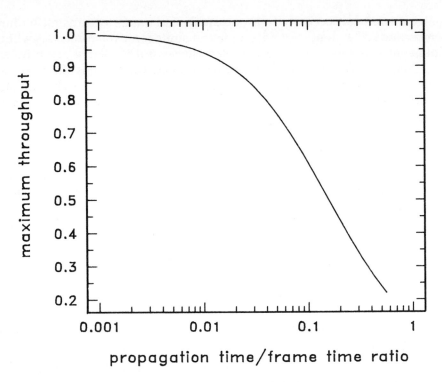

Figure 6.4. Maximum Network Throughput as a Function of α

$$T_{f2} = T_f{}^2 \tag{6.8a}$$

$$B^*(\lambda) = e^{-\lambda T_f} \tag{6.8b}$$

For exponentially-distributed frame lengths,

$$T_{f2} = 2T_f{}^2 \tag{6.9a}$$

$$B^*(\lambda) = 1/(1 + \lambda T_f) \tag{6.9b}$$

We can use (6.7) to compute the normalized mean delay D as a function of S and α by setting (arbitrarily) $\tau = 1$, $T_f = \tau/\alpha$, $\lambda = S/T_f$, obtaining T_d from (6.7), and computing $D = T_d/T_f$. (For an open system, $S = G$ for $S < S_{max}$.)

Lam's analysis assumes an infinite number of stations whose frame transmission requests collectively form a Poisson process (so inter-request

```
real delay(t,r,Tf,dis)
  real t,r,Tf; int dis;
    {
      real Tf2,B,f1,f2,f3,f4,f5,e=exp(1.0);
      if (dis==1)
        then {Tf2=Tf*Tf;      B=exp(-r*Tf);}
        else {Tf2=2.0*Tf*Tf; B=1.0/(1.0+r*Tf);}
      f1=Tf+t*(4.0*e+1.0)/2.0;
      f2=Tf2+t*Tf*(4.0*e+2.0)+t*t*(5.0+4.0*e*(2.0*e-1.0));
      f2*=r;
      f3=2.0*(1.0-r*(Tf+t*(2.0*e+1.0)));
      f4=(1.0-exp(-2.0*r*t))*(e+r*t-3.0*r*t*e);
      f5=r*e*(B*exp(-(1.0+r*t))+exp(-2.0*r*t)-1.0);
      return(f1+f2/f3-f4/f5);
    }
```

Figure 6.5. Function to Compute Lam's Mean Frame Delay

times are exponentially distributed), and assumes a "slotted" channel in which stations can begin transmissions only at the start of a time slot of length 2τ. As a consequence of the latter assumption, the mean delay approaches $Tf + \tau$ as the offered load approaches zero. Bux [1981] suggests that Lam's original formula be modified by reducing the mean delay by τ, and this modification is incorporated in (6.7).

A C function to compute Td is shown in Figure 6.5; its arguments are t, the propagation delay, r, the mean arrival rate, Tf, the mean frame transmission time, and dis, the frame length distribution type. dis is 1 for constant frame lengths or 2 for exponentially-distributed frame lengths. (This function is intended to be part of a program which includes *math.h* and defines $real$ and $then$.)

6.5 The *ether* Simulation Model

In *ether*, the network is viewed as a closed system with a single server (the channel) and a pool of request sources (stations). A simple variable is used to represent the state of the channel, and stations are represented by tokens. Stations, at random intervals, generate frame transmission requests, compete for the channel, and, on acquiring the channel, transmit a frame. When frame transmission is complete, another request is scheduled: inter-request intervals are exponentially distributed. The simulation event routines involved in transmission request processing are shown in Figure 6.6. Before we discuss the individual event routines, we'll look at the problems of representing the propagation delay effect and of efficiently modeling the request arrival process.

Representing propagation delay. The main problem in developing a simulation model of Ethernet is determining how to represent propagation delay. This isn't too difficult in a detailed model which distinguishes individual stations and knows their locations on the channel; in this case, timings can be computed deterministically using inter-station distances. In a macroscopic simulation model such as *ether*, stations are indistinguishable and timings are computed probabilistically.

ether assumes that the network has N identical stations distributed equidistantly along the channel. Suppose station i is the station last reserving or releasing the channel, and station j is the requesting station: what can we say about the distance between i and j? Since station inter-request times and frame transmission times are independently and identically distributed random variables, i and j can be considered to be random integers equiprobably selected from the set $[1, 2, .., N]$. Let d be the unit distance between stations i and j (i.e., $d = |i-j|$). Stations i and j are a pair (i,j) chosen from $N(N-1)$ possible pairs; the number of pairs with a distance d between them is $2(N-d)$. The factor 2 reflects the symmetry of the pairs: for example, a distance of N-1 occurs (only) for the pairs $(1,N)$ and $(N,1)$. Thus, the probability of a distance d between the two stations is

$$\Pr[x=d] = 2(N - d)/[N(N - 1)], \quad 1 \le d \le N\text{-}1 \tag{6.10}$$

and the probability of a distance equal to or less than d is

$$\Pr[x{\le}d] = \sum_{k=1}^{d} 2(N - k)/[N(N - 1)] \tag{6.11}$$

$$= \frac{2Nd - d(d + 1)}{N(N - 1)} \tag{6.12}$$

For large N, we can substitute N^2 for $N(N - 1)$ and d^2 for $d(d + 1)$ with small error ($1/N$ or less), and rewrite (6.12) as

$$\Pr[x{\le}d] = 1 - [1 - d/N]^2 \tag{6.13}$$

We can use the inverse of the distribution function of (6.13) to generate random inter-station distances, as discussed in Section 1.2. Also, for convenience, we'll treat the inter-station distance distribution as continuous, rather than discrete. The random distance generation function then becomes

$$d = N[1 - r^{1/2}] \qquad (6.14)$$

where r is a random variate uniformly distributed in [0,1]. Stations are equidistantly located on the channel; if d is the distance between two randomly-selected stations, the propagation delay dt between those two stations is $\tau d/(N - 1)$ or, for large N, approximately $\tau d/N$. Substituting in (6.14) gives us a function for generating a sample propagation delay between the requesting station and the station last reserving or releasing the channel:

$$dt = \tau[1 - r^{1/2}] \qquad (6.15)$$

where r, as before, is a uniform random variate.

Modeling the request arrival process. The easiest way to handle request arrivals is to schedule a first request for each of the N stations during model initialization, and then schedule a station's next request whenever it completes its current request. This, however, causes simulation run time to increase with increasing N because of the increased number of request arrival events in the event list. Given identical stations with exponential inter-arrival times, we can devise a more efficient scheme.

Suppose at a given instant there are n inactive stations.[4] Let T_i be the average inactive interval of any one station: this is the time between the station's completion of one request and its initiation of the next. However, because of the memoryless property of the exponential distribution, the distribution of the time remaining until initiation of the next request doesn't depend on when the previous request completed; at any instant, the distribution of the remaining inactive time y for any one station is defined by

$$\Pr[y{\le}t] = 1 - e^{-t/T_i} \qquad (6.16)$$

The remaining inactive times $y_1, y_2, ..., y_n$ of the n inactive stations are identically distributed random variables with distribution function $\Pr[y{\le}t]$. The remaining time until a request is next initiated by some one of the n stations is $x = \min[y_1, y_2, ..., y_n]$. The distribution function of x can be shown to be (see, for example, Chapter 3 in Trivedi [1982])

$$\Pr[x{\le}t] = 1 - \{1 - \Pr[y{\le}t]\}^n \qquad (6.17)$$

---

[4]from the channel's viewpoint.

Substituting (6.16) in (6.17) and simplifying gives

$$\Pr[x{\leq}t] = 1 - e^{-t/(T_i/n)} \qquad\qquad (6.18)$$

as the distribution function for the time remaining until the next request. Thus, at any instant, the time until the next request is initiated by one of a set of n stations is exponentially distributed with a mean equal to the mean inactive time per station divided by the number of inactive stations. (6.18), coupled with memoryless property of the exponential distribution, suggests the following algorithm for modeling request arrivals.

<u>model initialization</u>
- $n = N$, Ti = mean inactive time per station
- schedule first request arrival

<u>request arrival</u>
- schedule initiation of processing for arrival
- $n = n-1$
- schedule next arrival at time()+expntl(Ti/n)

<u>request completion</u>
- cancel currently-scheduled next request arrival
- $n = n+1$
- schedule next arrival at time()+expntl(Ti/n)

With this algorithm, only one arrival event is in the event list at any time, regardless of the value of N. There are a variety of other situations in which we may be able to use this approach, such as in modeling terminals in an interactive system simulation model.

Event routines. The *ether* simulation model comprises the six event routines shown in Figure 6.6. (We'll look at the simulation program itself in the next section.) As part of model initialization, the first transmission request is scheduled for event 1, TransmitFrame.

TransmitFrame. This event represents the arrival of a frame transmission request. The transmission attempt and backoff delay counts for the request are set to zero, the request's arrival time is recorded for use in computing the delay time when the transfer completes, and event 2, Defer, is scheduled for the request. The inactive station count is decremented and the next arrival scheduled.

Defer. This event routine determines a randomly-arriving request's view of the current state of the channel, and corresponds to the Deference

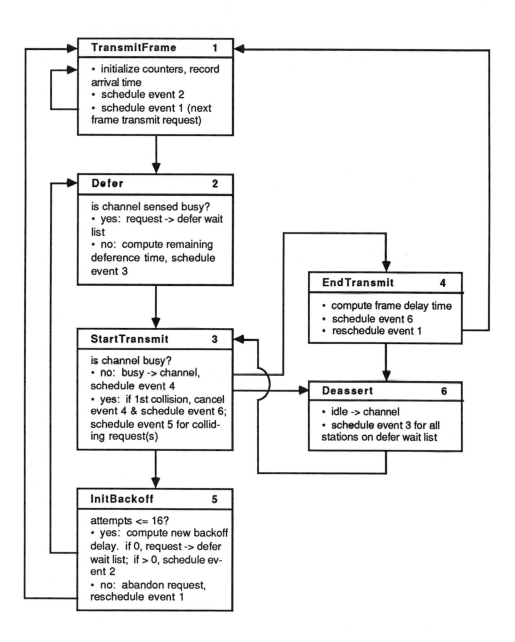

Figure 6.6. *ether* Simulation Model Events

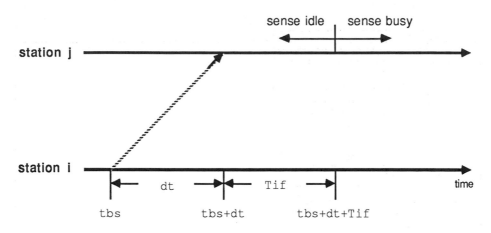

Figure 6.7 Channel State Sensing Timing

process of the Ethernet system (see the Ethernet specification or the IEEE 802.3 standard). The channel is represented by a simple variable whose value is busy or idle, depending on whether the most recent operation was transmission initiation or transmission completion. *ether* maintains two variables, `tbs` and `tis`, which record the time at which the facility last became busy and last became idle. These are used in conjunction with a sample propagation delay to determine if the channel's latest change of state has propagated to the requesting station.

The state of the channel is represented by the variable `chnl`, which is set to `busy` when a transmission is initiated and to `idle` when a transmission completes. To determine if the requesting station senses channel busy, Defer generates a variate `dt`, using (6.15), which represents the propagation delay between the requesting station and the station last reserving or releasing the channel. If `chnl = busy`, Defer determines if this state is sensed by the requesting station. The timing involved in this determination is illustrated in Figure 6.7. Station i is the station which initiated a transmission at time `tbs`, and station j is the requesting station. The transmission from station i reaches station j at time `tbs+dt`. A station continuously listens to the channel; when the channel goes from busy to idle (carrierSense signal is deasserted), the inter-frame gap delay is initiated. The station defers transmission until the end of this delay, and then starts transmitting without further checking of the state of the channel. In the extreme case, the transmission from station i reaches station j just as station j initiates its inter-frame gap delay and so station j does not sense channel busy. Thus, Defer assumes that the requesting station will sense channel busy

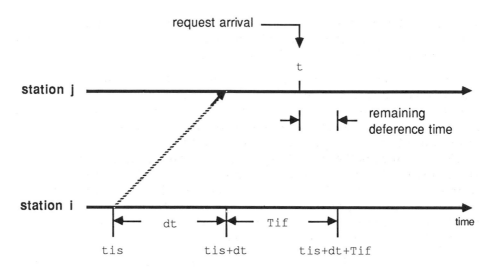

Figure 6.8 Remaining Deference Time Computation

if the time of its arrival is greater than `tbs+dt+Tif` (where `Tif` is the inter-frame gap delay), and will sense channel idle otherwise.

If the channel is sensed busy, Defer places the request on the *defer wait list*. Processing of requests on this list is reinitiated when the channel is released (by the Deassert event routine). If the channel is sensed idle, Defer computes the station's remaining deference time — the time until the end of the inter-frame gap delay — and schedules event 3, StartTransmit, to occur at the end of that time.

Figure 6.8 shows the times involved in computation of the remaining deference time. Station i is the station which completed transmission at time `tis` and station j is the requesting station; `t` is the arrival time of the request. The end of i's transmission is recognized by station j at time `tis+dt`, and j can begin transmitting at time `tis+dt+Tif`. The remaining deference time, then, is $(tis+dt+Tif)-t$.

StartTransmit. This event represents the start of a successful or unsuccessful transmission. StartTransmit first checks the state of the channel: if `chnl = idle`, then no other station has started a transmission, and it is not known whether or not a collision will occur. In this case, StartTransmit reserves the channel by setting `chnl = busy`, sets `tbs` to the current time, and schedules event 4, EndTransmit, to occur at the end of the frame transmission time. If the channel is busy, then some other station already has initiated a transmission (although this transmission has not yet propagated to the requesting station) and a collision will occur at some time in the future. Several stations may be involved in a collision: we'll consider first the initial collision in a collision interval.

Figure 6.3 helps envision the timing involved in a collision. Assume station 1 is the station originally reserving the channel, station n is the station initiating the current request, and `dt` is the propagation delay between these two stations (determined by StartTransmit using (6.15)). t1 corresponds to the busy period start `tbs`, and t2 corresponds to the transmission start time of the current request (and to the current simulation time). This request will recognize a collision at time t3, after it has transmitted for an interval of $\Delta t = t3 - t2$. Since t2 is the current simulation time and t3 = `tbs+dt`, Δt is the larger of 0 and `tbs+dt-time()`. The latter expression may be less than 0 because `dt` is a random variate. StartTransmit schedules event 5, Initbackoff, for this request after a delay of Δt+`Tjam`.

The transmission initiated by station n reaches station 1 at time t5 after a delay of `dt`. When the first collision in a collision interval occurs, StartTransmit cancels the EndTransmit event for this station's request, schedules Initbackoff for it after a delay of `dt+Tjam`, and schedules event 6, Deassert, also after a delay of `dt+Tjam`. However, this latter delay is elongated if necessary to make the busy period length at least equal to the propagation time. This keeps the channel state variable `chnl`, `tis`, and `tbs` from changing until all non-deferring stations have had a chance to transmit — and collide — in the current collision window.

For each colliding request arriving after the initial collision, StartTransmit computes a `dt` value and schedules backoff delay initiation after a delay of `Tjam`+Δt, where Δt is determined as described above. This is not an accurate representation, since these later arrivals potentially can collide with any one of several requests and `dt` over-estimates the propagation delay between the requesting station and the nearest (in time) collider; however, the effect on delay times is small.

EndTransmit. The EndTransmit event represents the successful completion of a transmission. The frame delay time is computed and accumulated and event 6, Deassert, is scheduled to release the channel. The next request arrival is rescheduled as described earlier; the currently-scheduled next request arrival event is cancelled, the count of inactive stations is incremented, and a new next request arrival event is scheduled.

InitBackoff. This event marks the end of jam transmission and the computation and initiation of a station's backoff delay. If the number of retransmission attempts for the current request is greater than 16, the request is abandoned and the next request arrival event is rescheduled exactly as done at the end of a successful transmission. If the number of attempts is 16 or fewer, the backoff delay is computed using the algorithm described in Section 6.2. If the backoff delay is 0, the request is placed on the defer wait list for reactivation when the channel is released; otherwise, the request is scheduled for event 2, Defer, at the end of its backoff delay.

Deassert. This event routine releases the channel after a successful or unsuccessful transmission by setting `chnl = idle` and setting `tis` to the current simulation time (these operations correspond to the deassertion of the carrierSense signal in the actual network). All requests on the defer wait list are removed and scheduled for event 3, StartTransmit, after a delay of `dt+Tif`. `dt` (computed separately for each request) represents the time required for transmission end to propagate through the network, and `Tif` is the inter-frame gap delay. Requests removed from the defer wait list are scheduled for StartTransmit, rather than Defer, since it is certain that they will sense channel idle following the end of transmission and so initiate their transmissions. Defer processes requests for which the state of the channel is uncertain (on arrival and after a non-zero backoff delay), and probabilistically determines the channel state sensed by these requests.

6.6 The *ether* Simulation Program

Figure 6.9 lists a **smpl** implementation of *ether*. To save space, model parameter values are specified in `#define` directives and in variable declarations. Event routine operations should be clear from the discussion of the preceding section; this section briefly examines some of the implementation details.

This program is designed to obtain estimates of the throughput S and mean normalized delay D as a function of the propagation time/mean transmission time ratio α, and the offered load G. (You may want to add some input statements to read values of α and G.) Network timing parameters — propagation time, inter-frame gap time, etc. — are specified by `#define` directives. Note that all times are in milliseconds. During model initialization, the mean inter-request time per station T_i, and the mean frame transmission time T_f, are computed using the relationships defined by (6.3) and (6.5), respectively. Inter-request (inactive) times are assumed to be exponentially distributed, and frame transmission times are assumed to be constant.

Transmission requests are represented by elements of the `request` structure array. These are linked into an available element list during model initialization, allocated by `TransmitFrame()` as requests arrive, and deallocated by `EndRequest()` as requests complete. If `TransmitFrame()`

```
#include <smpl.h>

#define busy    1
#define idle    0
#define Na      200         /* max. no. of active stations */
#define Tp      0.0225      /* propagation delay (ms.)     */
#define Tif     0.0096      /* interframe delay (ms.)      */
#define Tslot   0.0512      /* slot time (ms.)             */
#define Tjam    0.0032      /* jam time (ms.)              */

struct request             /* trans. request descriptor   */
  {
    int attempt;           /* no. retransmission attempts */
    int bkf;               /* current backoff count       */
    int lnk;               /* avail/defer wait list link  */
    real tin;              /* request initiation time     */
    real txf;              /* request's transmission time */
  } desc[Na+1];

int
  N=200,                   /* no. of stations in network  */
  chnl=idle,               /* channel status (busy/idle)  */
  avl=1,                   /* avail. descriptor list head */
  dfr=0,                   /* defer wait list head        */
  end=0;                   /* run termination flag        */

real
  a=0.05,                  /* propagation/transfer time ratio */
  G=0.50,                  /* offered load: G=N*Tf/(Ti+Tf)    */
  Tf,                      /* mean frame transmission time    */
  Ti,                      /* mean inter-request time/station */
  tbs=0.0,                 /* channel busy start times        */
  tis=0.0,                 /* channel idle start times        */
  tfsum=0.0;               /* frame transmission time sum     */
```

Figure 6.9. The *ether* Simulation Program

```
main()
  {
    int event,stn,nb; real hw,Td;
    Tf=Tp/a; Ti=Tf*((real)N/G-1.0);
    smpl(0,"Ethernet Local Area Network");
    for (stn=1; stn<=Na; stn++) desc[stn].lnk=stn+1;
    desc[Na].lnk=0;
    init_bm(2000,2000); schedule(1,Tp,0);
    while (!end)
      { /* run until 10% Td accuracy achieved */
        cause(&event,&stn);
        switch (event)
          {
            case 1:  TransmitFrame();    break;
            case 2:  Defer(stn);         break;
            case 3:  StartTransmit(stn); break;
            case 4:  EndTransmit(stn);   break;
            case 5:  InitBackoff(stn);   break;
            case 6:  Deassert();         break;
          }
      }
    civals(&Td,&hw,&nb);
    printf("S = %.3f\n",tfsum/time());
    printf("D = %.3f +/- %.3f\n",Td/Tf,hw/Tf);
  }

real dly()   {return(Tp*(1.0-sqrt(ranf())));}

real maxm(x,y)  real x,y;  {return(x>y? x:y);}

TransmitFrame()
  {
    int stn; struct request *p;
    if (avl) then
      { /* allocate & build request descriptor */
        stn=avl; p=&desc[stn]; avl=p->lnk;
        p->attempt=p->bkf=0; p->tin=time(); p->txf=Tf;
        schedule(2,0.0,stn); N--;
      }
    if (N) then schedule(1,expntl(Ti/N),0);
  }
```

Figure 6.9. The *ether* Simulation Program (continued)

```
Defer(stn)
  int stn;
    {
      real dt=dly(); struct request *p=&desc[stn];
      if (chnl==busy && time()>(tbs+dt+Tif))
        then {p->lnk=dfr; dfr=stn;}
        else schedule(3,maxm(tis+dt+Tif-time(),0.0),stn);
    }


StartTransmit(stn)
  int stn;
    {
      real tc,t=time(),dt; static int ncls;
      struct request *p=&desc[stn];
      if (chnl==idle)
        then
          { /* reserve channel & schedule EndTransmit */
            chnl=busy; tbs=t; ncls=0;
            schedule(4,p->txf,stn);
          }
        else
          { /* collision will occur in tc ms. */
            dt=dly(); tc=maxm(tbs+dt-t,0.0);
            if (++ncls==1) then
              { /* cancel EndTransmit event */
                schedule(5,Tjam+dt,cancel(4));
                schedule(6,maxm(Tjam+dt,tbs+Tp-t),0);
              }
            schedule(5,Tjam+tc,stn);
          }
    }


EndTransmit(stn)
  int stn;
    { /* end successful frame transmission */
      struct request *p=&desc[stn];
      tfsum+=p->txf; EndRequest(stn);
      schedule(6,0.0,0);
    }
```

Figure 6.9. The *ether* Simulation Program (continued)

```
InitBackoff(stn)
  int stn;
    {
       int k; struct request *p=&desc[stn];
       if (++p->attempt>16)
         then EndRequest(stn);   /* abandon request */
         else
           { /* compute and schedule backoff delay */
             if (p->attempt==1)
               then p->bkf=2;
               else if (p->bkf<1024) then p->bkf*=2;
             if ((k=random(0,p->bkf-1))==0)
               then {p->lnk=dfr; dfr=stn;}
               else schedule(2,Tslot*k,stn);
           }
    }


Deassert()
  {
    chnl=idle; tis=time();
    while (dfr)
      { /* activate requests on defer wait list */
        schedule(3,dly()+Tif,dfr); dfr=desc[dfr].lnk;
      }
  }


EndRequest(stn)
  int stn;
    { /* deallocate descriptor, reschedule next arrival */
      struct request *p=&desc[stn];
      end=obs(time()-p->tin);
      p->lnk=avl; avl=stn;
      N++; cancel(1);
      schedule(1,expntl(Ti/N),0);
    }
```

Figure 6.9. The *ether* Simulation Program (continued)

finds this list empty, it simply ignores the current arrival and schedules the next arrival. This is a rare occurrence, even with a large number of stations operating near channel saturation, and has no practical effect on results.

The batch means analysis module of Section 4.7 is used to terminate the simulation run when T_d, the mean delay time estimate, has been obtained with 10 percent accuracy at a 95 percent confidence level. In this particular implementation, frame transmission times are constant, so this confidence interval also applies to the normalized mean delay $D = T_d/T_f$ (this does not hold for variable transmission times). Note that delay time sample values are passed to the batch means analysis module via the obs() call in the EndRequest() function, and so include delays for transmissions abandoned because of too many transmission attempts as well as successful transmissions. Note also the relatively large initial deletion amount of 2000 observations. Initial transient effects become substantial as the network nears saturation; you may want to make the deletion amount a function of the offered load.

6.7 *ether* Verification and Validation

We'll now look at how the results produced by *ether* compare with those of Lam's model and with Ethernet measurement data reported by Gonsalves [1985]. Comparison of *ether* simulation results with results from Lam's analytic model provides a way of verifying the simulation model. Gonsalves' data lets us validate simulation model results against actual system measurements.

Comparison with Lam's results. *ether* simulations were carried out for a range of α and G values. Other model parameters (timings, number of stations) had the values shown in the *ether* program listing of Figure 6.9. Each simulation run produced estimates of S and D. α was varied from 0.01 to 0.25. (Note that the maximum Ethernet frame length is 1526 bytes: this corresponds to α = 0.147 at τ = 22.5 microseconds, so a α value of 0.01 is slightly outside the actual operating range of a network with these timing parameters.) For each of the chosen values of α, a set of simulation runs was made with G varied from 0.05 up to a value for which D became very large (on the order of 20). The value of S at that point was taken as S_{max}.

For small values of α, (< 0.075), the values of S_{max} produced by *ether* compare closely to Lam's bound (equation 6.6). For large values of α, *ether* estimates greater throughput than does (6.6): the difference is on the order of 20 percent at α = 0.25. This chiefly results from the assumption in Lam's analysis that a collision interval is equal to twice the propagation delay. (This assumption is needed for analytic tractability.) While the maximum collision interval in an actual network may be as large as 2τ, the average is

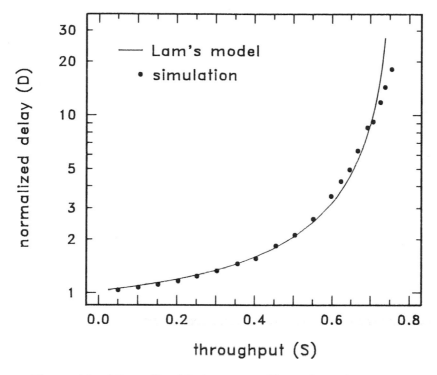

Figure 6.10. Normalized Delay versus Throughput at $\alpha = 0.05$

something less. For the parameters used here, 2τ is 45 microseconds; the mean frame transmission time is only twice that at $\alpha = 0.25$. At large α and high throughput rates with many collisions, this assumption results in over-estimating the channel time spent resolving collisions and consequently under-estimating throughput. For small α, 2τ is small relative to the frame transmission time, and the effect of this assumption diminishes.

To compare normalized mean delay times, the mean arrival rate of requests in the network was computed from the throughput of a simulation run ($\lambda = S/Tf$), the C function of Figure 6.5 used to compute the delay estimated by Lam's model, and that delay then compared with the delay estimate obtained from the simulation run. For other than large values of α and for throughputs not overly close to $Smax$, delay estimates produced by the two model agree very closely. Figure 6.10 compares delays from Lam's model and from *ether* for $\alpha = 0.05$. Differences in D for large α can be attributed to the effect on S of the collision interval length assumption discussed earlier. Differences arising as S approaches $Smax$ largely result from the different model types: Lam's model is an open model, *ether* is a closed model. (To examine the effect of the different model types, make some runs near saturation with N = 200, 500, and 1000, and see how D increases with N)

Comparison with Gonsalves' measurements. Gonsalves [1985] reports measurements of 3 Mbps and 10 Mbps Ethernet networks collected during execution of a controlled synthetic workload. Measurement data is presented in both graphical and numeric forms. The numeric throughput results for the 10 Mbps network given in Gonsalves' Table 4.6 are the most useful for our needs.

To compare *ether* simulation results with the data provided by Gonsalves, the simulation program of Figure 6.9 must be modified to reflect Gonsalves' measurement environment. Key parameters of this environment are

1. end-to-end propagation delay τ = 15 microseconds (the network length was 1500 meters with 2 repeaters),

2. number of station N = 32,

3. constant frame lengths, and

4. uniformly distributed inactive (inter-request) times.

Because of (4), we can't use the request scheduling algorithm devised for exponentially distributed inactive times, but instead have to schedule requests independently for each station. The impact of this change on simulation run times is not severe, since there are only 32 stations.

Gonsalves' Table 4.6 reports measured throughput as a function of the propagation time/mean frame transmission time ratio for various frame lengths. Throughput is computed using data bytes only, and mean frame transmission time is computed excluding the preamble. We'll use S' to denote throughput based on data bytes only, L' to denote the frame length in bytes exclusive of preamble, and α' to denote the propagation time/mean frame transmission time ratio for a frame length of L'. Note that

$$\alpha' = \alpha(1 + 8/L') \tag{6.19}$$

where α is the propagation time/mean frame transmission time ratio computed using the entire frame length including preamble.

Table 6.1 compares Gonsalves' throughput measurements with throughput estimates from *ether* simulations, with the *ether* simulation program modified to represent Gonsalves' environment. The simulation runs were made with G = 1. Measurement and simulation results are close: the largest difference is on the order of ten percent.

L'	α'	Gonsalves S'	ether S'
64	.280	.26	.28
200	.092	.60	.57
512	.026	.72	.72
1500	.012	.85	.83

Table 6.1. Measurement and Simulation Throughput Results

Gonsalves also provides a plot of normalized mean delay versus throughput which compares the normalized mean delay obtained from measurements with that estimated from Lam's model. You might like to try comparing *ether* delay estimates with delays obtained from this plot. Gonsalves concludes that Lam's model does not provide consistent accuracy because of differences between measurement and model results. These probably are due partly to the slotted channel and open model assumptions of Lam's analysis, discussed earlier in this section, and partly to measurement limitations: delays of a fraction of a millisecond could not be measured. Since the mean frame transmission time is less than 0.2 milliseconds at $\alpha = 0.1$, small delays were subject to considerable measurement error.

6.8 Applications and Extensions

ether provides a tool for estimating Ethernet performance under various loads and for evaluating network protocol and collision resolution variants. The literature abounds with proposals for enhancements to Ethernet and other CSMA/CD networks: a brief sampling of these follows.

Molloy [1984] briefly reviews several proposed mechanisms for collision resolution and presents a new method which can be integrated into CSMA/CD networks which follow the IEEE 802.3 standard. Wang and McGurrin [1985] suggest a fair share algorithm to protect the network from overload and describe a Markovian model for network analysis. Jackman and Medeiros [1984] propose a new backoff algorithm, describe the simulation model used in its evaluation, and compare the performance of their algorithm with the standard backoff algorithm. Chen and Li [1985] suggest varying the retransmission attempt limit to improve throughput and develop a probabilistic model of network operation for evaluating their scheme. Chlamtac and Eisenger [1983] discuss voice transmission in Ethernet and describe how voice performance can be improved by adjustment of the backoff algorithm. Many of these proposed extensions can be easily incorporated into *ether*.

For compactness, the simulation program of Figure 6.9 provides only constant frame transmission times. Actual networks have variable frame lengths, with a high frequency of short frames corresponding to request and acknowledge messages and a lower frequency of long frames representing data transmissions. Shoch and Hupp [1980] present measurements of several aspects of an Ethernet workload (measured on the original Ethernet), including request inter-arrival time and frame length distributions. They point out that frame lengths may be constrained by the environment in which the network operates. Variable frame transmission times can be incorporated into *ether* by modifying the `TransmitFrame()` event routine to generate a random frame transmission time from the appropriate distribution.

It is useful to extend *ether* to provide exponentially distributed frame transmission times, both to represent actual system variability and to provide a basis for comparison with certain analytic models. Depending on the application, you may want to truncate this distribution at the low end and possibly at the high end so that minimum and maximum transmission times correspond to Ethernet's minimum and maximum frame lengths. This may require adjusting the mean of the exponential distribution used to generate transmission times in order to obtained the desired mean time after truncation. To illustrate this, let's look at how to adjust the mean when sample times are truncated to a given minimum time (a similar approach can be used to limit sample times to a given maximum value).

Generating variates from a truncated exponential distribution. Suppose frame transmission times are assumed to be exponentially distributed except that the minimum transmission time is $tmin$, rather than 0, because of the minimum frame length requirement. The mean frame transmission time is Tf. To generate a sample frame transmission time in the simulation model, we generate a variate t from an exponential distribution and, if t is less than $tmin$, set t equal to $tmin$. (The distribution of t is called a *mixed* distribution, because it is part exponential and part constant.) The problem in generating t is determining the mean Tx of the exponential distribution which will result in a mean of Tf for the truncated variate.

For a random variable t distributed according to an exponential distribution with parameter u, the expected value of t is

$$E[t] = \int_0^\infty tue^{-ut}\, dt \qquad\qquad (6.20)$$

If we integrate (6.20) over the indicated integration period, we obtain $E[t] = 1/u$. Suppose, however, we divide the integration period into $[0, tmin]$ and $[tmin, \infty]$:

$$E[t] = \int_0^{tmin} tue^{-ut}\, dt \;+\; \int_{tmin}^\infty tue^{-ut}\, dt \qquad\qquad (6.21)$$

The left integral represents the contribution to the mean of values less than $tmin$, and the right integral represents the contribution of values greater than $tmin$. In generating sample frame transmission times, we essentially replace the contribution of the left integral by a quantity w

$$w = tmin\Pr[t<tmin] \;=\; tmin(1 - e^{-utmin}) \qquad\qquad (6.22)$$

i.e., variates with values less than $tmin$, whose relative frequency is $\Pr[t<tmin]$, are replaced by variates with value $tmin$. w is the contribution of these variates to the mean Tf of the truncated variate, which is

$$Tf = tmin(1 - e^{-utmin}) \;+\; \int_{tmin}^\infty tue^{-ut}\, dt \qquad\qquad (6.23)$$

Evaluating the integral and simplifying gives

$$Tf = tmin + u^{-1}e^{-utmin} \qquad\qquad (6.24)$$

Tf and $tmin$ are given (as model parameters), and we can determine from (6.23) the mean value $Tx = 1/u$ to use in generating the initial (not truncated) exponential variate. Unfortunately, we can't do this directly but have to use an iterative approach.

One possible approach is to use Newton's method (see, for example, Rice [1983]): write the equation in the form $f(x) = 0$, find the first derivative $f'(x)$, guess at an initial value $x0$, and compute an improved value $x1 = x0 - f(x0)/f'(x0)$. Repeat until the difference between successive values of x is less than some predetermined value. Applying Newton's method to (6.24) gives the following iterative relationship

$$u1 = u0 - \frac{Tf - tmin \ - u0^{-1} \ e^{-u0tmin}}{u0^{-1}e^{-u0tmin}\,(u0 \ ^{-1} + \ tmin\ )} \tag{6.25}$$

A reasonable starting point is $u0 = 1/Tf$. For typical *ether* model parameters, 4-digit accuracy typically is achieved with three or four iterations.

6.9 Summary

We have examined the construction of a macroscopic simulation model of Ethernet; this model employs analytic submodels to reduce the level of detail, and the resulting simulation program requires only 150 or lines of code. This model is not a hybrid model in the usual sense, but does illustrate how simple probabilistic analyses can be used to simplify a simulation mode'. O'Reilly and Hammond [1984] combine probabilistic and simulation analysis is a different way. Their approach partitions the network into a small number of priority stations and a large number of background stations: priority station operations are simulated, while the network load of background stations is probabilistically represented.

CSMA/CD networks, exemplified by Ethernet, represent one of the three local area network access methods for which IEEE standards have been developed: the other two methods are the token bus and token ring networks. Bux [1984] discusses and compares the performance of these three methods, and provides extensive references to performance analysis methods; Bux's references are a good starting point for exploring the literature on local area networks. A number of papers on simulation of token bus networks appear in the proceedings of a workshop on token bus modeling sponsored by the National Bureau of Standards [NBS 1985]. Token ring networks are the subject of this chapter's modeling project.

6.10 A Token Ring Modeling Project

The objective of this project is the development of a simulation model of a token ring local area network which can be used to determine how network configuration parameters (number of stations, station overhead, and ring length) and network load parameters (message lengths and rates) affect performance. Several different types of ring networks have been built or proposed, including token, slotted, and insertion rings, and there are several different protocols for token rings. This project is concerned with token ring

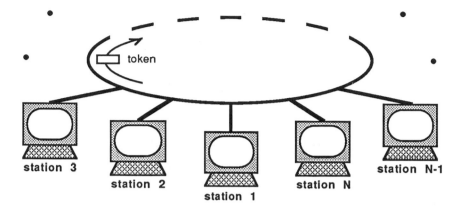

Figure 6.11. A Token Ring Network

networks of the type described in the ANSI/IEEE local area network standard 802.5 [IEEE 1985b]. Compared to CSMA/CD networks, token ring networks are less sensitive to workload characteristics, such as message length, and provide controlled delay under heavy load; CSMA/CD network delays are much more sensitive to load [Stuck 1983].

We'll begin our discussion of this project with a review of token ring operation. Next, we'll look at a simple analytic model of token ring performance which can be used to help verify the simulation model, and then discuss modeling assumptions and various aspects of simulation model construction.

Ring operation. A token ring network comprises a set of stations connected by a transmission medium such as twisted-pair cable. Information is transmitted in bit-serial fashion from one station to the next, circulating around the ring; each station reads, regenerates, and retransmits each bit. Data and control information is transmitted between stations in units called *frames*. Access to the ring is controlled by a *token*; a token is a specified bit pattern, one bit of which indicates whether the ring is free or busy. When the ring is free, the token continuously circulates from station to station. When a station has a frame to transmit, it waits until it the free token is received, changes the token status bit to mark the token busy, and transmits the frame; the token becomes part of the frame header. The bits of the frame circulate around the ring, are copied by the receiving station (or stations) as they pass, and are removed from the ring by the transmitting station.

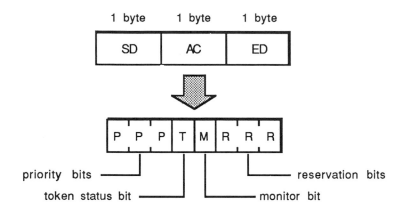

Figure 6.12. Token Format

A token comprises Starting Delimiter (SD), Access Control (AC), and Ending Delimiter (ED) bytes (Figure 6.12). Bits of the SD and ED bytes are transmitted in a way which insures that they can be distinguished from data and from other control fields. The Access Control (AC) byte contains priority, reservation, token status, and monitor bit fields. The priority and reservation fields are used to implement a network priority scheme; we won't be concerned with priorities in this project. The monitor bit is used in network error checking. When the ring is free, the token status bit is 0; on obtaining access to the ring, the sending station sets this bit to 1 and transmits the SD and AC fields as the first two bytes of a frame.

Token ring frame fields and field lengths (in bytes) are shown in Figure 6.13. The Frame Control (FC) byte distinguishes between data frames and network control message frames. Depending on the implementation, destina-tion (receiving station) and source (sending station) address fields may be either 2 bytes or 6 bytes in length. The maximum frame length, and consequently the maximum length of the information field, n, also depends on the implementation. The Frame-Check Sequence (FCS) field contains a cyclic redundancy check code similar to Ethernet's CRC code. Bits of the Frame Status (FS) byte are used to indicate that a receiving station has recognized its address and copied the frame from the ring.

When it finishes transmitting data, the sending station checks to see if it has received the frame header and, if it has, generates a new free token. If the frame header has not yet circulated back to the station, the station waits until the header is received before generating the free token. This insures that there is only one token on the ring at any given time, which

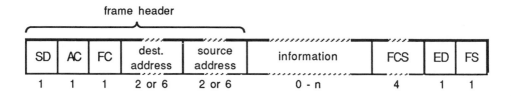

Figure 6.13. Token Ring Frame Format

helps in achieving reliable network operation Whether or not the sending station receives the token back before completing transmission depends on the relative values of frame transmission and network propagation times.

Application programs at a station generate messages and pass them to a network control program for transmission; the network program formats mes- sages into frames and queues them until the station can obtain access to the ring. Messages longer than the maximum frame length are broken down into multiple frames. The maximum time a station may use the ring on gaining access is determined by a Token Holding Timer (THT), which has a default timeout value of 10 milliseconds. When a station gains access to the ring, it transmits as many frames from its queue as it can in this interval.

The 802.5 token ring standard encompasses transmission rates of 1 and 4 Mbps, and specifies a ring capacity of at least 250 stations or repeaters. A repeater may be required for signal regeneration purposes when the distance between stations is very long. For ease of connection and maintenance, the physical form of a ring may resemble a star network, with inter-station connections made at a central point; this results in longer wire lengths than would be needed for point-to-point wiring. Rings can be interconnected via bridges, so very large networks can be constructed. Our analysis will assume a single ring and a transmission rate of 4 Mbps, which is equivalent to 4 bits per microsecond (us.).

Performance parameters and measures. The parameters of interest in token ring performance analysis are similar to those used in our Ethernet analysis. Network parameters are defined as follows.

N — number of stations in network

K — wire length in kilometers (km.)

B — station latency in bit times (discussed below)

R — transmission rate (4 bits/us.)

L — mean frame length in bits

The station latency B is the number of bit times required for a station to read, regenerate, and retransmit data on the ring. B can be as small as one bit time. The ring latency τ is the time (in us.) required for a signal to propagate around the ring; τ is equal to the propagation delay through the ring transmission medium plus the sum of the station latencies. Assuming a propagation delay of 5 us. per kilometer,

$$\tau = 5K + BN/R \qquad\qquad (6.26)$$

A minimum ring latency of 24 bit times (6 us. at a transmission rate of 4 Mbps) is provided by the network to insure that the first part of a token doesn't recirculate to a station while that station is still processing the last part.

The mean frame transfer time T_f is obtained by divided the mean frame length by the network transmission rate:

$$T_f = L/R \qquad\qquad (6.27)$$

Analogous to (6.5) for Ethernet, the ratio of the ring latency time to the mean frame transmission time is

$$\alpha = \tau/T_f \qquad\qquad (6.28)$$

For Ethernet, α was required to be less than 1. For the token ring network, α is less than 1 if the frame transmission time is greater than the ring latency, and greater than 1 if the frame transmission time is less than the ring latency.

In modeling the token ring network, we'll view it as an open system in which λ_i is the arrival rate of frame transmission requests at station i. For the present, we'll assume stations are identical and have the same arrival rate: $\lambda = \lambda_1 = \lambda_2 = \ldots = \lambda_N$. The *network throughput* is

$$S = N\lambda T_f \qquad\qquad (6.29)$$

See the comments on this definition of throughput in Section 6.3. The throughput in frames per unit time is $N\lambda$.

Define T_d as the mean frame delay time, measured from the time at which a frame transmission request is generated to the time at which the receiving station copies the last bit of the frame. The normalized mean delay D then is defined as

$$D = T_d/T_f \qquad\qquad (6.30)$$

For finite values of T_d and D, S must be less than 1.

An analytic model. The following analytic model is based on equation (1) in Bux [1981]. It employs the following assumptions.

- Each station has the same mean request arrival rate of λ frames per unit time; the request arrival process is Poisson (so inter-arrival times have a negative exponential distribution).

- The average distance between sending and receiving stations is one-half the ring length.

- Stations are located uniformly around the ring so that the propagation delay between adjacent stations is τ/N.

- Frame lengths are constant and equal to L bits for all requests.

- The mean frame transmission time Tf is greater than the ring latency τ, so that $\alpha < 1$.

Under these assumptions, the mean frame delay time is

$$Td = Tf + \frac{\tau}{2} + \frac{\tau(1 - S/N) + STf}{2(1 - S)} \qquad (6.31)$$

(6.31) provides a simple model for use in simulation model verification. Additional results can be found in the literature. Chapter 8 of Hammond and O'Reilly [1986] gives equations for Td in networks with both constant and exponential service times and with $\alpha > 1$. Bux [1984] provides references to a number of token ring queueing models. Networks in which all stations have identical arrival rates sometimes are called *symmetric* networks, while networks in which stations have differing arrival rates are called *non-symmetric* or *asymmetric* networks. Berry and Chandy [1983] present a simple iterative algorithm for computing Td for an asymmetric network in which all stations have the same frame length distribution. Everitt [1986] provides a relatively simple approximation for Td in asymmetric networks in which stations can have different frame length distributions.

Building the simulation model. The first version of your token ring simulation model should be based on the same assumptions as (6.31). However, to make extensions easier, plan for different arrival rates to different stations and for general frame length distributions; the latter requires proper representation of ring operation for frames whose transmission time is less than the ring latency time. Assume that messages correspond to frames regardless of length, so that message segmentation is not required, and that the timeout imposed by the Token Holding Timer can be ignored. The model should accept values of N, K, B, L, and λ as input parameters (R can be a compile-time parameter), and produce estimates of S, Td, and D. Assume that the frame length L includes overhead such as the frame header, and that S is computed using this total frame length. Since this is an open model, the estimated value of S should be very close to

$N\lambda L/R$. Use the batch means analysis module of Figure 4.7 to compute T_d with an accuracy of ten percent or better, and have the model report the confidence interval half-width for T_d.

A **smpl** facility can be used to represent the token; the utilization of this facility will be equal to S (as long as frame transmission times are greater than the ring latency). The state of the ring can be defined as the state of the token: non-busy when there is a free token on the ring, busy when there is not. It is possible to represent stations as **smpl** facilities, which may require increasing the size of the element pool (see Chapter 8). However, stations simply can be represented by an array of two-variable descriptors; each descriptor comprises a station state flag (idle or busy) and a pointer or index to the queue of requests for the station. A station is busy while it is transmitting frames and while it is removing its frame from the ring after completing transmission. For frames with transmission times greater than τ, then, the station remains busy for a time τ after completing its transmission and freeing the token.

Requests can be handled in the same way as the Ethernet model. During model initialization, a list of free request descriptors is constructed. As requests arrive in and depart from the system, request descriptors are allocated from and returned to this list. The request descriptor includes arrival time stamp, frame length (or frame transmission time), and link fields; the link field is used to link request descriptors on station queues or the free descriptor list.

Since station arrival processes are Poisson, the individual station arrival processes can be combined into a ring arrival process which also is Poisson and which, for a symmetric network, has mean rate $N\lambda$. The request arrival process, then, can be modeled by scheduling the next arriving request for the set of stations on the ring; inter-arrival times will have a negative exponential distribution with mean $1/N\lambda$. When a request "arrives", it is randomly assigned to one of the N stations; because a process created by random decomposition of a Poisson stream also is Poisson, the arrival process at each station will be Poisson. Generating request arrivals in this way means that, regardless of the number of stations in the ring, only one next arrival event is in the event list at any given time. For an asymmetric network, arrival processes for groups of stations with the same arrival rates can be combined, so that the number of next arrival events scheduled equals the number of different arrival rates.

The key problem in simulating the token ring network is determining how to compute (1) the delay between the time at which a request arrives in an idle ring and the time at which the token reaches the requesting station, and (2) the delay between the time at which a station places a free token on the ring and the time at which the token arrives at the closest station with an outstanding request. One way of approaching this problem is as follows.

Let t represent the current simulation time, and assume that, at time 0, the token has just left station N on its way to station 1. At time t, the token will have completed a fraction f of its current revolution, where f is the fractional part of t/τ. Assuming stations are equidistantly spaced around the ring, the position of station i corresponds to a fraction of a revolution $f_i = i/N$. From f and f_i, it is possible to compute the time t_i at which the token will arrive at station i. When a request arrives at station i in an idle ring, the time at which the token will arrive at that station can be computed and a Start Transmit event scheduled for that time, provided no Start Transmit event is scheduled for a station nearer the current token position. If a request arrives at station i and a Start Transmit event is scheduled for a station farther away from the token than station i, the Start Transmit event for that station is cancelled before scheduling that event for station i. Only one Start Transmit event, at most, is scheduled at a time, and the model keeps track of the number of the station for which that event is scheduled. An arriving request which finds a Start Transmit event scheduled for a station closer to the token, or which finds the ring busy, simply queues at its station.

When a transmission completes and a free token is placed on the ring, the model finds the closest station with a queued request, computes the time at which the token will arrive at that station, and schedules a Start Transmit event for that time. The simplest way to find the closest station is to search the station descriptor array, beginning with the next station, for a station with a queued request. This isn't as inefficient as it might seem; note that, as the network load increases, the average number of station descriptors examined decreases.

In this initial version of the model, it isn't necessary to represent the receiving station. Instrument the model to compute T_d', where T_d' is defined as the mean frame delay time measured from the time at which a request arrives at a station until the time at which its transmission is completed and the station either frees the token or dequeues and starts transmission of another frame. The mean frame delay time given by (6.31) is the sum of three terms: T_f, $\tau/2$, and a delay term. The $\tau/2$ term represents the average delay between sender and receiver, assuming that, on the average, the receiver is half way around the ring from the sender (i.e., the receiver is, equiprobably, any one of the other stations). With this assumption, $T_d = T_d' + \tau/2$. (If a confidence interval half-width of H is obtained for T_d', what is the confidence interval half-width for T_d?)

(a) Assume a network with 40 stations, a cable length of 1 kilometer, and a station latency of 1 bit time. For a constant frame size of 4000 bits, make a set of simulation runs with $\lambda = 2.5, 5.0, \ldots, 20$ frames per second per station. Plot $T_d + H$ and $T_d - H$, where T_d is the mean frame delay time esti - mated from simulation and H is its confidence interval half-width versus S. For the same parameter values and set of λ values, compute T_d from (6.31) and plot these values. What conclusion do you draw from this comparison? Do you consider your simulation model verified, at least in part?

Note that you can check model operation for short transfers ($T_f < \tau$) by making runs with a frame transmission time less than τ and with a frame transmission time equal to τ (or slightly larger, if necessary to assure proper event sequencing), using the same λ in both cases. Since a station does not free the token until it reads the frame header of its transmission, these two runs should produce comparable estimates for T_d.

(b) Suppose a network of 40 stations has a cable length of 4 kilometers and a station latency of 4 bit times. For a constant frame size of 4000 bits, make a set of simulation runs with $\lambda = 2.5, 12.5,$ and 20 frames per second per station. Compare the value of T_d with those obtained in (a); how does the increased ring latency affect delays?

(c) Investigate the effect of asymmetric operation on mean frame delay times in a network of 40 stations with $K = 1$ km., $B = 1$ bit time, and a fixed frame length of 4000 bits. Assume that stations in this network divide into two groups: a group of 36 stations with low arrival rates, and a group of 4 stations with high arrival rates. Set the relative arrival rates to stations in these groups as you deem appropriate. Compare your results with those obtained in (a).

(d) **A file server network**. A token ring local area network is composed of 50 diskless workstations and two file server stations, each with a single disk.[5] The network transmission rate is 4 Mbps, the network length is 1.5 km., and the station latency of each station is 4 bit times. A workstation performs a file read or write operation by sending a message to a file server; file information is transferred in fixed-size units of 4096 bytes called file blocks. To read from a file , a workstation sends a read request message to the appropriate server; the server reads the file block from its disk and transmits it to the workstation. To write to a file, the workstation constructs a write request which includes the file block and transmits it to a server, which writes it to the disk. Message traffic in the network divides into two

---

[5]See Lazowska et al [1986] for a discussion of performance issues in a network of diskless workstations.

types: read requests, which have a total frame length of 48 bytes, and file block read/write transfers, which have a total frame length of 4144 bytes. Reads are three times more frequent than writes. (Message traffic among workstations is small enough to be ignored.) Stations generate messages at a rate of 1 message per second per station; inter-message times are exponentially distributed.

Messages can be assumed to be directed randomly and equiprobably to the two file servers. On receipt of a message, the file server initiates a disk operation if its disk is free and otherwise queues the disk request; disk queues are first-in, first-out. Disk service times are distributed uniformly between 20 and 40 ms. Whenever the file server completes a disk read operation, it constructs a frame containing the file block and queues the frame for transmission. Because of the length of file block frames, a file server transmits only one file block each time it obtains access to the ring.

Extend the token ring simulation model to represent this file server network. You can position the file servers anywhere in the network (does it matter?). Instrument the model to obtain the mean response time T_r for workstation reads, measured from the time at which the workstation generates the read request to the time at which it receives the file block, and the mean network and disk queueing time components of this response time. Devise an approach to verifying the model. When verification is complete, use the model to estimate T_r for this system.

Determine how many workstations can be added to this network with an increase of no more than 30 percent in T_r. Next, suppose the file block size is doubled, increasing the file block transfer frame length to 8240 bytes, increasing the disk service time by 5 ms. and halving the station message rate. (Assume the token holding time limit is increased to permit transmission of frames of this length.) Determine how many stations can be supported in this modified network if a read response time equivalent to the original network (adjusted for file block size differences) is to be provided.

7. A Simulation Environment

7.1 Introduction

This chapter provides a user's view of a simulation environment called **SMPL**. **SMPL** comprises the **smpl** simulation subsystem described in Chapter 2, additional debugging, analysis, and reporting tools, and an interactive run-time interface called **mtr**. This description is based on an implementation of **SMPL** called **SMPL/PC**, which runs on one type of personal computer. Similar environments can be tailored to other systems; a design overview of **mtr** and some of the **SMPL** tools is given in Chapter 9.

The **SMPL** simulation environment is illustrated in Figure 7.1. Basic simulation operations are performed via simulation program calls to **smpl** functions, as discussed in Chapter 2. **mtr** provides an interface between the user, the simulation program, **smpl**, and other **SMPL** modules (most of these also can be used directly from the simulation program). These modules include the following.

> **dump.** This module displays the state (event list and queue contents, facility users and status) of the simulated system. This display can be invoked via **mtr** or by a simulation program function call.

> **table.** This module provides functions for table definition, data entry, reporting, and plotting. These can be invoked via mtr (for **SMPL** parameters) or by calls from the simulation program.

> **bma.** This is the batch means analysis module. A batch means analysis is used to determine the simulation run length required to achieve a specified accuracy for a model output parameter. It can be initiated from **mtr** (for **SMPL** parameters) or from the simulation program.

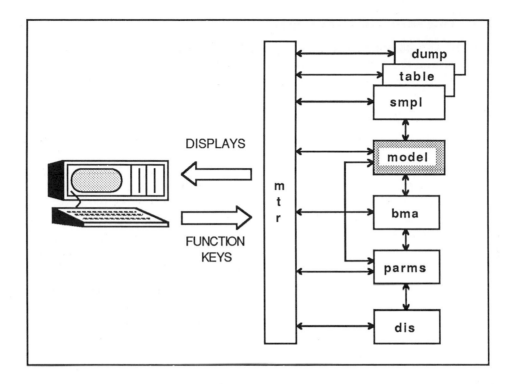

Figure 7.1. The **SMPL** Simulation Environment

parms. The **parms** module provides facilities for defining and naming **SMPL** parameters. These are selected model variables whose values can be assigned or displayed via **mtr** as well as by the simulation program. They also can be designated as inputs to table data entry, batch means analysis, and graphics display functions.

dis. This module uses the computer's bit-mapped graphics display to plot facility utilization, queue length, or a **SMPL** parameter versus time, or to plot one **SMPL** parameter versus another. This display can be initiated only from **mtr**.

Figure 7.1 provides a user-level view: lower-level **SMPL** modules, such as the screen/keyboard services module, are not shown.

Subsequent sections describe **mtr**, **SMPL** parameters and the **parms** module, and the **dump, table, bma,** and **dis** modules. These last four modules are optional components of a **SMPL** system "build".

7.2 The Run-Time Interface

The simulation program specifies whether or not **mtr** is to be activated by assigning the appropriate value to a `smpl()` call parameter (see Section 2.3). Thus, the overhead and user attendance associated with **mtr** can be bypassed if desired, as when we're in "production mode" and the simulation program is set up to perform multiple runs during one execution.

Once activated, **mtr** pauses at two points during model initialization. The first pause occurs on completion of **smpl** initialization; this provides an opportunity to set **SMPL** parameters from the keyboard, possibly including parameters specifying the number of facilities to be defined, or to define a table. The second pause occurs when the first event is scheduled. At this point, all facilities have been defined; the pause provides an opportunity to specify a value associated with a facility, such as its utilization or queue length, as an input to the graphics display. At each pause, the user performs the desired operations and then presses a function key to resume execution.

After these two pauses, execution continues until the simulation program terminates, an error is encountered, or execution is paused by the program, by a **SMPL** display, or by the user. As the model executes, **mtr** displays the current simulation time on the screen. During execution, a pause can be initiated by the simulation program, via a function call, or by the user, via a function key. Also, **SMPL** modules typically initiate a **mtr** pause after generating a display. If an error is detected by **smpl**, the error message is displayed on the screen, and **mtr** pauses to permit the user to invoke the dump and report displays (and possibly a simulation program display). The simulation program usually displays the simulation report before terminating; **mtr**, as a subprogram of **smpl**, terminates when the simulation program terminates.

Monitoring operations are performed by a **mtr** function which is called by **smpl** whenever an event occurs. This function checks to see if a breakpoint match has occurred, updates any displays or analysis functions invoked from **mtr**, and checks the keyboard to see if a function key has been pressed since the last **mtr** entry (no other keys are recognized by **mtr** at this point).

The function key assignments of **SMPL/PC** are shown in Figure 7.2.[1] The notes next to each key describe the key functions; the upper note indicates the function executed when the key is pressed by itself, while the lower note indicates the function executed when the key is pressed together with the shift key. We'll refer to the normal functions keys as **Fn**, the shifted function

---

[1]In this implementation, user-model interaction is based on function keys; other implementations may use pull-down (or pop-up) menus.

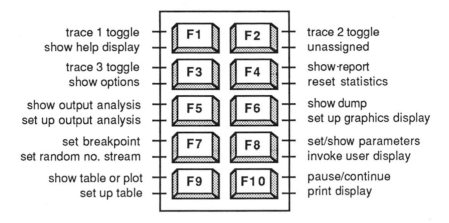

trace 1 toggle — F1
show help display —

trace 2 toggle — F2
unassigned —

trace 3 toggle — F3
show options —

show·report — F4
reset statistics —

show output analysis — F5
set up output analysis —

show dump — F6
set up graphics display —

set breakpoint — F7
set random no. stream —

set/show parameters — F8
invoke user display —

show table or plot — F9
set up table —

pause/continue — F10
print display —

Figure 7.2. SMPL/PC Function Keys

keys as **sFn**. By using the appropriate function key, the user can pause execution (or resume execution after a pause), turn tracing on and off, generate any output display, invoke an initialization panel (screen display) for the table, batch means, or graphics display functions, and display or modify SMPL parameter values.

The **F10** key is used to pause execution, resume execution after a pause, and exit from displays. Pressing **F10** while the simulation is running pauses execution in a state called *monitor pause* state. Any display may be invoked from this state, and exit from displays is to this state. Pressing **F10** while in monitor pause state causes execution to be resumed. However, it is not necessary to use **F10** to pause execution prior to invoking a display; any function key can be pressed at any time while the simulation is running. Also, it is possible to invoke one display from another. As an example of display sequencing, suppose the simulation is running and **F6** is pressed. This invokes the dump display, which may require stepping through several panels. When the final panel is reached, the user can print the dump by pressing **sF10**, exit to monitor pause state by pressing **F10**, or invoke another display, such as the simulation report, by pressing the appropriate function key.

Certain keys provide access to **smpl** functions. Keys **F1-F3** turn **smpl** tracing on and off. Trace 1 is free-running, trace 2 pauses after each full screen, and trace 3 pauses after each trace message. These keys are toggles; pressing a key once turns tracing on, pressing it again turns tracing off.

Execution is resumed after a pause by pressing **F10**. The **F4** key displays the **smpl** simulation report which, depending on the number of facilities defined in the model, may comprise more than one panel. When the final panel is reached, the user can print the report, invoke another display, or exit to monitor pause state and, from there, resume execution.

sF4 invokes the **smpl** reset function (described in Section 2.9). This can be used to effect multiple simulation runs in a single instance of simulation program execution, even though the program is not designed to do so. One way to do this is to set a breakpoint specifying when the run is to end; when the breakpoint pause occurs, output parameter values are noted, accumulated measures are cleared with the reset key, a breakpoint set for the end of the next run, and execution resumed. Another way involves use of the graphics display in an ad hoc determination of simulation run length. The graphics display is used to monitor the output parameter of interest, such as mean queue length. When the display indicates that the value of this parameter has stabilized, this sample value is recorded, the reset key used to clear accumulated measures, and the process repeated to obtain another sample value. A similar approach can be used to discard measurements collected during model "warm-up".

The **sF7** key generates a screen message which shows the number of the currently-specified random number generator stream and permits entry of a new stream number. This makes it easy to obtain independent runs — replications — of a model without building run control into the simulation program. To obtain n sample values of an output parameter, the simulation program is executed n times; on the initial pause of each execution, a new random number stream is selected. The stream selection and reset keys let the user accomplish a lot of experimental work without programming effort.

Keys **sF1**, **sF3**, and **F7** invoke functions local to **mtr**. **sF1** invokes the help display; this display shows function key assignments, and looks very much like Figure 7.2. The inclusion of the **dump**, **table**, **bma**, or **dis** modules in a SMPL system is a system "build" option; other options include data structure sizes, table plot routine selection, and graphics print driver selection. The **sF3** key invokes a display listing the options used to build the currently-executing version of SMPL. The **F7** key requests entry of a breakpoint time or a breakpoint parameter number and value: **mtr** will pause when the break-point time or breakpoint parameter value is reached.

It is possible to invoke a simulation program display by a function key; **sF8** is used for this purpose. To do this, the simulation program first passes a pointer to the display function to **mtr** via a call to **mtr**'s user () function; **mtr** then calls that display function whenever **sF8** is pressed.

The remaining function keys invoke displays of particular **SMPL** modules; we'll look at the functions of these keys when we discuss the modules with which they're associated.

7.3 Parameters

The **SMPL** parameter mechanism provides a very simple, yet very effective, means of communication between the simulation program, **SMPL**, and the user. The simulation program defines a (real) variable as a parameter via a call to a **parms** module function, specifying the parameter number, a pointer to the variable, and a pointer to a string to be used as the parameter name. **parms** maintains an array of parameter variable pointers via which other **SMPL** modules obtain and assign parameter values.

The **F8** key invokes the **SMPL** parameter display. which shows the current values of parameters and permits keyboard assignment of parameter values. This display also provides a print option. Typically, both model input and model output parameters are defined as **SMPL** parameters. Defining model input parameters as **SMPL** parameters eliminates the need to code input processing routines for many simulation programs. Similarly, defining model output parameters as **SMPL** parameters can eliminate (or at least reduce) the need to code reporting routines, since output parameters can be displayed and printed from the keyboard. In addition, a **SMPL** parameter can be specified as input to the batch means analysis function, the table function, and the graphics display, and a breakpoint can be set to pause execution when a parameter reaches a specified value, such as a completion count.

7.4 The dump Module

The **dump** module displays the state of the simulated system as **smpl** knows it. For each facility in the system, **dump** shows the status of each server together with the number of the reserving token if the server is busy, and lists the contents of the facility's queue. This display can be invoked from the simulation program via a dump() function call or from **mtr** via function key **F6**. It also is invoked by **smpl** when a simulation error is detected. When invoked from the simulation program, dump output is sent to the current output destination, so it can be printed by changing the output destination to the printer prior to the call. When invoked via a function key, a print option is provided on the final panel of the display.

An abbreviated example of dump output is shown in Figure 7.3. This was generated during execution of the queueing network model presented in

```
MODEL:  central server model                    TIME:     6616.087


      ---------------- FACILITIES and QUEUES ----------------

f  --- facility ---   server     status    token    pri.  busy start
1  CPU                  1         busy       8        1     6614.613

                      queue       event     token    pri.  time left
                        1           3         5        1        8.101

                  last queue entry/exit time = 6614.613

              .             .         .         .         .
              .             .         .         .         .
              .             .         .         .         .

f  --- facility ---   server     status    token    pri.  busy start
10 disk                 1         busy       7        0     6608.084

                      queue       event     token    pri.  time left
                        1           4         4        0        0.000
                        2           4         3        0        0.000

                  last queue entry/exit time = 6608.084

              .             .         .         .         .
              .             .         .         .         .
              .             .         .         .         .

              -------------- EVENT LIST -----------
              entry      event      token      to occur at
                1          5          1          6619.292
                2          5          6          6639.710
                3          5          7          6641.656
                4          5          2          6650.744
              last event caused = 3 for token 3
```

Figure 7.3. dump Module Output Example

Section 2.8. The display heading gives the model name and current simulation time. For each facility, the facility descriptor, facility name, and state of each server are shown, and the facility queue contents are listed. For each busy server, the number and priority of the reserving token are shown; for all servers, the time at which the facility last became busy is shown.

The facility queue listing shows, for each queued request, the queue position, token number and priority, and the event to be rescheduled when the facility becomes available. If the entry represents a preempted facility request, the remaining event time ("time left") is shown, as for the CPU queue entry in Figure 7.3. At the end of the queue listing, the time of the most recent queue or dequeue operation for the facility is shown; this sometimes is useful in deciding when tracing should be turned on.

The event list display shows the event number, token, and event occurrence time for each entry in the event list, followed by the number and associated token of the event last caused. Since **smpl** invokes **mtr** at the end of `cause()` function execution, this "last event caused" will not have been returned to the simulation program at the time the display is generated when invoked from **mtr**.

7.5 The table Module

Tables are used to collect distributions of output parameters such as system residence times or queueing times. The **table** module provides functions for table definition, data entry, reporting, and plotting. A table definition specifies a range of values and a number of intervals into which this range is to be divided; it results in the creation of a data structure which includes a counter for each interval. When a value is entered into a table, the interval into which the value falls is determined and the corresponding counter is incremented. The number of values falling in a given interval divided by the total number of values entered in the table gives the proportion of values falling in that interval. The table report includes the mean and standard deviation of entered values and the count, proportion, and cumulative proportion of values for each interval and of values outside the specified range. An example of a table report is shown in Figure 9.4.

Tables can be defined via function calls from the simulation program and from **mtr** via an input display invoked by function key **sF9**. When a table is defined from the simulation program, values are entered by `enter()` function calls. When a table is defined from **mtr**, a **SMPL** parameter is specified as the table entry parameter, and values are entered by **mtr** without simulation program action. A second **SMPL** parameter, an entry count, also must be specified; it is used to determine when a new value has been assigned to the entry parameter. Similar entry and count parameters are used by the **bma** and **dis** modules. Thus, by specifying appropriate simulation program variables as **SMPL** parameters, a number of analysis and display functions can be invoked from **mtr** without additional programming.

The total number of tables which can be defined as limited only by the size of certain data structures; however, only one table can be defined from **mtr**. This limitation is based on a combination of efficiency and simplicity considerations. The count parameter is checked on each **mtr** entry to determine if a table entry should be made: this imposes a certain amount of overhead. Checking for only one table keeps this overhead at a minimum, and the single table seems to meet most needs.

Tables and table plots can be displayed from **mtr** via function key **F9** or by a function call from the simulation program; the **mtr**-invoked display provides a print option. The simulation program can print individual table reports if desired; also, when the current output destination is the printer, a `report()` function call will print reports and plots (if specified) for all tables as well as printing the simulation report.

7.6   The Batch Means Analysis Module

The batch means analysis module, **bma**, determines the simulation run length required to estimate the mean value of a discrete-time simulation output variable with specified accuracy and confidence level. It is based on the approach proposed by Adam [1983]. We'll briefly review the method before describing **bma** inputs and outputs.

The analysis begins by discarding the first l values to minimize model "warmup" effects. Next, k batches, each comprising m values, are collected. The batch means, the grand mean, and the variance of the batch means are computed. Autocorrelation coefficients of the batch means are computed for a specified number of lags. If none of the autocorrelation coefficients is significant at a specified level of significance, the batch means are assumed to be independent. If any of the coefficients is significant, the independence hypothesis is rejected, existing pairs of batches are combined (halving k) and m is doubled, $k/2$ more batches are collected, and the test for independ-ence repeated. The batch size is increased by doubling because **bma** retains only the batch sums, not individual values.

When the independence hypothesis has been satisfied, the second phase of the analysis is initiated. The relative confidence interval half-width is computed and compared with the specified relative half-width. If the estimated relative half-width is greater than that specified, k is incremented, another batch is collected, a new confidence interval is estimated, and the comparison repeated. If adding another batch will exceed the batch sum storage space of **bma**, the batch size is doubled and the number of batches halved, and k then incremented.

When the specified relative confidence interval half-width has been achieved, **bma** reduces the number of batches to 30 or fewer to improve coverage of the mean (see Schmeiser [1982]). The number of batches is halved and the batch size doubled (another batch is collected first if the original number is odd), and the relative confidence interval half-width is recomputed and compared with the specified value. If the estimated value is greater than the specified value, another batch is collected and the comparison repeated. This process continues until the specified accuracy is achieved with 30 or fewer batches.[2]

A batch means analysis can be initiated from the simulation program or from **mtr**. When initiated from the simulation program, sample values of the output parameters are transmitted to **bma** via an `accum()` function call: this function returns a code indicating when the analysis is complete. When initiated from **mtr**, the output parameter must have been defined as a **SMPL** parameter by the simulation program, and a count of the number of sample values must be maintained by the program: this also must be a **SMPL** parameter.

The **bma** input display, shown in Figure 7.4(a), is invoked by key **sF5**. The output parameter and count parameter are specified (by SMPL parameter number) on the first two lines. Analysis control parameters are specified on subsequent lines; these are initialized to default values (shown in the figure) and can be modified as desired. These include the number of initial values to be discarded, the initial batch size, the initial number of batches to be collected, the desired relative half-width, and the confidence level. (Estimation of autocorrelation requires a large number of batches, relative to the number recommended for the method of Section 4.7.) The number of lags and the significance level to be used in autocorrelation coefficient computation and testing also can be specified.

One of the analysis control parameters is the maximum number of values to be collected. If doubling the batch size or increasing the number of batches will require collecting more than this number of values, **bma** asks that the

---

[2]This differs somewhat from Adam's algorithm, which reduces the number of batches to ten and so must either collect additional values to make the number of batches before reduction a multiple of ten or exclude some data from this step of the analysis.

```
        Simulation Output Analysis Definition

  parameter no. of obs. value . . . . . . . . . . 1
  parameter no. of obs. count . . . . . . . . . . 2
  initial observations discarded  . . . . . . . 100
  max. no. of observations  . . . . . . . . . . 32000
  starting batch size . . . . . . . . . . . . . 200
  starting no. of batches . . . . . . . . . . . 50
  relative c.i. halfwidth (%) . . . . . . . . . 10.0
  confidence level (%)  . . . . . . . . . . . . 90.0
  max. no. of lags  . . . . . . . . . . . . . . 12
  r significance level (%)  . . . . . . . . . . 5.0


        trace analysis decisions? (y/n):
```

(a) input display

```
          Simulation Output Analysis

  central server model                    time:   167948.625

          variable:  class 0 tour time

  confidence interval . . . . . . . . . . . . . 99.677 +/- 0.986
  confidence level (%)  . . . . . . . . . . . . . . . . 90.0
  estimated relative c.i. half-width (%)  . . . . . . . 1.0
  specified relative c.i. half-width (%)  . . . . . . . 10.0
  no. of initial observations discarded . . . . . . . . 100
  total no. of observations . . . . . . . . . . . . . 10100
  batch size  . . . . . . . . . . . . . . . . . . . . . 400
  no. of batches  . . . . . . . . . . . . . . . . . . . 25
```

(b) output display

Figure 7.4. **bma** Input and Output Displays

maximum be raised (or the analysis terminated). Since various **smpl** counters are int variables (**bma** counters either are long int or real variables), counts in excess of 32767 will result in overflow in implementations where ints are 16-bit quantities. This can be avoided by setting this maximum count to an appropriate initial value (based on the maximum number of operations on any one facility per sample value) and, if the maximum is reached, using the reset key to clear **smpl** counters before increasing it.

bma provides an optional trace facility which shows intermediate results and analysis decisions. During the batch size determination phase, the analysis trace display shows the grand mean, batch mean variance, autocorrelation coefficients for each lag, and the significant autocorrelation coefficient value. During the confidence interval computation phase, the mean and variance are shown together with the estimated and specified confidence interval half-widths, and changes in the batch size and the number of batches are shown.

An example of the **bma** report is shown in Figure 7.4(b). When **bma** is invoked from **mtr**, this display is generated automatically when the analysis is complete, and can be recalled to the screen via function key **F5**. This key also will display the report at any time during the analysis after the batch size has been determined, showing the current estimates of the output values. When **bma** is invoked from the simulation program, the report is displayed or printed via a function call.

The report of Figure 7.4(b) was generated from a batch means analysis of class 0 tour times in the queueing network model of Section 2.7. The first line of the body of the report gives the mean value and the absolute confidence interval half-width, the second line states the specified confidence level, and the third and fourth lines show the estimated and specified relative half-widths. The last three lines gives the total number of values collected (including those discarded), the final batch size, and the final number of batches. In this case, both batch independence and initial confidence interval requirements were satisfied by the starting values of l, k, and m, and the confidence interval remained satisfactory when k was halved to 25. Note that the estimated half-width is much smaller than that specified; it might have been possible to achieve the desired confidence interval and level with a smaller starting value of m.

Batch means methods are empirical and cannot be guaranteed to work under all circumstances: no particular method has become widely accepted. **bma** has been used to analyze output from a variety of simulations of queueing systems for which exact analytic results are available with good results; nevertheless, it should be regarded as an experimental tool. The survey of output analysis methods by Law [1983] — recommended reading — includes some results of testing batch means (and other) methods.

7.7 The Graphics Display Module

dis, the graphics display module, provides five time series plot options: facility utilization, average queue length, current queue length, or a **SMPL** parameter value can be plotted against simulation time, or a **SMPL** parameter value can be plotted against a count.

The **dis** input display is invoked by **sF6**. This display has two parts: the first part is used to select the plot option, and the second part, which is option-dependent, is used to specify plot parameters. These include the facility name for utilization and queue length plots, the **SMPL** parameter number (or numbers) for **SMPL** parameter plots, the interval of time to be spanned by the plot (X axis length), minimum and maximum Y axis values, and the plotting mode (e.g., point mode, step mode). When a **SMPL** parameter is plotted against a count, the count also must be a **SMPL** parameter; here, **dis** inputs are defined in the same way — and may be the same — as **table** and **bma** module inputs. It also is possible to specify that data points are to be written to a file as they are plotted.

When all plot parameters required by the selected option have been specified, plotting is initiated immediately and continues until execution is interrupted (by a function key or some program action) or until the specified time period has been covered. In the latter case, **dis** asks if the display is to be printed (**SMPL/PC** provides graphics print drivers for several popular printers), and then asks if the plot is to be continued. If it is, plotting is resumed with a new plot interval continuing from the end of the previous interval and of the same duration as the previous interval; otherwise, **dis** exits to monitor pause state.

Figure 7.5 shows a plot of current queue length versus time generated during an **M/M/1** queueing system simulation. This is a "step" mode plot, reminiscent of Figure 1.5b. There are several other modes, two of which are illustrated by Figures 4.1 ("line" mode) and 4.2 ("point" mode). Figure 7.5 is a representation of the **dis** screen display. Most of the figures in Chapter 4 were drawn using the data file optionally produced by **dis** as input to a special X-Y plotter driver program.

The time series plots produced by **dis** have several uses. Examination of queue lengths and residence times during the early part of a simulation run provides an ad hoc way of assessing warm-up effects. For example, the user can plot mean queue length and, when the value begins to stabilize, use the

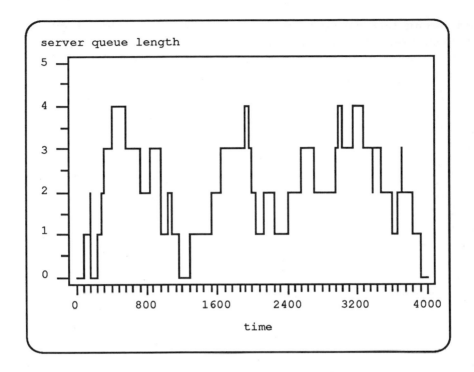

Figure 7.5. **dis** "step mode" Plot

reset key to clear accumulated measures. When the analysis doesn't require the precision offered by **bma**, simulation run length can be determined by plotting the mean value of interest and letting the simulation run until this value stabilizes. Simply observing the dynamic behavior of a simulated system is interesting; also, casual observation sometimes reveals bugs that otherwise might go unnoticed, as evidenced by, for example, unexpected growth — or lack of growth — of queues.

7.8 Summary

The goal of **SMPL** is to speed the development, testing, and use of small- and medium-scale simulation models. Defining key input and output parameters as **SMPL** parameters reduces implementation time by eliminating the need to code input processing and report generation functions and, at the same time, defines potential inputs to the **table, bma,** and **dis** modules. These modules then can be invoked as desired, without coding function calls and recompiling the model when model parameter values need to be changed. Run termination, trace control, and other supporting code can be omitted from the initial version of the simulation program, letting the user concentrate on the model itself.

Once coding is completed, keyboard control of debugging and reporting aids via **mtr** expedites the debugging process and minimizes the number of times the program has to be recompiled to insert debugging code. When the program generates its own output report, defining the report function as a mtr user function (see the discussion of the **sF8** key) makes it possible to display that report at any time, which helps the debugging process. Problem analysis often can be carried out from the keyboard without program changes if model parameters are defined as **SMPL** parameters; **bma** can be used to determine the run length, and reports can be displayed and printed via **mtr** function keys. Independent replications can be obtained by repeated program execution with the random number stream changed at the start of each execution. (Direct user control of each run isn't always desired; when many runs are needed, implementing run control in the simulation program saves the user's time and eliminates **mtr** overhead.)

We've been looking at a particular **SMPL** implementation, **SMPL/PC**. However, the machine dependencies of this implementation largely are limited to two areas. There is a screen and keyboard services module (**svc**) which provides functions for keyboard input and character or graphics screen output, and **dis** contains machine-dependent display coordinate mapping functions. Consequently, transportation of **SMPL** to other systems should be straightforward. If you're developing your own simulation system, the key modules to get in place are **parms** and **mtr**; we'll look at the general design of these and some other **SMPL** components in Chapter 9.

8. Implementing smpl

8.1 Introduction

In this chapter, we'll take a close look at the design and implementation of **smpl**. A detailed understanding of how **smpl** works will plug any gaps left by Chapter 2, help you fix it if it breaks, and provide a basis for tailoring and extending it to meet needs unique to your environment. We'll look at some possible extensions in the next chapter.

This implementation of **smpl** uses the C language as described by Kernighan and Ritchie in *The C Programming Language* [K&R].[1] If C is a new programming language for you, you may find a more extensive introduction, such as that provided by Gehani [1985], to be a helpful supplement to [K&R]. For reference purposes, the book by Harbison and Steele [1984] is excellent. The implementation presented here is straightforward: the code should be easy to read even for the reader new to C. Traditional arrays and indexes are used for data structures, rather than C structures and pointers, to maintain correspondence between this version of **smpl** and versions implemented in other languages.

The Appendix provides C source code listings for the following files:

smpl.c — the **smpl** simulation subsystem except for random variate generation functions,

rand.c — random variate generation functions,

smpl.h — **smpl** external name declarations and various user-level directives, and

stat.c — normal and *t* distribution quantile functions.

---

[1]This departure from our usual reference notation is in deference to the industry-wide recognition of "K&R".

initialization

smpl()*	initialize simulation subsystem
reset()*	clear measurement counters and accumulators

namespace and element pool allocation

save_name()	save model or facility name
mname()*	return model name pointer
fname()*	return facility name pointer
get_blk()	allocate block of elements
get_elm()	allocate single element
put_elm()	deallocate single element

event scheduling

schedule()*	schedule event
cause()*	cause event and advance simulation time
time()*	return current simulation time
cancel()*	cancel scheduled event
suspend()	remove event list entry of preempted token

list processing

enlist()	enter element in queue or event list

facility definition, operation, and query

facility()*	define facility
resetf()	clear facility and queue measurements
request()*	reserve facility (non-preemptive)
enqueue()	build facility queue entry
preempt()*	reserve facility (preemptive)
release()*	release facility and reinitiate queued request
status()*, inq()*	return current facility status, current queue length
U()*, B()*, Lq()*	return utilization, mean busy period, mean queue length

debugging and reporting

trace()*	turn trace on/off
msg()	display/print trace message
end_line()	trace line end: test for and process page end
pause()*	pause execution
error()*	print/display error message and halt
report()*	generate simulation report
reportf()*	generate facilities report
rept_page()	generate facility report page
lns()*	count output lines used on current page
endpage()*	advance (pause) on full page (screen)
newpage()*	initialize line count for new page or screen
sendto()*	set/get current output destination

Figure 8.1. *smpl.c* Functions

The random variate functions are logically part of **smpl**, but are maintained in a separate file and separately compiled as a matter of convenience. The *smpl.h* file is provided for inclusion in simulation programs; in addition to external name declarations, it contains #include's for *stdio.h* and *math.h*, and typedef and #define for real and then. The *stat.c* file is used by the batch means analysis module of Section 4.7, and won't be discussed here. If you have **smpl** in machine-readable form, you may want to print the source files to avoid flipping back and forth between this chapter and the Appendix as we look at what the various **smpl** functions do.

smpl.c contains 37 functions, 26 of which can be called from a simulation program. Function names are listed in Figure 8.1, categorized by use. Names of user-callable functions (names not declared static) are marked with an asterisk: most of these were discussed in Chapter 2 and should be familiar. Function names in Figure 8.1 appear in the same order as functions in the *smpl.c* listing in the Appendix. Our discussion will stray from this order somewhat to follow order of use: we'll begin with a look at the basic building block used to form **smpl** data structures.

8.2 The Element Pool and Namespace

One of the design goals for **smpl** was compactness. This was motivated in part by the limited memory sizes — as small as 32K bytes — available for some implementations, and in part by the use of **smpl** as a "kernel" of a larger application-oriented simulation system. Examples of the latter include highly-parameterized configurable local area network and computer system simulation models.

Compactness is achieved in part through the use of a single basic data element for all **smpl** data structures. This element comprises five fields, typed and named as shown below.[2]

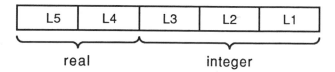

smpl maintains a pool of these elements; elements are allocated from this pool to construct facility descriptors, queue entries, and event list entries.

---

[2]In the source code, these fields are named using a lower-case "l". In the text and figures, an upper-case "L" is used to avoid confusion between "l" and "1".

They also are used to construct *table* and *storage* descriptors, as we'll see in the next chapter.

smpl.c declares the integer fields L3 - L1 to be of type int. On some machines, ints are 16-bit quantities (15 bits plus sign) and the maximum value which can be represented by this type is only 32767: on other machines (or in other C implementations), ints are 32-bit quantities. Certain fields are used for counts (e.g., in a facility descriptor, L3 is a count of the number of releases): the maximum count is limited to the maximum int value, which may limit the length of a simulation run. While reset() can be used to re-initialize counts when this limit is reached, you may want to consider defining integer fields as type long in this case. This concern, of course, applies to the simulation program as well as to *smpl.c*. In the author's environment, simulation models can be run on both microcomputers with 16-bit ints and mainframe computers with 32-bit ints; long runs can be done on the mainframe system, so everything works out nicely.

Elements are declared as a set of arrays of fields (see the global declarations in *smpl.c*); element Ln[0] is unused. The element pool takes two forms, as shown in Figure 8.2: each has its own mode of allocation. During model initialization, the pool is viewed as an array of elements from which contiguous blocks are allocated to construct facility (or table or storage) descriptors; blk is the index of the next available element. When model initialization is complete, the remaining elements in the pool are linked together in a list: avl is the index of the element at the head of this list. During simulation, elements from this list are dynamically allocated and deallocated as events are scheduled and caused and tokens are queued and dequeued.

The size of the element pool is determined by the value defined for nl. A facility descriptor for an *n*-server facility requires *n*+2 elements, each queue entry requires 1 element, and each scheduled event requires 1 element. Generally, a token either will have an event scheduled for it or will be queued, so the maximum number of elements needed for queue and event list entries is equal to the maximum number of tokens. Thus, a value for nl of 128 is sufficient for models with 16 single-server facilities and up to 79 tokens.

One other global array is declared in *smpl.c*: the character array name[]. This array, called *namespace*, is used to record model and facility (and table or storage) name strings. avn is the index of the next available namespace position, and ns determines namespace size. smpl limits model names to 50 characters, single-server facility names to 17 characters, and multi-server facility names to 14 characters. (The shorter limit for a multi-server facility name is to insure space to append the number of servers in the facility report.)

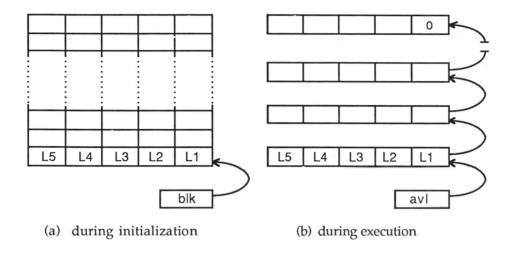

(a) during initialization   (b) during execution

Figure 8.2. The **smpl** Element Pool

8.3 Initialization

The simulation subsystem is initialized via a call to smpl() with parameters m and s: m controls **mtr** activation and s is a pointer to a character string containing the model name. **mtr** is part of the **SMPL** simulation environment; some of its facilities were described in the previous chapter. While its implementation isn't included here, an overview of its design is given in Chapter 9, and you may want to build similar facilities into your system. The "hooks" between **smpl** and **mtr** have been left in place (in the form of comments) in the source code in the Appendix, and their functions will be noted as we encounter them.

smpl() initializes various indexes, sets the simulation time (clock) and the start of the current measurement interval (start) to zero, clears the element pool, and saves the model name in namespace. Names are stored in namespace by save_name(), which limits a name to a specified length, copies it to namespace, and returns its namespace index. The namespace index of the model name isn't saved, since the model name always is the first namespace entry (mname() provides a pointer to the model name for report generation). stream() is called to select the random number stream for the current run and the stream number then incremented so the next run will use a different stream.

When **mtr** is present (and its activation specified by m), smpl() insures that its current output destination is the screen display and makes the first of two **mtr** initialization calls: mtr pauses execution, permitting parameter values to be assigned from the keyboard, tracing to be turned on, or the random number stream to be changed.

Reinitialization of **smpl** measurement variables (as when deleting initial observations of a simulation run) is effected via a call to reset(), which calls resetf() to clear facility and facility queue measurement counters and accumulators, and sets the start of the current measurement interval, start, to the current simulation time. resetf() uses the facility chain described in the next section to locate facility descriptors.

As you add extensions such as storages or tables to **smpl**, calls to reinitialize measurement data collection variables associated with these entities should be added to reset().

8.4 Facility Definition

A facility is defined by a call to the facility() function, which creates a data structure called a facility descriptor and returns the index of the first element of that structure to the caller. This facility descriptor index, denoted as f (and called simply a *facility descriptor* in Chapter 2) is used to designate the facility in subsequent facility operations. The facility descriptor (and queue) structure is shown in Figure 8.3. A descriptor for a facility with *n* servers requires *n*+2 contiguous elements: a 2-element facility header followed by *n* server elements.

The parameters of a facility definition call are s, a pointer to the facility name, and n, the number of servers. facility() calls get_blk() to get a block of pool elements for the descriptor, records the number of servers in L1[f], and saves the facility name. At this stage of execution, the element pool is viewed as an array of elements (Figure 8.2), with blk — initialized to 1 by smpl() — pointing to the next available element. get_blk() simply returns the current value of blk and increments it by the block size.

Facility descriptors are chained together into a list for use in facility/queue reinitialization and report generation. fchn — initialized to 0 by smpl() — is the index of the descriptor at the head of the list, and L2[f+1] is either the index of the next descriptor on the list or 0, marking the end of the list. This list is ordered in accordance with the order in which facilities are defined, so the facility currently being defined is placed at the end of the list: L2[f+1] for this facility was initialized to zero by smpl(). resetf() follows this chain in clearing facility and queue measurement counters and accumulators.

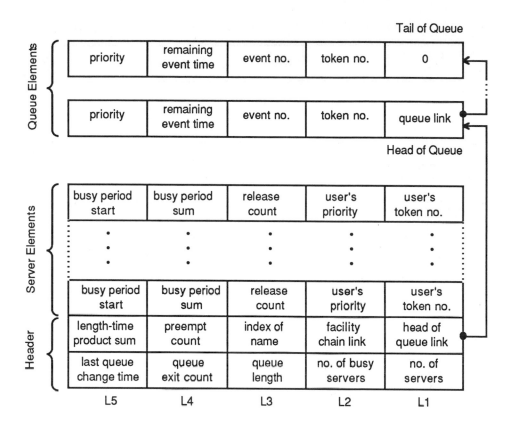

Figure 8.3. smpl Facility Descriptor and Queue Structure

If tracing is active, msg() is called to generate a trace message: fname() provides a pointer to the facility name. The index of the first element of the facility descriptor is returned to the caller.

8.5 Event Scheduling

Simulation model initialization includes initializing **smpl**, defining facilities, and scheduling the initial events. An event is scheduled via a call to the schedule() function with parameters ev, te, and tkn. ev is the event number, te is the inter-event time, and tkn is the token number associated with the event. After verifying that the inter-event time is not negative, schedule() calls get_elm() to get an element from the element pool, constructs an event list element containing the token number, event number, and event occurrence time (the sum of the current time clock and the

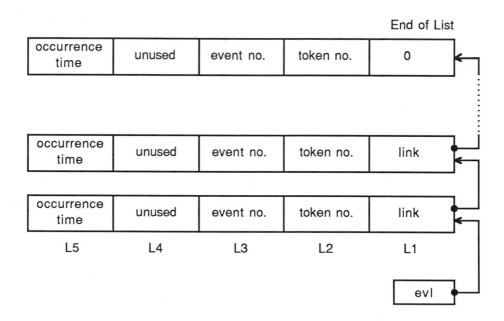

Figure 8.4. smpl Event List Structure

inter-event time `te`), and calls `enlist()` to enter this element in the event list. A trace message is generated if tracing is active, and control returned to the user.

   `get_elm()` allocates a single element from a linked list of available elements. Before this list can be used, however, it has to be built: `get_elm()` does this the first time it is called. `smpl()` initializes `avl` to −1 and `blk` to 1. As facilities are defined, blocks of elements are allocated for facility descriptors by `get_blk()`, and `blk` advanced accordingly. smpl requires that all facilities be defined before the first event is scheduled (or the first queue entry is made). On the first call to `get_elm()`, indicated by `avl` = −1, the elements remaining in the pool after facility definition are linked into a list. `avl` is set to the index of the element at the head of the list: the link field of the last element in the list, `L1[nl]`, is zero, marking the end of the list. `blk` is set to zero so that any subsequent call to `get_blk()` will result in an error. After transforming the element pool into a list (or on calls after the first), `get_elm()` unlinks the element at the head of the list and returns its index to the caller.

   When **mtr** is present (and active), the second **mtr** initialization call is made on the first call to `get_elm()`. All facilities have been defined at this point, and **mtr** pauses execution again so that displays involving facilities can be invoked.

The event list is a simple singly-linked list, ordered in ascending values of event occurrence times; its structure is shown in Figure 8.4. `evl` is the index of the element at the head of the list.

The event list element constructed by `schedule()` is entered in the event list by `enlist()`, which also is used to enter elements in queues. Queues are singly-linked lists structured very much like the event list. `enlist()` is called with two parameters: a pointer to the head of the list (i.e., to the variable containing the index of the first element in the list), and the index of the element to be entered in the list. For event list entry, `arg` is set to the event occurrence time of the event being scheduled. `enlist()` then threads its way through the event list, comparing `arg` with the occurrence times of already scheduled-events. `succ` is the index of the event list entry whose occurrence time currently is being compared, and `pred` is the index of the preceding entry (if there is one). The end of the list is indicated by an element whose link field contains 0. When the end of the list is reached, or when an existing entry with an occurrence time greater than `arg` is found, the new element is linked into the list. Its link field is set to `succ`, which is 0 if the element is being linked to the end of the list. Depending on the position of the new element in the list, either the link field of the preceding element — `Ll[pred]` — or the head of list is set to its index.

Generally, elements for events with the same occurrence time are placed on the event list in first-in, first-out order. There is one exception: when an event is rescheduled for a dequeued token which was queued because of a blocked request or preempt operation, it is placed (directly, by `release()`) at the head of the event list.

The simulation program calls `cause()` to obtain the next event to occur together with the token associated with that event: call parameters are pointers to the program's event number and token number variables. `cause()` verifies that the event list is not empty, returns the token number and event number from the element at the head of the event list, sets `event` to this event number, and sets the current simulation time `clock` to the event occurrence time from this element. It then delinks the element from the event list, calls `put_elm()` to return the element to the pool, and generates a trace message if tracing is active.

smpl uses `event`, the current event, to keep track of the event routine currently being executed by the simulation program. If a token's facility request is blocked or its reservation of a facility is preempted, **smpl** queues the token and records the current event in the queue entry. When the token is dequeued, this event is rescheduled for it. Consequently, the simulation program should not directly transfer control between event routines: if it does, `event` will not be valid.

The `cause()` function is the primary point of interaction between **smpl** and **mtr**. If **mtr** is present and active, `mtr()` is called on every execution of `cause()` (unless trace mode 3 has been selected, in which case a monitor pause occurs after every trace message). `mtr()` performs any necessary updates of **mtr**-initiated displays or analyses (such as **bma**), checks for and processes keyboard interrupts (from **SMPL** function keys), and updates the simulation time displayed on the screen before returning. We'll take a closer look at **mtr** in Chapter 9.

Occasionally, as in the Ethernet model of Chapter 6, events occurring after a particular event has been scheduled make it necessary to cancel the occurrence of that event. The `cancel()` function searches the event list for event `ev` and, if an entry for that event is found, unlinks the entry from the list, deallocates it, and returns the token number from the entry to the caller. The `suspend()` function is called by `preempt()` when a token's use of a facility is being preempted. `suspend()` searches the event list for an event scheduled for that token, unlinks the entry from the list, and returns the element index of the entry to `preempt()`.

Event scheduling in **smpl** is based on a simple singly-linked list about which Reeves [1984] says "... it may be thought scandalous if the simple linear linked list remains in common use ...". We'll revisit this subject in the next chapter.

8.6 Facility Reservation and Release

Request function processing. A simulation program makes a non-preemptive facility reservation request via a `request()` call: call parameters are the facility descriptor index `f`, the requestor's token number `tkn`, and the request's priority `pri`. `request()` compares the number of busy servers for the facility, `L2[f]`, with the total number of servers `L1[f]`. If at least one server is free, the server element set is searched for a free server (a server element whose `L1` field is 0); `i` is set to the index of the free server's element. The server is reserved by setting `L1[i]` to the requestor's token number, and recording the request's priority and the server's current busy period starting time in the server element. The facility's busy server count is incremented, and `r` is set to 0 so that the function return will indicate to the caller that the facility has been reserved. Note that since a server is marked busy by setting the `L1` field of the server element to the requestor's token number, 0 is not a valid token number for facility operations: you may want to add a check for this in reserve/preempt processing.

If all servers of a facility are busy, request() calls enqueue() to build a facility queue entry and sets r to 1 so that the function return will indicate that the request has been blocked. enqueue() call parameters in this case are the request parameters, the current event event, and the remaining event time, which is 0 for a blocked request. enqueue() updates the queue length-time product accumulator L5[f+1],[3] increments the current queue length L3[f], and sets the last queue entry/exit time L5[f] to the current simulation time. get_elm() is called to allocate an element from the pool for the queue entry, and the requestor's token number and priority, the current event, and the remaining event time are recorded in the entry. enlist() is called to insert this entry in the facility's queue: call parameters are a pointer to the head of the queue L1[f+1] (which contains either 0 or the index of the first element in the queue) and the index of the queue entry.

A facility queue is a singly-linked list ordered in descending priority values: the highest-priority entry, then, is at the head of the list. enlist() is used to enter elements in queues as well as in the event list; it determines where an entry should be inserted by comparing the argument field L5 of the new entry with those of existing entries. (Note that in constructing a queue entry, enqueue() converts the request's priority from int to real in assigning it to L5.) The only difference in enlist() execution between event list entry and queue entry is in argument comparison: the event list is ordered in ascending values of L5, queues in descending order. For a blocked facility request, the entry's L4 field is 0, and enlist() inserts the entry after existing entries of the same priority.

If tracing is active, request() generates a trace message before returning to the caller. The trace msg() function uses r to determine if a reserve or a queue message should be issued.

Preempt function processing. A preemptive facility reservation request is issued via a call to preempt(): call parameters are the same as those of request(). When the requested facility is nonbusy, reservation processing is the same for both preemptive and non-preemptive requests (although the code is slightly different). The server element set is searched for a free server, the requestor's token number and priority, together with the busy

---

[3]This sum, divided by the length of the measurement period, gives the mean queue length: see Section 1.5.

period starting time, are recorded in the server element, the busy server count for the facility is incremented, and 0 is returned to the caller.

If all the servers are busy, preempt() searches the server element set for the server with the lowest priority user. If the request's priority is not higher than that of the lowest priority user, the request is queued in just the same way as a blocked non-preemptive facility request: enqueue() builds the queue entry, enlist() inserts the entry in the queue, and 1 is returned to the caller.

If the request's priority is greater than that of the lowest priority user (whose element index is k), that user is preempted and the facility reserved for the requestor. This is done as follows.

1. suspend() is called to search the event list for an entry with the same token number as the user, unlink the element from the list, and return its index i. **smpl** assumes that the user has one and only event scheduled, and that event represents completion of the user's current facility reservation.

2. The event number ev of the suspended event is noted and the remaining event time te — the difference between the event occurrence time and the current simulation time — is computed. If preemption happens to be taking place at the same instant in time that the facility was to be released, so that the remaining event time is 0, te is set to a very small but non-zero value. enlist() and release() distinguish between blocked and preempted requests on the basis of zero or non-zero remaining event times.

3. put_elm() is called to deallocate the element removed from the event list, and enqueue() is called to construct a queue entry for the preempted user. enqueue() calls enlist() to insert the entry in the queue. In this case, with L4[elm] (the remaining event time) greater than 0, enlist() inserts the new queue entry ahead of other entries of the same priority. Thus, the most recently preempted request will be returned to execution before other preempted (or blocked) requests of the same priority. Note that, if desired, two function calls could be eliminated here by having preempt() use the element removed from the event list to build the queue entry and calling enlist() directly to insert the entry in the queue.

4. The release count L3[k] and busy period sum L4[k] for the interrupted server are updated, the number of busy

servers L2[f] decremented, and the facility's preempt count
L4[f+1] incremented.

5. The interrupted server is reserved for the requestor.

If tracing is active, trace messages are generated showing the actual
operations performed. Figure 2.3 shows an example of the messages
generated when preemption takes place.

Release function processing. release() is called to release a server of a
facility: call parameters are the facility descriptor index f and the token
number tkn associated with the original reservation. release() searches
the server element set, beginning with element 1, for a server reserved for
tkn: j is the index of this element. An error exit occurs if no element
reserved for tkn is found. Note that the servers of a facility are identical
and indistinguishable; it is possible for multiple servers to be reserved by a
single token (as, for example, when a facility is used to represent a buffer
pool) and selection of a particular server for release essentially is arbitrary.

The server to be released is marked nonbusy by setting L1 of the server
element to 0. The server release count L3 is incremented, the length of the
busy period just completed is computed and added to the server's busy period
accumulator L4, and the number of busy servers for the facility, L2[f+1], is
decremented. If tracing is active, a trace message is generated and, if the
facility queue is empty, release() then returns to its caller.

If the facility queue is not empty, release() dequeues the element at
the head of the queue: k is the index of this element. The queue length-time
product accumulator L5[f+1] is updated, the current queue length L3[f]
decremented, the queue exit count L4[f] incremented, and the last queue
entry/exit time L5[f] set to the current simulation time. The dequeued
request may be either a blocked or a preempted facility reservation request:
the remaining event time L4[k] of a blocked request is zero, while that of a
preempted request is greater than zero.

If the dequeued request originally was blocked, release() reschedules
execution of the event routine which originally generated the request
(remember that the current event number was recorded when the queue entry
was made). Queue elements have the token number and event number
recorded in the same fields (L2 and L3) as event list elements; release()
sets the L5 field to the current simulation time and inserts the element at the
head of the event list. This insures that, even though there may be other
requests for the facility scheduled for this same instant in simulation time,
reinitiation of this facility request will be successful since its event routine
will be selected on the next cause() call (provided, of course, that the simu-

lation program itself does not schedule a facility request after the release). m is set to select a "reschedule" trace message.

If the dequeued request is being returned to execution after preemption, the server just released is reserved for it. The token number and priority are copied from the element of the dequeued request to the server element (note that the priority is converted back to int in the process), the server's busy period start time is set to the current simulation time, and the busy server count for the facility is incremented. If tracing is active, a "reserve" trace message is generated. The dequeued request's element is used for the event list entry: release() computes the event occurrence time for the request, stores it in the L5 field, and calls enlist() to insert the element in the event list. m is set to select a "resume" trace message.

A preempted request is rescheduled for execution at a time equal to its remaining event time plus the current simulation time. In preemption processing, if preemption takes place at the same instant in time that the preempted request was scheduled to release the facility (so that its actual remaining event time is zero), preempt() sets the remaining event time to a very small non-zero value. release() doesn't bother to do anything about this, so the actual facility execution interval in this situation will be very slightly greater than that scheduled. For most models, this doesn't matter: the situation rarely occurs, and the small increment has no real effect on simulation results. There is, however, one class of models for which this increment is a problem: hardware-level models in which times are multiples of machine clock cycles, and so are integer-valued (although not ints). In this case, adding a very small fractional value to an execution interval can upset model timing. If your applications include models of this class, you should revise release() to check and correct the remaining event time.

8.7 Facility Query Functions

The status(), inq(), U(), B(), and Lq() functions return instantaneous or average facility measures; all are called with the facility descriptor index f as the single parameter. Operation of these functions should be clear from looking at the code together with Figure 8.3.

status() returns 1 if all servers of a facility are busy, and 0 otherwise: some modelers prefer to have it return the number of free servers. The U(), B() and Lq() functions are used in generating the smpl simulation report: they can be used to generate reports tailored to a particular model, or to accumulate measures across multiple simulation runs. If you need to develop model-specific reports, you may want to add functions to return release and queue exit counts.

8.8 Debugging and Reporting Functions

Output and page control. trace and error messages, and the simulation report, are directed to the current output destination specified by the file pointer opf (which is initialized to stdout). The simulation program can change the output destination (or get the current destination) via a call to sendto(). The output produced by **smpl** usually will be sent either to a printer or to the screen. **smpl** defines two values, pl and sl, as the number of output lines which can be written to a printer page or a screen "page", and maintains a variable, lft, which is a count of the number of lines remaining on the current page. The program can coordinate line counting with **smpl** by calling trace() (with a parameter value of 4) to count program-generated trace lines and lns() to count program-generated output lines.

Page end processing is done by endpage(), which is called by lns() when there are no more lines left on the current page, and by other functions on completion of output (e.g., end of report). If the current output destination is the screen, endpage() pushes the output to the top, displays a message, and pauses. When the user responds, endpage() clears the screen if **mtr** is available and active and otherwise generates an inter-display spacer. If the current output destination is the printer, endpage() issues a form feed (if not at top-of-page). Before returning to its caller, endpage() calls newpage() to reset the line count to top-of-page.

Trace functions. The simulation program calls trace() to turn tracing on or off, or to count a program-generated trace line. The call parameter n determines the operation to be performed. Tracing is turned off (n = 0) by setting the trace control flag tr to 0. It is turned on (n = 1–3) by setting the trace control flag to n: the last trace message issue time tl is set so that the first trace message issued will be time-stamped, and newpage() is called to set the output line count to correspond to top of page or top of screen. (The simulation program should issue a form feed before initiating a trace when output is to the printer.)

Trace messages are generated via calls to msg() made by various simulation functions when tracing is active. Call parameters are a message number n, an optional token number i, a character string pointer s, and qualifying parameters q1 and q2 (which provide additional information, such as event numbers and current queue lengths). A trace message comprises four segments:

n	i	s	q1	q2	message phrase string - m[n]	qualifier
1	tkn	0	ev	0	SCHEDULE	EVENT q1
2	tkn	0	ev	0	CAUSE	EVENT q1
3	tkn	0	ev	0	CANCEL	EVENT q1
4	-1	0	ev	0	RESCHEDULE	EVENT q1
5	-1	0	ev	0	RESUME	EVENT q1
6	-1	0	ev	0	SUSPEND	EVENT q1
7	tkn	*fn	0	0	REQUEST	: RESERVED
7	tkn	*fn	1	L3[f]	REQUEST	: QUEUED (inq=q2)
8	tkn	*fn	0	0	PREEMPT	: RESERVED
8	tkn	*fn	1	L3[f]	PREEMPT	: QUEUED (inq=q2)
8	tkn	*fn	2	0	PREEMPT	: INTERRUPT
9	tkn	*fn	0	0	RELEASE	
10	-1	0	tn	L3[f]	QUEUE	token q1 (inq=q2)
11	-1	0	tn	L3[f]	DEQUEUE	token q1 (inq=q2)
12	-1	*fn	tn	0	RESERVE	for token q1
13	-1	*fn	f	0	FACILITY	: f=q1

Figure 8.5. Trace Message Parameters and Phrases

<time stamp> <token number> <basic message> <qualifier>

The time stamp segment is generated only when the current simulation time is greater than the time (t1) at which the last message was generated. The token number segment is generated only when i is non-negative. The basic message is formed by concatenating the message phrase string m[n] and the parameter string s (which is null for some messages). For most messages, a qualifier is appended: its form depends on the message number and, for facility request and preempt operations, on the value of q2.

Figure 8.5 shows the various msg() parameter combinations and the corresponding message phrase strings and qualifiers. In this figure, tkn represents a token number, ev represents an event number, and *fn represents a facility name pointer. f is a facility descriptor index, and L3[f] is the current queue length field from the facility descriptor. The trace message sequence of Figure 2.3 shows most of the message formats.

end_line() is called by msg() after a **smpl** trace message has been printed and by trace() when the latter is called to count a program-generated trace line (i.e., with n = 4). It decrements the line counter lft and, if the count is reduced to zero, performs page end processing as determined by the trace mode. In trace mode 1, endpage() is called to generate a form feed if output is not to the screen: otherwise, the line count simply is reset (in this mode, output to the screen is generated without pause). In trace mode 2, **smpl** pauses execution on each full screen: if **mtr** is available and active, pause() is called to initiate a monitor pause. In the absence of **mtr**, endpage() is called to pause execution for screen output or generate a form feed for printer output. In trace mode 3, execution is paused after each trace message is printed.

Error processing. When **smpl** detects an error, such as an empty event list, it calls error() to issue a diagnostic message, print the simulation report (if output is to the printer), and halt execution. This function also can be called from the simulation program if desired. error() is called with two parameters: an error number n and a character string pointer s. For errors detected by the functions in *smpl.c*, error() is called with n = 1-8 and s null. For errors detected by other modules (such as *rand.c* or the simulation program), it is called with n = 0 and s pointing to a diagnostic message.

If the current output destination is the printer, error() sends the error message both to the screen and the printer, and prints the simulation report. If **mtr** is available and active, a monitor pause is initiated. This provides an opportunity to examine various displays, such as the simulation dump or report, before execution is terminated via a call to exit().

Report generation. The simulation report is generated by a call to report() from the simulation program or from error(). In this version of **smpl**, report() simply calls reportf() to produce the facility report; in an extended version, report() might include calls to generate table or storage reports. Note that you can call reportf(), rather than report(), to avoid the form feed or screen pushup generated by endpage().

reportf() traces the facility chain constructed by facility(), and calls rept_page() until the end of the chain is reached. rept_page() prints the report heading, followed by a report line for each facility, until the page is full or the chain end reached. Generation of the facility report lines is straightforward: review the code together with Figure 8.3. Figure 2.4 shows an example of the simulation report format.

8.9 Random Variate Generation

smpl random variate generation functions are contained in the *rand.c* file: a listing for this file follows that of *smpl.c* in the Appendix. *rand.c* function names are listed in Figure 8.6: all of these functions can be called from the simulation program.

ranf()	generate uniform random variate
stream()	set/get random number stream
seed()	set/get seed for stream n
random()	generate random integer
expntl()	generate exponentially-distributed random variate
erlang()	generate Erlang-distributed random variate
hyperx()	generate hyperexponentially-distributed random variate
normal()	generate normally-distributed random variate

Figure 8.6. *rand.c* Functions

Uniform random variate generation. smpl uses the venerable multiplicative congruential random number generator

$$I_{n+1} = \alpha I_n \mod M \tag{8.1}$$

with $\alpha = 7^5 = 16807$ and $M = 2^{31}\text{-}1 = 2147483647$ (a prime). It has a period (number of values generated before the sequence repeats) of M–1. This generator originally was described by Lewis et al [1969], and has been extensively tested (testing results can be summarized as "good: not great"). It is discussed in our simulation texts and by Kobayashi [1978]. A frequently-referenced implementation is called LLRANDOM [Learmonth and Lewis 1973].

smpl's random number generator function, ranf(), uses the recursion of (8.1) to generate integer variates uniformly distributed in the range 1, M–1, then converts these to floating-point variates uniformly distributed in $0+\varepsilon$, $1-\varepsilon$ (where ε is a very small value). Both of the arithmetic operations required to compute I_{n+1} present problems: the divide operation frequently is very slow, and the multiply operation usually requires double precision.

$\varepsilon = 1/m$

The use of division to perform the modulo operation in (8.1) can be avoided using the simulated division method described by Payne et al [1969]. (This method also is described in several of our simulation texts, by Kobayashi [1979], and by Schrage [1979].) The method works as follows. Define

$$Z = 16807 I_n \mod 2^{31} \tag{8.2}$$

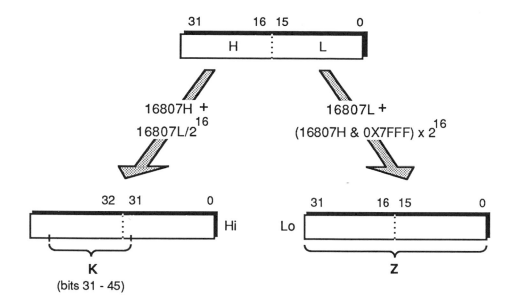

Figure 8.7. Simulated Double Precision Multiply Operands and Operations

and

$$K = \lfloor 16807 I_n / 2^{31} \rfloor \tag{8.3}$$

where $\lfloor x \rfloor$ denotes the floor function of x — the largest integer equal to or less than x. The product $16807I_n$ comprises a maximum of 46 bits: Z represents the low-order 31 bits and K represents the higher-order bits, treated as a number. It can be shown (see the references cited above) that

$$I_{n+1} = Z + K, \text{ if } Z + K < M$$
$$\tag{8.4}$$
$$I_{n+1} = Z + K - M, \text{ if } Z + K > M$$

In implementing (7.4) with 32-bit arithmetic, M should be pre-subtracted from Z to avoid possible overflow: that is, compute $Z - M + K$ (in that order: you may have to outwit your compiler) and, if the result is less than zero, add M back in to form I_{n+1}.

For many systems, `long`s are 32 bits and `int`s are either 16 or 32 bits in length: consequently, formation of the 46-bit product $16807I_n$ requires a double precision integer multiply. The versions of `ranf()` in the Appendix are designed for systems with 32-bit `long` and 16-bit `short` integers, and use a simulated double precision multiply to generate this product. The method is illustrated in Figure 8.7. The `long` seed is viewed as the concatenation of two 16-bit `short`s called `L` (the integer corresponding to the low-order 16 bits) and `H` (the integer corresponding to the higher-order 16-bits). The product 16807In is formed in two `long`s, `Lo` and `Hi`, as shown in the figure. `Lo`, with its sign bit is set to zero by the mask `0X7FFF`, is equal to 16807In mod 2^{31}, or **Z**, as defined in (8.2). The high-order bits of the product are formed in `Hi`: note that bits 16-31 of the product are contained in both `Lo` and `Hi` (except that bit 31 is set to zero in `Lo`). Bits 31-45 of `Hi`, extracted and shifted, form **K** as defined in (8.2). In+1 then is computed as described earlier.

This implementation of `ranf()`, while coded in **C** and semi-portable (to systems with the stated `long` and `short` lengths), is not very pretty. Generally, a cleaner and more efficient implementation can be obtained by coding the random number generator in assembly language and taking advantage of machine features, such as integer double precision multiply, which are not accessible directly from **C**.

In implementing **smpl** on your system, `ranf()` should be the only function that requires changes. *rand.c* contains two versions of `ranf()`: one for CPUs of or similar to the Intel 808x family, and one for CPUs of or similar to the Motorola 680x0 family. Both versions assume 32-bit `long` and 16-bit `short` integers: however, the relative positions of `Hi` and `Lo` are different in the two families and require different pointer access.

Your math library may provide a random number generator function (usually called `rand()`) which you may elect to use in place of `ranf()`. This will require replacing `ranf()` calls with `rand()` calls in the other random variate functions of *rand.c*, and revising stream and seed handling. Before deciding to use the library's random number generator, find out what algorithm is used. It is not uncommon for library generators to use shift-and-add generators because of their speed; however, generators of this type show departures from randomness (see Chapter 8 in Fishman [1978]). If you decide to implement `ranf()`, the two sequences listed below will help check your implementation.

starting seed I0	1	1973272912
I1	16807	1207871363
I2	282475249	531082850
I3	1622650073	967423018

If your random number generator is functionally identical to `ranf()`, and identical seeds are used, your simulations of the **M/M/1** and central server queueing models should produce results identical to those presented in Chapters 1 and 2.

Seeds and streams. The In[] array declared at the start of *rand.c* provides seeds for 15 different random number streams; strm is the index of the currently-selected stream. strm is initialized to 1, and can be changed via a call to the stream() function (which also can be used to obtain the current stream index). ranf() uses the current value of In[strm] to generate a new random variate and stores the new variate in In[strm] prior to converting it to a real in [0,1]. Thus, each starting seed initiates a unique subset of the sequence generated by the recursion of (8.1). Starting seeds for the 15 streams are taken from Table A.2 in Fishman [1978], and represent values of the generator sequence spaced 100,000 values apart. Seeds for additional streams can be obtained from Fishman's Table A.2 (which provides 400 seeds) or by extracting every 100,000th value of In[15] produced by ranf().

The seed() function is called to set the seed for a given stream or to obtain a stream's current seed. Its uses include saving the current seed as part of a model's state when a simulation is interrupted and is to be restarted later.

Uniform variate and random integer generation. ranf() returns a real value uniformly distributed in [0,1]; uniform() simply maps this value into the range [a,b]. random() works in much the same way, but deals with integer, rather than real, values.

Exponential, Erlang, and hyperexponential variate generation. The expntl() function returns a variate from a negative exponential distribution with mean x: its implementation was discussed in Section 1.2. erlang() returns a variate from a Erlang distribution with mean x, standard deviation (approximately) s, and number of stages $k = \lfloor x/s \rfloor^2$. A k-stage Erlang-distributed random variable with mean X can be viewed as the sum of k exponentially-distributed random variables, each with mean X/k. This suggests the following approach to generating Erlang-distributed variates. Define v as a random variate from a k-stage Erlang distribution with mean X and define y as a random variate from an exponential distribution with mean X/k. Then,

$$v = \sum_{i=1}^{k} y_i \qquad (8.5)$$

$$v = \sum_{i=1}^{k} -(X/k) \ln r_i \qquad (8.6)$$

where r_i is the uniform random variate from `ranf()` used to produce y_i. Since $\ln a + \ln b = \ln ab$,

$$v = -(X/k) \ln \left(\prod_{i=1}^{k} r_i \right) \tag{8.7}$$

`erlang()` computes k from the specified mean and standard deviation and then computes a variate value using (8.7). When x/s is not integer-valued, the standard deviation of values produced by `erlang()` will be less than s.

The `hyperx()` function returns a variate from a two-stage hyperexponential distribution with mean x and standard deviation s. The distribution sampled by this function is a special case of a two-stage hyperexponential distribution, described by Morse [1963]: it requires only two parameters (mean and standard deviation) for characterization. The cumulative distribution function for this distribution is

$$\Pr[s{\leq}x] = 1 - pe^{-2px/X} - (1{-}p)e^{-2(1-p)x/X} \tag{8.8}$$

where X is the distribution's mean. The squared coefficient of variation c^2 is

$$c^2 = [1 - 2p(1-p)]/[2p(1-p)] \tag{8.9}$$

and the standard deviation is cX. This distribution can be viewed as being produced by a mechanism which has two parallel stages. Stage 1, selected with probability p, generates an exponential variate with mean $X/2p$; stage 2, selected with probability 1–p, generates an exponential variate with mean $X/[2(1{-}p)]$. We can use this approach to generate variates from this distribution. By appropriately specifying p, any desired standard deviation (equal to or greater than X) can be obtained. Alternatively, we can specify the standard deviation and compute the value of p required to produce it. The coefficient of variation c is equal to the standard deviation divided by the mean; solving (8.9) for p gives

$$p = \left[1 - [(c^2{-}1)/(c^2{+}1)]^{1/2}\right]/2 \tag{8.10}$$

`hyperx()` computes the coefficient of variation and uses it to compute p, uses p to randomly select one of two exponential distributions, and returns a variate from the selected distribution.

`hyperx()` has several drawbacks: it is slow, and it represents only one member of the family of two-stage hyperexponential distributions. In any particular application, it is much faster to precompute c, p and the stage means, so that variate generation simply requires random selection of one stage mean or the other as the mean of an exponentially distributed variate. Some form of gamma distribution generation variate function (described in most of our simulation texts) will provide more representational flexibility. However, hyperx() does have one virtue: it requires specification of only the mean and standard deviation. With erlang(), expntl(), and hyperx(), variates can be generated from distributions with coefficients of variation less than one, equal to one, and greater than one, using only the mean and standard deviation to characterize the distribution.

Normal variate generation. normal() returns a variate from a normal distribution with mean x and standard deviation s. It generates a unit normal variate using the polar method of Marsaglia and Bray [1964] (see Section 7.3.6 in Law and Kelton [1982]). This method generates a pair of unit variates, and so is invoked only on alternating calls. A unit variate is transformed into a variate from the specified distribution by multiplying it by the distribution's standard deviation and adding the mean.

8.10 The *smpl.h* File

The *smpl.h* file is intended to be included in all **smpl** simulation programs. It provides #includes for *stdio.h* and *math.h*, typedef and #define definitions for real and then, and extern declarations for those **smpl** functions which return other than an integer value. As you add functions to the simulation subsystem, add the appropriate declarations to *smpl.c*.

8.11 Summary

We've examined the workings of the **smpl** simulation subsystem in considerable — perhaps tedious — detail. An intimate understanding of how **smpl** works helps avoid modeling errors and puts you in control of your simulation environment: if you don't like the way something works, you can change it!

In implementing your version of **smpl**, it is best to start with a straight copy of the source code as listed in the Appendix, changing only ranf() if necessary. If your version of ranf() is functionally the same as the Appendix version and uses the same initial seed for stream 1, you should obtain results for the **M/M/1** queue and central server queueing network simulations identical to those presented in earlier chapters. If you do not, analyzing trace sequences for these models should provide some insight into the problem; first, however, determine that it is a functional problem and not a report generation error. If you use a different random number generator, results will agree only in a statistical sense, so don't be concerned if there is a difference between your results and the book's results for a single run. To verify your implementation, use simple M/M/1 queue and preemptive priority queue models with known analytic solutions. set parameters to obtain moderate utilizations, and compare simulation and analytic results using the methods described in Chapter 4. Once you've checked your implementation, revisions to match your programming style and environment can be made more confidently. However, before making substantial revisions, take a look at the extensions discussed in the next chapter to see if and how they would fit in your revised subsystem.

9. Extending smpl

9.1 Introduction

This chapter discusses various modifications and extensions to the basic smpl simulation subsystem. These include queue management variants and some additional queue operations, alternative event scheduling mechanisms, and three new simulation constructs: storages, tables, and distributions. A *storage* is a static entity analogous to a facility, representing perhaps a computer memory or a communication buffer pool; storage operations include storage definition, space allocation (with implicit queueing if space is unavailable) and deallocation. *Tables* provide a means of collecting the distributions of simulation output variables such as response times or queueing times. *Distributions* separate distribution sampling and definition operations; this helps in constructing parametric models, aids debugging, and has some statistical advantages. We'll also look at the design of mtr, the **SMPL** interactive interface, and related **SMPL** parameter handling functions.

Although source code is not provided for the extensions discussed in this chapter, the design (and, in some cases, data structure) descriptions presented should give you a starting point for your own implementation.

9.2 Queueing

In most event-oriented simulation languages, queueing is *explicit*. The programmer must test the status of a facility before reserving it, and explicitly queue the request if the facility is busy. When a facility is released, the programmer must explicitly examine the facility queue and, if there are waiting requests, dequeue one and reserve the facility for it. In smpl, queueing is *implicit*: the simulation subsystem queues a request for a busy facility and dequeues it when the facility becomes free. Implicit queueing can substantially reduce the number of simulation operations which have to be coded in implementing a simulation model.

This implicit queue management works well for many, but not all, modeling applications. Queueing situations in which different or added capabilities are needed include the following.

> **simultaneous reservation.** Sometimes two or more facilities must be simultaneously available before an operation can be performed. In an IO subsystem, for example, transfer of data between a disk and memory requires that both the disk control unit and the channel be free before the transfer can be initiated. In modeling this subsystem, we can't simply code

```
request(controller, …); request(channel, …);
```

> since the request might be queued for one and not the other, and this can block transfers for other requests.

> **exit-time queueing disciplines. smpl** provides priority queueing, with first-in, first-out ordering within a priority class. Priorities can be used to synthesize a variety of queue-ing disciplines, such as last-in, first-out. Not all disciplines can be represented in this way: in particular, disciplines in which ordering is determined at queue exit time, rather than queue entry time, require another approach. An example of this type of queue discipline is the shortest seek time first (SSTF) ordering sometimes used in scheduling disk requests.

> **unqueueing.** It is sometimes necessary to remove an entry from a queue for reasons other than reserving a newly-released facility for the head–of–queue entry. For example, in representing swapping in a timesharing system model, it may be necessary to remove a token from the CPU queue and transfer it to the memory queue.

We may be motivated to implement an alternative queue structure in order to closely represent the queue structure of the system being modeled (for reasons discussed in Section 3.7). Also, it may be desired to provides queues without facilities, as in the case of the token ring model of Section 6.10 or in some software modeling situations.

One way of dealing with the first two situations is to bypass **smpl**'s implicit queueing and implement the required queueing structure and opera-tions directly in the model. Consider, for example, an IO subsystem with several *strings* of disk units. Each string comprises *n* disk units connected to a

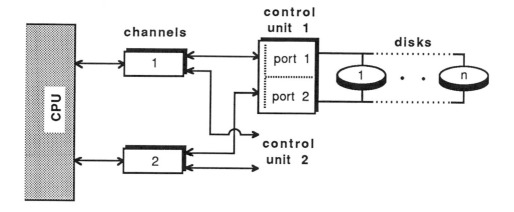

Figure 9.1. Multi-Path Disk String

control unit which in turn is connected to two data channels, as illustrated in
Figure 9.1. The control unit has two independent ports and can support two
simultaneous operations, so there are two paths between the CPU and each
disk unit. To transfer data to or from a disk unit, a sequence of commands must
be transmitted to the unit, requiring that a path be reserved between it and
the CPU; if a path is not available when a command is issued, the command
is queued. (Queueing of requests for a busy disk unit is done by the operating
system; we won't worry about it here.) Transfer of data when the disk
completes rotational positioning also requires that a path be available;
otherwise, the disk waits a revolution and tries to obtain a path once again.

Let's look at some pieces of a model of this system, beginning with the
connect() function which reserves a path for commands or data transfers.

```
connect(req)
  int req;
  {
    int i=0;
    if (status(CTLR)!=busy) then
      {
        if (status(CHNL[1]!=busy) then i=1;
        else if (status(CHNL[2]!=busy) then i=2;
        if (i) then
          {request(CTLR,req,0); request(CHNL[i],req,0);}
      }
    return(i);
  }
```

Assume that channels are defined as single-server facilities so that CHNL[i] is the facility specifier for channel i, and that the control unit is defined as a two-server facility whose facility specifier is CTLR. (We'll consider just a single string: extension to a multi-string system largely is a matter of dimensioning.) If both a control unit port and a channel are free, connect() reserves a port and a channel for the disk request (whose token number is req), and returns the channel number to its caller; otherwise, it returns 0. Note that the request statements are executed only if they are both certain to be successful: the requesting token never will be queued.

In initiating disk command processing, the model attempts to reserve a path and, if none is available, queues the request. The request will be dequeued by disconnect() when a path is released.

```
if ((path[req]=connect(req))!=0)
  then schedule(xcmd,…,req);   /* execute command */
  else
    { /* queue request in string path queue */
      link[req]=0;
      if (tq==0) then hq=tq=req; else link[tq]=req;
```

A request descriptor is assumed to take the form of a set of array elements, two of which are path[] and link[]. req is the index of the request currently being processed. hq and tq are, respectively, indexes of the request descriptors at the head and tail of the string path queue, which is a simple, singly-linked list of request descriptors.

A "reconnect" event is scheduled at the end of rotational positioning. This event routine calls connect() to reserve a path for data transfer. If no path is available, the "reconnect" event is rescheduled after a delay of one revolution time.

```
/* event "reconnect" */
if ((path[req]=connect(req))!=0)
  then schedule(endxfer,txfr,req);
  else {schedule(reconnect,tr,req); rps++;}
```

tr is the disk revolution time, and rps counts the number of revolutions lost trying to reserve a path. Data transfer requests that find all paths busy are not queued, but rather are periodically reinitiated.

When command processing or a transfer completes, the disconnect() function is called to release the path. If the string path queue is not empty, disconnect() dequeues the command at the head of the queue, reserves a path for it via a call to connect(), and schedules its next event.

```
disconnect(req,i)
   int req,i;
     {
       release(CTLR,req);  release(CHNL[i],req);
       if (hq) then
         { /* dequeue request from string path queue */
           req=hq;  hq=link(hq);  if (hq==0) then tq=0;
           path[req]=connect(req);  schedule(xcmd,…,req);
         }
     }
```

These brief sketches illustrate several points: simultaneous reservation of facilities (the port and channel comprising a path), explicit queueing implemented in the simulation model (the string path queue), and a queueing situation not representable by a conventional data structure (path reservation on completion of rotational positioning). Note that, while smpl provides facility utilizations for the channels and control units, code would have to be added to the model to obtain the mean queue length for the string path queue. The rps count can be used to compute the mean delay time of path requests for data transfers.

The level of detail of your models and the type of models you build determine how often you'll have to bypass smpl's queueing and implement queues in the model itself. The need tends to increase with increasing level of detail; also, software models often need queues which are not directly tied to facilities. If this need arises frequently in your environment, you may want to add a *queue* construct, with *enq* and *deq* operations, to smpl.

Explicit smpl queues. These can be implemented with relative ease by adapting the facility descriptor data structure of Figure 8.3; the server elements are not needed, and some of the header fields are unused. A queue is defined by a call to the queue(s) function. This function saves string s as the queue name, calls get_blk() to get a two-element block for the queue header, initializes header fields, links the header to a queue chain, and returns the index of the header as the queue specifier q. The model calls enq(q,j,pri) to enter token j in queue q; pri is j's priority. enq() calls smpl's enqueue() function to build a queue entry, update queue measurement data, and link the entry into the queue. The deq(q) function returns the entry at the head of the queue, and is constructed using three or four lines of code from release(). report() will have to be expanded; the Lq() and inq() functions can be used with explicit queues as well as facility queues.

It is hard to devise a general mechanism for queues with exit-time ordering: each instance of this type of queue usually requires a unique approach. Some care in designing data structures for these queues can help reduce search times. However, before spending much time worrying about structures and algorithms, try to estimate an upper bound on the mean queue length, and then decide if anything more than a simple search is needed.

An "unqueue" function. A model may need the ability to remove an arbitrary entry from a queue, as in the task swapping situation mentioned earlier. Implementation of an `unqueue(f,tkn,@te)` function is straight-forward. This function unlinks and deallocates `tkn`'s queue entry, updates queue measurement accumulators, and returns its remaining event time `te`; the unlinking code is much the same as the event list entry unlinking code in `cancel()`. Also of occasional use is a `qentry(f,n)` function, which returns the token number of the nth entry in the queue for facility `f`.

Data structures for queues. For generality, all queues are assumed by **smpl** to be priority-ordered, which requires a queue search on each entry. The most common queue discipline, however, is FIFO (first-in, first-out), in which a new entry always is placed at the end of the queue. By maintaining an index to the tail, as well as the head, of the queue, searching can be elim-inated. We can — potentially — improve simulation run times by adding a queue type parameter to `facility()` calls, adding a queue type indicator and a queue tail index to facility descriptors, and selecting queue entry code according to the queue type. Alternative and potentially more efficient data structures also can be considered for priority queues. The extent to which we actually realize improved performance from these changes depends on the average lengths of queues in our individual modeling environments.

Constructive power. Many of our modeling difficulties would be elim-inated if we had more powerful simulation constructs. For example, the disk subsystem model sketched earlier would be much simpler if we could define a facility "path" as a composite of the control unit and channel facilities, with its state derived from their states. In the process-oriented simulation language SIML/I (MacDougall [1979]), the states of static entities such as facilities are defined as *basic signals*; *compound signals* can be defined as logical combinations of other signals, and processes can queue on either basic or compound signals. Most simulation languages, however, provide only simple constructs for representation of static entities; while there is considerable room for innovation in this area, research into simulation constructs has centered primarily on event scheduling mechanisms.

9.3 Event Scheduling

The performance of event scheduling mechanisms has been the subject of many studies and occasionally heated debate. Many simulation languages, including **smpl**, use simple time-ordered linked lists for event scheduling.

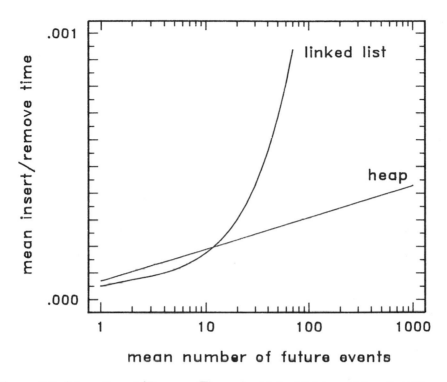

Figure 9.2. Mean Insert/Remove Times for Linked Lists and Implicit Heaps

The average time to insert one entry in and remove one entry from an ordered linked list is proportional to n, where n is the mean number of entries in the list — the mean number of future events.. Other data structures, such as *implicit heaps*,[1] provide an mean insert/remove time proportional to log n, and so offer a potential improvement in simulation run time. Figure 9.2 shows how insert/remove times for a linked list compare with those of a heap. This relative performance has resulted in the labeling of the use of linked lists as "scandalous" [Reeves 1984].[2] However, before replacing smpl's event list, there are several points to consider.

FIFO ordering of same-time entries. Many event-oriented simulation languages require that events with the same event occurrence time be ordered

---

[1]For a brief, very readable, introduction to heaps, see Bentley [1985]. Also, see Section 5.2.3 in Knuth [1971].

[2]Reeves compares simple linked lists, adaptive lists, and heaps: see O'Keefe [1985] for comments on Reeves's paper.

first-in, first-out. Since transfers between event routines are effected by scheduling events with an inter-event time of 0, events with the same occurrence time are not uncommon. Heap-based mechanisms cannot guarantee FIFO ordering of such events without the addition of secondary keys.

Event cancellation. It sometimes is necessary to search the set of future events for a particular event or for a particular token and remove that event from the set. This is a simple task with an event list like smpl's, but can require additional pointers in other data structures.

Need. The efficiency of smpl's event list is on a par with that of other data structures when the mean number of future events is small, say 20 or less. Alternative data structures certainly should be considered when the number of future events is large. First, however, ask if this number must necessarily be large. In many cases, it is possible to revise our modeling approach so as to reduce the potential number of future events, just as we did in the Ethernet model (Section 6.5). The same question should be asked if queue lengths tend to be very long.

Further reading. Specific recommendations in this area are hard to make (for reasons not excluding some trepidation). There is a substantial body of literature on the analysis of event scheduling mechanisms; two papers provide a good starting point for a review of this literature. McCormack and Sargent [1981] analyze a dozen different mechanisms; their results include relative execution times for a number of actual simulation models. Jones [1986] presents insert/remove code size and execution times for a number of mechanisms using various argument (i.e., event time) distributions, and provides an annotated set of references to earlier work.

9.4 Storages

Storages, like facilities, are static entities. Storages can be used to model such things as memory allocation in a multiprogramming computer system or message buffer allocation in a communication network node. While it is hard to devise a generally-applicable form for storages (because of the wide variety of allocation algorithms), they are useful in some types of models, and you may want to tailor some form of storage construct to meet the needs of your environment. This section sketches a simple implementation which you can use as a starting point.

Storages can be constructed as a variation on smpl's facility/queue structure. Operations on storages are analogous to facility operations, and include the following.

```
s = storage(p,n);
```

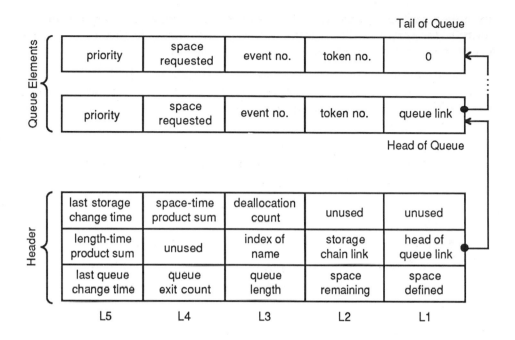

Figure 9.3. Storage Descriptor and Queue Structure

```
r = alloc(s,tkn,m);
dealloc(s,k);
m = avail(s);
```

storage() builds a descriptor for a storage with a capacity of n units and returns the index of the first element of the descriptor for use in other storage operations; p is a pointer to the storage name. alloc() is called to allocate m units on storage s for token tkn. If space is available, it is allocated and 0 returned to the caller; otherwise, the allocation request is queued and 1 returned. dealloc() deallocates k units on storage s; if this frees sufficient space to satisfy the needs of a queued request, that request is dequeued and rescheduled. The avail() function returns the number of units currently available on storage s.

For simplicity, this implementation does not permit specification of a token's priority on an allocation request. Note that dealloc(), unlike release(), does not have a token number as a parameter. It is desirable to permit multiple allocation and deallocation requests to be made for a single token, and keeping track of the space allocated to a particular token would add unwarranted complexity. Also, a storage is not viewed as a multi-server entity in the way a facility is (although we could view a facility of n servers as a storage of capacity n).

The structure of a storage descriptor and its associated queue is shown in Figure 9.3; note the similarity between it and the facility descriptor structure of Figure 8.3. A storage() call is processed very much like a facility() call;

- get_blk() is called to allocate a three-element block from the element pool for the descriptor header (s is the index of the first element of the block),

- the descriptor is linked to a storage descriptor chain via L2[s+1],

- the storage size is stored in L1[s] and L2[s],

- the storage name is stored in namespace and the namespace index saved in L3[s+1], and

- s is returned to the caller.

Remember that smpl() clears the element pool, so that fields not specifically initialized by storage() will contain 0.

The L5[s] and L5[s+1] fields are used to accumulate data for mean queue length computation in exactly the same way as the corresponding fields of a facility descriptor. The L5[s+2] and L4[s+2] fields are used in a very similar way to compute the utilization of the storage. Whenever space is allocated or deallocated, the amount of space allocated prior to the change is multiplied by the time elapsed since the last change, and this product added to the space–time product sum. The mean utilization of the storage at simulation time t is computed by dividing this sum by $n \times t$, where n is the total space defined for the storage. A count of dealloc() calls also is maintained for inclusion in the simulation report.

The simulation program calls alloc() to request allocation of n units on storage s. alloc() execution is similar to that of request(). n is compared with the available storage space (in L2[s]); if the request can be satisfied. the available space is decremented by n, the space-time product sum and last storage change time fields are updated, and 0 returned to the caller. If the request cannot be satisfied, it is queued. Even in our simple implementation, there are several different ways of managing storage queues.

Pure first-in, first-out queueing can be mechanized by assigning one of the unused storage descriptor fields (e.g., L4[s+1]) as a queue entry count. This count is initialized to a large value by alloc(). When a request is queued, the current value of this count is assigned as the request's priority and the count decremented. We also may want to do this for best-fit queueing (which requires a search at deallocation time) so that, if there are several comparable candidates for dequeueing, the earliest queued request will be selected. Alternatively, we may want to order the queue in ascending order of space requests; we can effect this by setting the request's priority equal to total storage space minus requested space: L1[s]-n. In any case, some modifications to enlist() and, consequently, its callers, are needed. A list type parameter (facility queue, storage queue, or event list) should be added to the enlist() call so that enlist() can distinguish between facility queues, in which a non-zero L4 field indicates an entry for a preempted token and causes head-of-class queueing, and storage queues, in which L4 simply is a requested space holder. enqueue() — with the addition of a queue type parameter — then can be used by alloc() to update queue measurement accumulators and allocate and build queue entries.

dealloc() frees k storage units on storage s. It updates the space-time product sum and last storage change time fields, adds k to L2[s], and, if the storage queue is empty, returns to the caller. If the queue is not empty, dealloc() determines if a request can now be dequeued; note that, depending on the amount of storage freed, it may be possible to dequeue more than one request. For a first-in, first-out or priority-ordered queue, dealloc() examines the entry at the head of the queue and, if the storage request of that entry can now be satisfied, dequeues it, updates queue measurement accumulators, and reschedules the event associated with the dequeued request. It then repeats this process for the new head-of-queue entry, and continues until the storage request at the head of the queue cannot be satisfied. Other storage queue disciplines, such as best-fit, may require a search of the queue.

Some additional things need to be done to complete storage implementation; these include error checking (e.g., for an attempt to deallocate more than the available space), clearing of measurement accumulator fields on a reset() call, trace message generation, and report generation. Use the appropriate facility function as a model for coding these details.

9.5 Tables

Tables provide a means of collecting and reporting distributions of simulation variables such as queueing times and response times; they also are useful in debugging random variate generators and in analyzing measurement data. Figure 9.4 shows the report produced for a table used to collect the

```
                        CPU execution times

       mean   7.8657                        minimum   0.0000
  std. dev.   8.5659                        maximum  93.4733

   interval                                       cumulative
  upper limit        frequency      proportion    proportion
        5              4967           0.4964        0.4964
       10              2363           0.2362        0.7326
       15              1160           0.1159        0.8485
       20               656           0.0656        0.9141
       25               339           0.0339        0.9479
       30               215           0.0215        0.9694
       35               134           0.0134        0.9828
       40                85           0.0085        0.9913
       45                33           0.0033        0.9946
       50                17           0.0017        0.9963
     > 50                37           0.0037        1.0000
                total  10006
```

Figure 9.4. smpl Table Report

distribution of CPU execution times in the queueing network simulation model of Section 2.7. This section outlines the design of the table facility used to collect and report this data; like the other **smpl** extensions we've examined, the table mechanism uses a block of elements from the element pool as the principal part of its data structure.

A table is defined via the following function call:

```
t = table(from,to,n,opt,s);
```

from and to specify the table range, n specifies the number of intervals into which this range is to be divided, opt specifies various reporting options (e.g., plot), and s is a pointer to the table name. table() creates a table descriptor and returns the index of the first element of the descriptor for use in data entry and reporting operations. n divides the table range into a set of intervals, each representing an increment $\Delta = (\text{to}-\text{from})/n$. A table descriptor includes an array of n cells, representing the intervals from $\rightarrow$ from$+\Delta$,

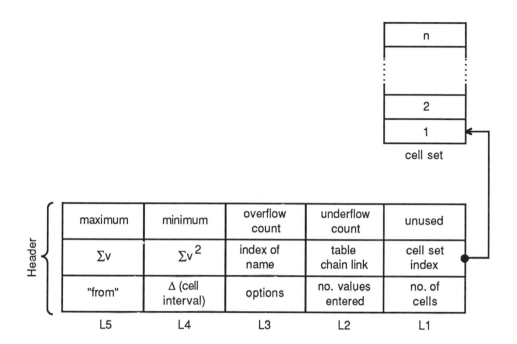

Figure 9.5. Table Descriptor

$\texttt{from}+\Delta \rightarrow \texttt{from}+2\Delta, ..., \texttt{from}+(n{-}1)\Delta \rightarrow \texttt{to}$. A value is entered in a table via the function call

$$\texttt{enter(v,t);}$$

where $\texttt{v}$ is the value to be entered and $\texttt{t}$ is the table descriptor index. The $\texttt{enter()}$ function determines into which interval the value $\texttt{v}$ falls and increments the corresponding cell. When the table report is generated, the number of values in that cell divided by the total number of values entered in the table gives the proportion of values falling in that interval.

Figure 9.5 shows the structure of a table descriptor. $\texttt{table()}$ calls $\texttt{get\_blk()}$ to get a three-element block from the element pool for the header ($\texttt{t}$ is the index of the first element in this block), sets $\texttt{L5[t]}$ to $\texttt{from}$, $\texttt{L4[t]}$ to $\texttt{(to-from)/n}$, $\texttt{L3[t]}$ to $\texttt{opt}$, and $\texttt{L1[t]}$ to $\texttt{n}$. The table name is stored in namespace and its namespace index saved in $\texttt{L3[t+1]}$, and the descriptor is linked to a table descriptor chain similar to a facility (or storage) chain. A set of n contiguous integer cells is allocated and the header linked to the first cell of the set via $\texttt{L1[t+1]}$. The simplest way to define cell space for tables is to add the declaration $\texttt{static int cell[nc]}$ to the declarations for the element pool and namespace at the start of *smpl.c*, with nc defined large enough to accommodate the requirements for the anticipated number and sizes of tables, and allocate blocks of cells from this array in the same way namespace is allocated. (Alternatively, you can use the malloc() function available in most systems to allocate a cell set for a table.) After clearing the cell set to 0, table() returns t to its caller.

The enter() function is quite simple; it takes less space to list it than it does to describe it (only the function body is shown — v is the value being entered and t is the table descriptor index).

```
int i; real c;
L1[t]++;                             /* no. of entries */
L5[t+1]+=v; L4[t+1]+=v*v;        /* sum, sum of squares */
if (v>L5[t+2]) then L5[t+2]=v;         /* new maximum */
else if (v<L4[t+2]) then L4[t+2]=v;    /* new minimum */
c=((v-L5[t])/L4[t])+0.00001;           /* cell index */
if (c<0.0) then L2[t+2]++;             /* underflow */
else if (c>=(real)L1[t]) then L3[t+2]++;    /*overflow */
else {i=L1[t+1]+(int)c; cell[i]++;}   /* increment cell */
```

In translating v into a cell index, a small constant is added so that when v−from is an multiple of the cell interval, the higher cell is incremented.

Most of the work in implementing tables is in coding the table report function; the code is straightforward, but formatting is tedious! In addition to the report function, you'll need a table clear function (to re-initialize tables on a reset() call), and you may want to implement a plot function to plot histograms like that of Figure 4.8.

A similar mechanism can be constructed to tabulate queue length distributions. In this case, we need a set of real-valued cells in which the *ith* cell is used to accumulate the time during which there were i entries in the queue; dividing this accumulated time by the simulation interval gives the desired queue length probability.

One disadvantage of our table mechanism is that we have to specify the table range in advance; if we don't have some idea of the location and shape of the distribution, we may end up making several simulation runs simply to determine the best range (and interval). Jain and Chlamtac [1985] describe an algorithm for collecting a histogram with equiprobable (rather than equal interval) cells which does not require storing observations (and doesn't require a range specification).

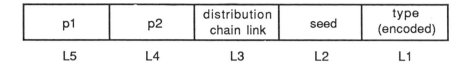

p1	p2	distribution chain link	seed	type (encoded)
L5	L4	L3	L2	L1

Figure 9.6. Distribution Descriptor

9.6 Distributions

The *distribution* construct separates random variate generation into two parts: distribution definition and distribution sampling. A distribution is defined via a function call of the form

```
d=distr(type,p1,p2);
```

where p1 and p2 are parameters of the distribution specified by type. For most distributions, p1 and p2 specify the mean and standard deviation; for the uniform distribution, p1 and p2 specify the lower and upper limits. distr() creates a simple data structure to hold the distribution type and parameters, and returns the structure's index d to its caller. A sample variate v then is generated by the function call

```
v=sample(d);
```

Separating the definition and sampling functions makes it easy to specify the distribution type as a model parameter, speeding both model debugging and experimentation. In addition, by providing each defined distribution with its own random number stream seed, it is easy to exploit two of the variance reduction techniques discussed in Section 4.8: common random numbers and antithetic variates. This section briefly sketches the design of a distribution definition and sampling mechanism using the continuous distribution random variate generation functions of *rand.c*.

If ints are 32-bit quantities in your environment, you can use an element from the element pool to construct a distribution descriptor, as shown in Figure 9.6. If ints are 16-bit quantities, then another data structure must be devised which will provide long storage for the 31-bit random number stream seed. We'll assume here that a standard smpl element can be used. When a distribution is defined, distr() calls get_blk() to get a one-element block whose index is d, stores p1 and p2 in L5[d] and L4[d], links the descriptor on a distribution chain, gets the seed for the current random number stream and stores it in L2[d], stores a distribution type code in L1[d], and returns d to the caller.

The simplest way to provide an independent random number stream for each distribution is to use the `seed()` function in *rand.c* to obtain the seed of the currently-selected stream when defining a distribution and again to set the seed when a sample value is to be generated from that distribution. To improve performance, you can have `sample()` set a pointer to the active seed for use by `ranf()`, thus avoiding a `seed()` call on each `sample()` call. Distribution descriptors are chained together so that, on a stream switch, descriptors can be accessed and their seeds changed; this requires that `stream()` be moved to *smpl.c* and the appropriate changes made.

The distribution type stored by `distr()` may be identical to the `type` value specified by its caller, or may be some encoding of that value, depending on how you choose to define types. One possibility is to define four distribution types by adding the following definitions to *smpl.h*.

```
#define constant  1
#define uniform   2
#define normal    3
#define expntl    4
```

A `constant` distribution is handy in debugging; a sample variate from this distribution always is equal to p1. A sample variate from the `uniform` distribution is distributed uniformly in [p1,p2]. For `normal` distributions, p1 and p2 specify the mean and standard deviation.[3] p1 and p2 also specify the mean and standard deviation for an `expntl` distribution. An `expntl` sample value is generated from the Erlang distribution if p1<p2, from the negative exponential distribution if p1=p2, and from the hyperexponential distribution if p1>p2. With this definition for distributions of this family, the distribution type doesn't have to be changed as the standard deviation changes. The `distr()` function encodes the distribution type to whatever form provides the fastest `sample()` call. In the case of a hyperexponential distribution (Section 8.9), it precomputes p and stage mean values.

The provision of an independent random number stream for each distribution provides the basis for the common random number method of variance reduction. The antithetic variate method can be implemented by complementing the random number seed before establishing it as the active seed. A function can be provided to appropriately mark the descriptor for the distribution whose random numbers are to be complemented.

The `sample()` function establishes the seed for distribution d as the active seed, calls the random variate generation function specified by `L1[d]`

---

[3]The `normal()` function in *rand.c* saves values between calls and will need to be modified if multiple normal distributions will be defined.

with parameters L5[d] and L4[d], and passes along the value returned by that function to its caller. You can eliminate a function call by incorporating the variate generation code directly in sample().

9.7 A Run-Time Interface

A run-time interface, such as **SMPL/PC**'s **mtr**, is the most useful addition you can make to your simulation system; the time spent in its implementation will pay substantial dividends in reducing debugging and experiment setup times. The detailed design of this interface will largely depend on your hardware and software environment. This section gives a brief sketch of the **mtr** module of **SMPL/PC** and associated **SMPL** parameter handling functions, and is intended to provide a starting point for your own design. In **SMPL/PC**, interactions between the modeler and the model are controlled by function keys, and the operating system is required only to deliver key codes. In other systems, interactions may be controlled via pop-up or pop-down menus, and the system may provide facilities for creating, controlling, and obtaining input from these menus. The operations you should get in place first are trace control, report display, and parameter handling; other operations can be added as needed. A user's view of **SMPL/PC** was given in Chapter 7, and you may find it useful to review that chapter in considering run-time interface design.

smpl communicates with **mtr** via calls to two functions: the **mtr** initialization function init_mtr(), and the main **mtr** control function, mtr(). Simplified flow charts of these functions are shown in Figure 9.7.

smpl makes two calls to init_mtr(), first from smpl() with mr=1, and later from get_elm() with mr=2. (smpl's calls to **mtr** functions are shown in the source code listing in the Appendix in the form of comments.) On the first call, init_mtr() initializes **mtr** variables, clears the screen and generates the standard **mtr** display, displays initialization and pause messages, and waits for a function key to be pressed. The **mtr** display comprises a heading — model name, etc. — at the top of the screen, and left and right message lines at the bottom of the screen. The left message line is used for pause messages and certain input prompts; the right one is used for messages such as the initialization and facility definition messages, as well for the simulation time display. This first call, which is made before any facilities have been defined, provides an opportunity for the modeler to change the values of parameters which affect facility definitions, such as the number of servers for a facility. The second call, from get_elm(), is made when the first event is scheduled (and after all facilities have been defined); it provides an opportunity for the user to set up displays involving facilities,

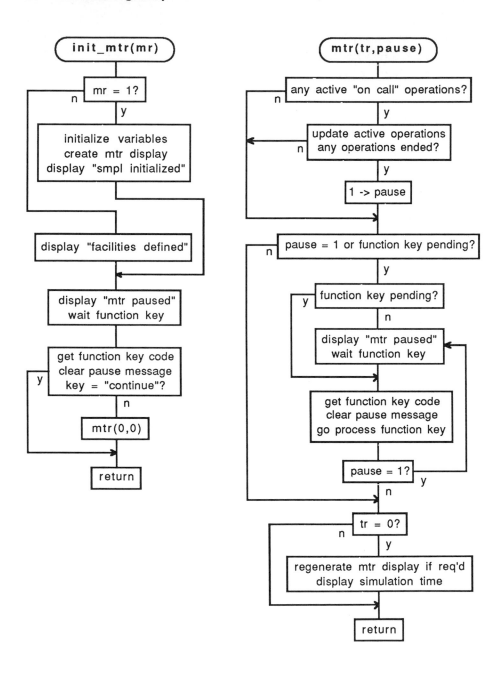

Figure 9.7. mtr Initialization and Control Functions

such as queue length plotting. On either call, if no **mtr** display is to be invoked, the modeler presses function key **F10** to continue, and init_mtr() returns to smpl(); otherwise, mtr() is called to process the selected function.

mtr() is the main **mtr** control function; it is called from cause(), pause(), and error(). A mtr() call has two parameters: tr, a copy of **smpl**'s trace mode flag, and pause, which is 1 if a monitor pause is requested and 0 otherwise.

When tracing is active and trace mode 2 or 3 has been selected, **smpl**'s trace message end_line() function calls mtr() — via pause() — to pause execution after each full screen (trace mode 2) or after each trace message (trace mode 3). On returning to **smpl**, mtr() uses tr to determine if **mtr** screen display generation should be bypassed. error() calls mtr() to pause execution when an error occurs, giving the modeler the opportunity to invoke displays which may help determine the cause and location of the error.

During normal execution, with tracing inactive, mtr() is called from cause() on every event. On each call, mtr() performs three tasks: it updates active "on-call" operations, checks the keyboard for **mtr** function invocation, and displays the current simulation time. "On-call" operations involve **mtr** functions which, in SMPL/PC, include breakpoints, **mtr**-defined tables, simulation output analysis, and time series display (see Chapter 7). Each of these has its own updating function; for some, the operation may terminate as the result of an update. For example, when breakpointing is active, mtr() compares the current simulation time or the current value of the **SMPL** parameter designated as the breakpoint parameter with the breakpoint value and, if the breakpoint condition is met, turns breakpointing off, displays a message and pauses.

When a function key has been pressed, mtr() transfers to the corresponding function key processor. Many of these are very simple. For example, processors for **F1-F3**, the trace toggles, simply call **smpl**'s trace function with the appropriate parameter, the F4 processor calls report(), and the sF4 processor calls reset(). Processors for **F7** and sF7 use the left message area of the **mtr** display to request entry of a breakpoint value or stream number. Some function key processors, such as the **SMPL** parameter display, involve full screen displays with display editing capability.

Simulation time is displayed in the lower right message area. Since generating this message involves floating point to character conversion, **mtr** overhead can be reduced by generating this message only on every n^{th} **mtr** call, where n is on the order of 50.

Parameters. An important adjunct to **mtr** is the SMPL parameter mechanism, which provides a very simple but effective means of communication between the simulation program, **mtr**, and the modeler. This mechanism comprises a few simple function and data structures packaged in the **parms** module. The simulation program defines a variable as a parameter via a call to **parms'** `pdef()` function; `pdef()` parameters are the parameter number, a pointer to the variable being defined as a parameter, and a pointer to a character string to be used as the parameter name in **mtr** displays. The character string is stored in a parameter namespace array; a pointer to the string and a pointer to the variable are stored in a **parms** data structure. The size of this data structure, and hence the number of parameters which can be defined, np, is fixed at compile time; 8–12 parameters are sufficient for most models.[4] Other **parms** functions return the name or the variable pointer of a parameter, given its number, and the parameter number, given its variable pointer.

mtr provides a display, invoked by function key **F8**, which lists the names and values of all defined parameters and permits their values to be changed. This display processor loops through the set of np possible parameters, calling **parms** functions to get the name and variable pointer of each defined parameter; it then loops through the set of defined parameters, permitting their values to be changed, and assigns any changed values to the parameter variable using its pointer. In addition to these facilities for displaying and modifying parameter values, **mtr** uses parameter numbers as input parameters for various displays, and a breakpoint can be set on a parameter value. In these applications (described in Chapter 7), **mtr** reads the specified parameter number, calls **parms** functions to verify that the parameter has been defined and to get its variable pointer, and uses the pointer for subsequent data access.

9.8 In Conclusion

In this chapter, we've looked at a variety of possible extensions to the basic **smpl** simulation subsystem described in Chapter 8. You may want to implement some of these, and you'll probably develop others to fit the needs of your modeling environment. First, though, develop a run-time interface along the lines of that described in Section 9.7; other extensions then can be developed to be compatible with this interface.

---

[4]SMPL system parameters, such as the sizes of data structures, are defined in a configuration file. Modules requiring access to this information (**mtr** and **parms** in this case) `#include` this configuration file.

smpl is a useful tool for building small- to medium-scale simulation models. For large-scale models, a process-oriented simulation language is strongly recommended.[5] This is not to say that process-oriented languages aren't useful for small models; they are. At any scale, the process view offers more descriptive power than the event view; for large models, this power, and the way it impacts model design, can be crucial. However, the implementation of a process-oriented simulation language is — relative to an event-oriented "language" like smpl — complex, and usually involves machine-dependent functions which limit portability.

Regardless of language, the development of a high-detail, large-scale simulation model in support of a system design effort is a high-risk task. It is very easy to under-estimate the effort required to develop a large model and keep it current. The effort required to get an initial version of a large model running may keep the modeler from contributing to the analysis of early design decisions; in any case, the nature of the model is such that much of the design has to be in place before the model can be built. Consequently, the main use of such a model — even if it is successfully constructed — may be the analysis of relatively low-level design decisions. Perhaps this is important enough to justify model development costs; in the early stages of design, though, small-scale models frequently are the most useful tools. Such models can be small-scale in the sense of either providing a very high level representation of the overall system design or providing a detailed representation of a small part of the system. In the ideal case, the high-level model developed in the early stages of a design would be extended in hierarchical fashion through increasing levels of detail as the design evolves. (This is easier said than done, partly because designing usually is done both "top down" and "bottom up", and both approaches raise issues requiring analysis.) A process-oriented simulation language provides the most natural vehicle for hierarchical model development.

Because of its compactness, smpl lends itself to use as the simulation "kernel" of specialized modeling packages. Such packages can take the form of models tailored for specific applications, such as a communication network simulator, or may provide a specialized user interface. The latter is exem-plified by the Research Queueing (RESQ) package in which models are described as queueing networks. (See MacNair and Sauer [1985] for examples and references.) Developments in visual programming may result in new ways to build simulation models and examine simulation results; see Melamed and Morris [1985] for an example.

---

[5]Schwetman [1986] has developed a process-oriented simulation language which is an extension of C.

Appendix

The following pages contains C source code listings for four files:[*]

> *smpl.c* — the **smpl** simulation subsystem except for random variate generation functions,
>
> *rand.c* — random variate generation functions,
>
> *smpl.h* — **smpl** external name declarations and various user-level directives (for inclusion in simulation programs), and
>
> *stat.c* — normal and *t* distribution quantile computation functions `Z()` and `T()` (used by the batch means analysis module of Section 4.7).

An executable instance of a **smpl** simulation model is formed by

> 1. compiling *smpl.c* and *rand.c* (and, if desired, creating a library module from their object modules),
>
> 2. compiling the simulation program, which contains `main()` (and which `#includes` *smpl.h*), and
>
> 3. linking the simulation program's object module to the *smpl* and *rand* object modules (or their library module) to form an executable file.

Note that there are two versions of `ranf()` in *rand.c*; the version compiled is determined by the value `#defined` for CPU (8086 or 68000). You may want to compile the batch means analysis module of Section 4.7 (which `#includes` *stat.c*) and add its object module to your library.

---

[*]These files, together with source code files for the other programs in this book, are available on diskette; see note in Preface.

```
/**********************************************************************/
/*                                                                    */
/*                        File "smpl.c"                               */
/*                  smpl Simulation Subsystem                         */
/*                                                                    */
/*                                   (c) 1987  M. H. MacDougall    */
/*                                                                    */
/**********************************************************************/

#include <stdio.h>

typedef double real;
#define then

#define nl 256          /* element pool length                    */
#define ns 256          /* namespace length                       */
#define pl 58           /* printer page length    (lines used     */
#define sl 23           /* screen page length       by 'smpl')    */
#define FF 12           /* form feed                              */

static FILE
  *display=stdout,      /* screen display file                    */
  *opf=stdout;          /* current output destination             */

static int
  event,                /* current simulation event               */
  token,                /* last token dispatched                  */
  blk,                  /* next available block index             */
  avl,                  /* available element list header          */
  evl,                  /* event list header                      */
  fchn,                 /* facility descriptor chain header       */
  avn,                  /* next available namespace position      */
  tr,                   /* event trace flag                       */
  mr,                   /* monitor activation flag                */
  lft=sl;               /* lines left on current page/screen      */

static real
  clock,                /* current simulation time                */
  start,                /* simulation interval start time         */
  tl;                   /* last trace message issue time          */

static int
  l1[nl],
  l2[nl],               /*          facility descriptor,          */
  l3[nl];               /*               queue, &                 */
static real             /*             event list                 */
  l4[nl],               /*             element pool               */
  l5[nl];

static char
  name[ns];             /* model and facility name space          */
```

```
/*--------------      INITIALIZE SIMULATION SUBSYSTEM  -----------------*/
smpl(m,s)
  int m; char *s;
    {
      int i; static int rns=1;
      blk=1; avl=-1; avn=0;         /* element pool & namespace headers */
      evl=fchn=0;                 /* event list & descriptor chain headers */
      clock=start=tl=0.0;   /* sim., interval start, last trace times */
      event=tr=0;                 /* current event no. & trace flags */
      for (i=0; i<nl; i++)   {l1[i]=l2[i]=l3[i]=0; l4[i]=l5[i]=0.0;}
      i=save_name(s,50);                     /* model name -> namespace */
      rns=stream(rns); rns=++rns>15? 1:rns;  /* set random no. stream */
      mr=(m>0)? 1:0;                           /* set monitor flag */
  /* if (mr) then {opf=display; init_mtr(1);} */
    }

/*----------------------  RESET MEASUREMENTS  ----------------------*/
reset()
  {
    resetf(); start=clock;
  }

/*------------------------- SAVE NAME --------------------------*/
static save_name(s,m)
  char *s; int m;
    {
      int i,n;
      n=strlen(s); if (n>m) then n=m;
      if (avn+n>ns) then error(2,0); /* namespace exhausted */
      i=avn; avn+=n+1; strncpy(&name[i],s,n);
      if (n==m) then name[avn++]='\0';
      return(i);
    }

/*------------------------ GET MODEL NAME -------------------------*/
char *mname()
  {
    return(name);
  }

/*------------------------ GET FACILITY NAME ---------------------*/
char *fname(f)
  int f;
    {
      return(&name[l3[f+1]]);
    }

/*------------------------- GET BLOCK ----------------------------*/
static get_blk(n)
  int n;
    {
      int i;
      if (blk==0) then error(3,0);    /* block request after schedule */
      i=blk; blk+=n;
      if (blk>=nl) then error(1,0);            /* element pool exhausted */
      return(i);
    }
```

```
/*------------------------- GET ELEMENT -------------------------*/
static get_elm()
  {
    int i;
    if (avl<=0) then
      {
        if (avl==0) then error(1,0);      /* empty element list */
    /* if (mr && !tr) then init_mtr(2); */
        /* build the free element list from the block of elements */
        /* remaining after all facilities have been defined      */
        for (i=blk; i<(nl-1); i++) l1[i]=i+1;
        avl=blk; blk=0;
      }
    i=avl; avl=l1[i];
    return(i);
  }

/*------------------------- RETURN ELEMENT -------------------------*/
static put_elm(i)
  int i;
    {
      l1[i]=avl; avl=i;
    }

/*------------------------- SCHEDULE EVENT -------------------------*/
schedule(ev,te,tkn)
  int ev,tkn; real te;
    {
      int i;
      if (te<0.0) then error(4,0); /* negative event time */
      i=get_elm(); l2[i]=tkn; l3[i]=ev; l4[i]=0.0; l5[i]=clock+te;
      enlist(&evl,i);
      if (tr) then msg(1,tkn,"",ev,0);
    }

/*------------------------- CAUSE EVENT -------------------------*/
cause(ev,tkn)
  int *ev,*tkn;
    {
      int i;
      if (evl==0) then error(5,0);           /* empty event list  */
      i=evl; *tkn=token=l2[i]; *ev=event=l3[i]; clock=l5[i];
      evl=l1[i]; put_elm(i);  /* delink element & return to pool */
      if (tr) then msg(2,*tkn,"",event,0);
    /* if (mr && (tr!=3)) then mtr(tr,0); */
    }

/*------------------------- RETURN TIME -------------------------*/
real time()
  {
    return(clock);
  }
```

```
/*------------------------   CANCEL EVENT   --------------------------*/
cancel(ev)
   int ev;
      {
        int pred,succ=evl,tkn;
        while((succ!=0) && (l3[succ]!=ev)) {pred=succ; succ=l1[pred];}
        if (succ==0) then return(-1);
        tkn=l2[succ]; if (tr) then msg(3,tkn,"",l3[succ],0);
        if (succ==evl)
           then evl=l1[succ];                  /* unlink  event */
           else l1[pred]=l1[succ];             /* list entry &  */
        put_elm(succ);                         /* deallocate it */
        return(tkn);
      }

/*------------------------   SUSPEND EVENT   -------------------------*/
static suspend(tkn)
   int tkn;
      {
        int pred,succ=evl;
        while((succ!=0) && (l2[succ]!=tkn)) {pred=succ; succ=l1[pred];}
        if (succ==0) then error(6,0);    /* no event scheduled for token */
        if (succ==evl)
           then evl=l1[succ];          /* unlink  event */
           else l1[pred]=l1[succ];     /* list entry    */
        if (tr) then msg(6,-1,"",l3[succ],0);
        return(succ);
      }
```

```
/*-------------- ENTER ELEMENT IN QUEUE OR EVENT LIST  --------------*/
static enlist(head,elm)
  int *head,elm;
    { /* 'head' points to head of queue/event list */
      int pred,succ; real arg,v;
      arg=l5[elm]; succ=*head;
      while(1)
         { /* scan for position to insert entry:  event list is order- */
           /* ed in ascending 'arg' values, queues in descending order */
           if (succ==0)
             then break;   /* end of list */
             else
                {
                  v=l5[succ];
                  if (*head==evl)
                    then
                       { /* event list  */
                         if (v>arg) then break;
                       }
                    else
                       { /* queue:  if entry is for a preempted token    */
                         /* (l4, the remaining event time, >0), insert   */
                         /* entry at beginning of its priority class;    */
                         /* otherwise, insert it at the end              */
                         if ((v<arg) || ((v==arg) && (l4[elm]>0.0)))
                           then break;
                       }
                }
           pred=succ; succ=l1[pred];
         }
      l1[elm]=succ; if (succ!=*head) then l1[pred]=elm; else *head=elm;
    }

/*----------------------- DEFINE FACILITY ----------------------------*/
facility(s,n)
  char *s; int n;
    {
      int f,i;
      f=get_blk(n+2); l1[f]=n; l3[f+1]=save_name(s,(n>1 ? 14:17));
      if (fchn==0)
        then fchn=f;
        else {i=fchn; while(l2[i+1]) i=l2[i+1]; l2[i+1]=f;}
      l2[f+1]=0;
      if (tr) then msg(13,-1,fname(f),f,0);
      return(f);
    }
```

```
/*--------------     RESET FACILITY & QUEUE MEASUREMENTS   --------------*/
static resetf()
  {
    int i=fchn,j;
      while(i)
        {
           l4[i]=l4[i+1]=l5[i+1]=0.0;
           for (j=i+2; j<=(i+l1[i]+1); j++) {l3[j]=0; l4[j]=0.0;}
           i=l2[i+1];  /* advance to next facility */
        }
    start=clock;
  }


/*----------------------   REQUEST FACILITY   -----------------------*/
request(f,tkn,pri)
  int f,tkn,pri;
    {
      int i,r;
      if (l2[f]<l1[f])
        then
          { /* facility nonbusy - reserve 1st-found nonbusy server    */
            for (i=f+2; l1[i]!=0; i++);
            l1[i]=tkn; l2[i]=pri; l5[i]=clock; l2[f]++; r=0;
          }
        else
          { /* facility busy - enqueue token marked w/event, priority */
            enqueue(f,tkn,pri,event,0.0); r=1;
          }
      if (tr) then msg(7,tkn,fname(f),r,l3[f]);
      return(r);
    }


/*----------------------   ENQUEUE TOKEN   ---------------------------*/
static enqueue(f,j,pri,ev,te)
  int f,j,pri,ev; real te;
    {
      int i;
      l5[f+1]+=l3[f]*(clock-l5[f]); l3[f]++; l5[f]=clock;
      i=get_elm(); l2[i]=j; l3[i]=ev; l4[i]=te; l5[i]=(real)pri;
      enlist(&l1[f+1],i);
    }
```

```
/*----------------------- PREEMPT FACILITY ------------------------*/
preempt(f,tkn,pri)
  int f,tkn,pri;
    {
      int ev,i,j,k,r; real te;
      if (l2[f]<l1[f])
        then
          { /* facility nonbusy - locate 1st-found nonbusy server    */
            for (k=f+2; l1[k]!=0; k++); r=0;
            if (tr) then msg(8,tkn,fname(f),0,0);
          }
        else
          { /* facility busy - find server with lowest-priority user  */
            k=f+2; j=l1[f]+f+1;  /* indices of server elements 1 & n  */
            for (i=f+2; i<=j; i++) if (l2[i]<l2[k]) then k=i;
            if (pri<=l2[k])
              then
                { /* requesting token's priority is not higher than   */
                  /* that of any user: enqueue requestor & return r=1 */
                  enqueue(f,tkn,pri,event,0.0); r=1;
                  if (tr) then msg(7,tkn,fname(f),1,l3[f]);
                }
              else
                { /* preempt user of server k.  suspend event, save   */
                  /* event number & remaining event time, & enqueue   */
                  /* preempted token.  If remaining event time is 0   */
                  /* (preemption occurred at the instant release was  */
                  /* to occur, set 'te' > 0 for proper enqueueing     */
                  /* (see 'enlist').  Update facility & server stati-  */
                  /* stics for the preempted token, and set r = 0 to  */
                  /* reserve the facility for the preempting token.   */
                  if (tr) then msg(8,tkn,fname(f),2,0);
                  j=l1[k]; i=suspend(j); ev=l3[i]; te=l5[i]-clock;
                  if (te==0.0) then te=1.0e-99; put_elm(i);
                  enqueue(f,j,l2[k],ev,te);
                  if (tr) then
                    {msg(10,-1,"",j,l3[f]); msg(12,-1,fname(f),tkn,0);}
                  l3[k]++; l4[k]+=clock-l5[k];
                  l2[f]--; l4[f+1]++; r=0;
                }
          }
      if (r==0) then
        { /* reserve server k of facility */
          l1[k]=tkn; l2[k]=pri; l5[k]=clock; l2[f]++;
        }
      return(r);
    }
```

```
/*----------------------- RELEASE FACILITY ------------------------*/
release(f,tkn)
  int f,tkn;
    {
      int i,j=0,k,m; real te;
      /* locate server (j) reserved by releasing token */
      k=f+1+l1[f];      /* index of last server element */
      for (i=f+2; i<=k; i++) if (l1[i]==tkn) then {j=i; break;}
      if (j==0) then error(7,0); /* no server reserved */
      l1[j]=0; l3[j]++; l4[j]+=clock-l5[j]; l2[f]--;
      if (tr) then msg(9,tkn,fname(f),0,0);
      if (l3[f]>0) then
        { /* queue not empty:  dequeue request ('k' =  */
          /* index of element) & update queue measures */
          k=l1[f+1]; l1[f+1]=l1[k]; te=l4[k];
          l5[f+1]+=l3[f]*(clock-l5[f]); l3[f]--; l4[f]++; l5[f]=clock;
          if (tr) then msg(11,-1,"",l2[k],l3[f]);
          if (te==0.0) then
            then
              { /* blocked request:  place request at head of event  */
                /* list (so its facility request can be re-initiated  */
                /* before any other requests scheduled for this time) */
                l5[k]=clock; l1[k]=evl; evl=k; m=4;
              }
            else
              { /* return after preemption:  reserve facility for de- */
                /* queued request & reschedule remaining event time   */
                l1[j]=l2[k]; l2[j]=(int)l5[k]; l2[f]++;
                if (tr) then msg(12,-1,fname(f),l2[k],0);
                l5[k]=clock+te; enlist(&evl,k); m=5;
              }
          if (tr) then msg(m,-1,"",l3[k],0);
        }
    }

/*----------------------- GET FACILITY STATUS -----------------------*/
status(f)
  int f;
    {
      return(l1[f]==l2[f]? 1:0);
    }

/*-------------------- GET CURRENT QUEUE LENGTH --------------------*/
inq(f)
  int f;
    {
      return(l3[f]);
    }
```

```
/*-------------------- GET FACILITY UTILIZATION --------------------*/
real U(f)
  int f;
    {
      int i; real b=0.0,t=clock-start;
      if (t>0.0) then
        {
          for (i=f+2; i<=f+l1[f]+1; i++) b+=l4[i];
          b/=t;
        }
      return(b);
    }

/*--------------------- GET MEAN BUSY PERIOD ---------------------*/
real B(f)
  int f;
    {
      int i,n=0; real b=0.0;
      for (i=f+2; i<=f+l1[f]+1; i++) {b+=l4[i]; n+=l3[i];}
      return((n>0)? b/n:b);
    }

/*-------------------- GET AVERAGE QUEUE LENGTH --------------------*/
real Lq(f)
  int f;
    {
      real t=clock-start;
      return((t>0.0)? (l5[f+1]/t):0.0);
    }

/*--------------------- TURN TRACE ON/OFF -----------------------*/
trace(n)
  int n;
    {
      switch(n)
        {
          case 0: tr=0; break;
          case 1:
          case 2:
          case 3: tr=n; tl=-1.0; newpage(); break;
          case 4: end_line(); break;
         default: break;
        }
    }
```

```
/*------------------- GENERATE TRACE MESSAGE ----------------------*/
static msg(n,i,s,q1,q2)
  int n,i,q1,q2; char *s;
    {
      static char *m[14] = {"",  "SCHEDULE", "CAUSE", "CANCEL",
       "  RESCHEDULE"," RESUME", " SUSPEND", "REQUEST", "PREEMPT",
       "RELEASE", "  QUEUE", " DEQUEUE", "  RESERVE", "FACILITY" };
      if (clock>tl)      /* print time stamp (if time has advanced) */
        then {tl=clock; fprintf(opf," time %-12.3f  ",clock);}
        else fprintf(opf,"%21s",m[0]);
      if (i>=0)          /* print token number if specified */
        then fprintf(opf,"--  token %-4d -- ",i);
        else fprintf(opf,"--           -- ");
      fprintf(opf,"%s %s",m[n],s);  /* print basic message */
      switch(n)
        { /* append qualifier */
          case 1:
          case 2:
          case 3:
          case 4:
          case 5:
          case 6:  fprintf(opf," EVENT %d",q1); break;
          case 7:
          case 8:  switch(q1)
                     {
                       case 0: fprintf(opf":  RESERVED"); break;
                       case 1: fprintf(opf,":  QUEUED  (inq = %d)",q2);
                               break;
                       case 2: fprintf(opf,":  INTERRUPT"); break;
                       default: break;
                     }
                   break;
          case 9:  break;
          case 10:
          case 11: fprintf(opf," token %d  (inq = %d)",q1,q2); break;
          case 12: fprintf(opf," for token %d",q1); break;
          case 13: fprintf(opf,":  f = %d",q1); break;
          default: break;
        }
      fprintf(opf,"\n"); end_line();
    }
```

```
/*----------------------- TRACE LINE END  --------------------------*/
static end_line()
  {
    if ((--lft)==0) then
      { /* end of page/screen.  for trace 1, advance page if print- */
        /* er output;  screen output is free-running.  for trace 2, */
        /* pause on full screen;  for trace 3, pause after line.    */
        switch(tr)
          {
            case 1: if (opf==display)
                      then lft=sl;
                      else endpage();
                    break;
            case 2: if (mr)
                      then {putchar('\n'); lft=sl; pause();}
                      else endpage();
                    break;
            case 3: lft=sl; break;
          }
      }
    if (tr==3) then pause();
  }

/*-------------------------- PAUSE  -----------------------------*/
pause()
  { /* pause execution via 'mtr' call (if active) */
 /* if (mr) then mtr(tr,1); else */ getchar();
  }

/*------------------- DISPLAY ERROR MESSAGE & EXIT  ------------------*/
error(n,s)
  int n; char *s;
    {
      FILE *dest;
      static char
          *m[8]= { "Simulation Error at Time ",
                   "Empty Element Pool",
                   "Empty Name Space",
                   "Facility Defined After Queue/Schedule",
                   "Negative Event Time",
                   "Empty Event List",
                   "Preempted Token Not in Event List",
                   "Release of Idle/Unowned Facility" };
      dest=opf;
      while(1)
        { /* send messages to both printer and screen */
          fprintf(dest,"\n**** %s%.3f\n",m[0],clock);
          if (n) fprintf(dest,"    %s\n",m[n]);
          if (s) fprintf(dest,"    %s\n",s);
          if (dest==display) then break; else dest=display;
        }
      if (opf!=display) then report();
  /* if (mr) then mtr(0,1); */
      exit(0);
    }
```

```
/*---------------------- GENERATE REPORT  -------------------------*/
report()
  {
    newpage();
    reportf();
    endpage();
  }


/*------------------- GENERATE FACILITY REPORT  --------------------*/
reportf()
  {
    int f;
    if ((f=fchn)==0)
      then fprintf(opf,"\nno facilities defined:  report abandoned\n");
      else
        { /* f = 0 at end of facility chain */
          while(f) {f=rept_page(f); if (f>0) then endpage();}
        }
  }


/*-------------------- GENERATE REPORT PAGE  ----------------------*/
static rept_page(fnxt)
  int fnxt;
    {
      int f,i,n; char fn[19];
      static char *s[7]= {
      "smpl SIMULATION REPORT", " MODEL: ", "TIME: ", "INTERVAL: ",
      "MEAN BUSY     MEAN QUEUE         OPERATION COUNTS",
      " FACILITY            UTIL.     ",
      " PERIOD          LENGTH      RELEASE    PREEMPT    QUEUE" };
      fprintf(opf,"\n%51s\n\n\n",s[0]);
      fprintf(opf,"%-s%-54s%-s%11.3f\n",s[1],mname(),s[2],clock);
      fprintf(opf,"%68s%11.3f\n\n",s[3],clock-start);
      fprintf(opf,"%75s\n",s[4]);
      fprintf(opf,"%s%s\n",s[5],s[6]);
      f=fnxt; lft-=8;
      while(f && lft--)
        {
          n=0; for (i=f+2; i<=f+l1[f]+1; i++) n+=l3[i];
          if (l1[f]==1)
            then sprintf(fn,"%s",fname(f));
            else sprintf(fn,"%s[%d]",fname(f),l1[f]);
          fprintf(opf," %-17s%6.4f %10.3f %13.3f %11d %9d %7d\n",
            fn,U(f),B(f),Lq(f),n,(int)l4[f+1],(int)l4[f]);
          f=l2[f+1];
        }
      return(f);
    }


/*------------------------- COUNT LINES  -------------------------*/
lns(i)
  int i;
    {
      lft-=i;  if (lft<=0) then endpage();
      return(lft);
    }
```

```
/*-------------------------- END PAGE --------------------------*/
endpage()
  {
    int c;
    if (opf==display)
      then
        { /* screen output: push to top of screen & pause */
          while(lft>0) {putc('\n',opf); lft--;}
          printf("\n[ENTER] to continue:");  getchar();
       /* if (mr) then clr_scr(); else */ printf("\n\n");
         }
      else if (lft<pl) then putc(FF,opf);
    newpage();
  }

/*-------------------------- NEW PAGE --------------------------*/
newpage()
  { /* set line count to top of page/screen after page change/screen  */
    /* clear by 'smpl', another SMPL module, or simulation program    */
    lft=(opf==display)? sl:pl;
  }

/*----------------------- REDIRECT OUTPUT -----------------------*/
FILE *sendto(dest)
  FILE *dest;
    {
      if (dest) then opf=dest;
      return(opf);
    }
```

```
/*******************************************************************/
/*                                                                 */
/*                       File "rand.c"                             */
/*                  Random Variate Generation                      */
/*                                                                 */
/*                              (c) 1987  M. H. MacDougall         */
/*                                                                 */
/*******************************************************************/

#include <math.h>

#define CPU 8086

typedef double real;
#define then

#define A 16807L            /* multiplier (7**5) for 'ranf' */
#define M 2147483647L       /* modulus (2**31-1) for 'ranf' */

static long In[16]= {0L,    /* seeds for streams 1 thru 15  */
   1973272912L,  747177549L,   20464843L,  640830765L, 1098742207L,
     78126602L,   84743774L,  831312807L,  124667236L, 1172177002L,
   1124933064L, 1223960546L, 1878892440L, 1449793615L,  553303732L};

static int strm=1;          /* index of current stream */


#if CPU==8086
/*------------   UNIFORM [0, 1] RANDOM NUMBER GENERATOR  -------------*/
/*                                                                 */
/* This implementation is for Intel 8086/8 and 80286/386 CPUs using */
/* C compilers with 16-bit short integers and 32-bit long integers.  */
/*                                                                 */
/*-----------------------------------------------------------------*/
real ranf()
  {
    short *p,*q,k; long Hi,Lo;
    /* generate product using double precision simulation  (comments  */
    /* refer to In's lower 16 bits as "L", its upper 16 bits as "H")   */
    p=(short *)&In[strm]; Hi=*(p+1)*A;                    /* 16807*H->Hi */
    *(p+1)=0; Lo=In[strm]*A;                             /* 16807*L->Lo */
    p=(short *)&Lo; Hi+=*(p+1);    /* add high-order bits of Lo to Hi */
    q=(short *)&Hi;                        /* low-order bits of Hi->LO */
    *(p+1)=*q&0X7FFF;                               /* clear sign bit */
    k=*(q+1)<<1; if (*q&0X8000) then k++;      /* Hi bits 31-45->K */
    /* form Z + K [- M] (where Z=Lo): presubtract M to avoid overflow */
    Lo-=M; Lo+=k; if (Lo<0) then Lo+=M;
    In[strm]=Lo;
    return((real)Lo*4.656612875E-10);            /* Lo x 1/(2**31-1) */
  }
#endif
```

```
#if CPU==68000
/*------------ UNIFORM [0, 1] RANDOM NUMBER GENERATOR -------------*/
/*                                                                  */
/* This implementation is for Motorola 680x0 CPUs using C compilers */
/* with 16-bit short integers and 32-bit long integers.            */
/*                                                                  */
/*------------------------------------------------------------------*/
real ranf()
   {
     short *p,*q,k; long Hi,Lo;
     /* generate product using double precision simulation  (comments */
     /* refer to In's lower 16 bits as "L", its upper 16 bits as "H") */
     p=(short *)&In[strm]; Hi=*(p)*A;                /* 16807*H->Hi */
     *(p)=0; Lo=In[strm]*A;                          /* 16807*L->Lo */
     p=(short *)&Lo; Hi+=*(p);       /* add high-order bits of Lo to Hi */
     q=(short *)&Hi;                  /* low-order bits of Hi->LO */
     *(p)=*(q+1)&0X7FFF;                          /* clear sign bit */
     k=*(q)<<1; if (*(q+1)&0X8000) then k++;      /* Hi bits 31-45->K */
     /* form Z + K [- M] (where Z=Lo): presubtract M to avoid overflow */
     Lo-=M; Lo+=k; if (Lo<0) then Lo+=M;
     In[strm]=Lo;
     return((real)Lo*4.656612875E-10);            /* Lo x 1/(2**31-1) */
   }
#endif

/*------------------- SELECT GENERATOR STREAM ---------------------*/
stream(n)
   int n;
     { /* set stream for 1<=n<=15, return stream for n=0 */
       if ((n<0)||(n>15)) then error(0,"stream Argument Error");
       if (n) then strm=n;
       return(strm);
     }


/*----------------------- SET/GET SEED ---------------------------*/
long seed(Ik,n)
   long Ik; int n;
     { /* set seed of stream n for Ik>0, return current seed for Ik=0 */
       if ((n<1)||(n>15)) then error(0,"seed Argument Error");
       if (Ik>0L) then  In[n]=Ik;
       return(In[n]);
     }

/*----------- UNIFORM [a, b] RANDOM VARIATE GENERATOR -------------*/
real uniform(a,b)
   real a,b;
     { /* 'uniform' returns a psuedo-random variate from a uniform */
       /* distribution with lower bound a and upper bound b.       */
       if (a>b) then error(0,"uniform Argument Error: a > b");
       return(a+(b-a)*ranf());
     }
```

```
/*------------------- RANDOM INTEGER GENERATOR  -------------------*/
random(i,n)
  int i,n;
    { /* 'random' returns an integer equiprobably selected from the   */
      /* set of integers i, i+1, i+2, . . , n.                        */
      if (i>n) then error(0,"random Argument Error: i > n");
      n-=i; n=(n+1.0)*ranf();
      return(i+n);
    }


/*------------- EXPONENTIAL RANDOM VARIATE GENERATOR  -------------*/
real expntl(x)
  real x;
    { /* 'expntl' returns a psuedo-random variate from a negative    */
      /* exponential distribution with mean x.                       */
      return(-x*log(ranf()));
    }


/*---------------- ERLANG RANDOM VARIATE GENERATOR  ----------------*/
real erlang(x,s)
  real x,s;
    { /* 'erlang' returns a psuedo-random variate from an erlang     */
      /* distribution with mean x and standard deviation s.          */
      int i,k; real z;
      if (s>x) then error(0,"erlang Argument Error: s > x");
      z=x/s; k=(int)z*z;
      z=1.0; for (i=0; i<k; i++) z*=ranf();
      return(-(x/k)*log(z));
    }


/*---------- HYPEREXPONENTIAL RANDOM VARIATE GENERATION  ----------*/
real hyperx(x,s)
  real x,s;
    { /* 'hyperx' returns a psuedo-random variate from Morse's two-  */
      /* stage hyperexponential distribution with mean x and standard */
      /* deviation s, s>x.  */
      real cv,z,p;
      if (s<=x) then error(0,"hyperx Argument Error: s not > x");
      cv=s/x; z=cv*cv; p=0.5*(1.0-sqrt((z-1.0)/(z+1.0)));
      z=(ranf()>p)? (x/(1.0-p)):(x/p);
      return(-0.5*z*log(ranf()));
    }
```

```
/*----------------- NORMAL RANDOM VARIATE GENERATOR  ----------------*/
real normal(x,s)
  real x,s;
    { /* 'normal' returns a psuedo-random variate from a normal dis-  */
      /* tribution with mean x and standard deviation s.              */
      real v1,v2,w,z1; static real z2=0.0;
      if (z2!=0.0)
        then {z1=z2; z2=0.0;}   /* use value from previous call */
        else
          {
            do
              {v1=2.0*ranf()-1.0; v2=2.0*ranf()-1.0; w=v1*v1+v2*v2;}
            while (w>=1.0);
            w=sqrt((-2.0*log(w))/w); z1=v1*w; z2=v2*w;
          }
      return(x+z1*s);
    }
```

```
/**********************************************************************/
/*                                                                    */
/*                        File "smpl.h"                               */
/*   Includes, Defines, & Extern Declarations for Simulation Programs */
/*                                                                    */
/*                                      (c) 1987  M. H. MacDougall    */
/*                                                                    */
/**********************************************************************/

#include <stdio.h>
#include <math.h>

typedef double real;
#define then

extern real Lq(), U(), B(), time();
extern char *fname(), *mname();
extern FILE sendto();

extern real ranf(), uniform(), expntl(), erlang(), hyperx(), normal();
extern long seed();
```

```
/*********************************************************************/
/*                                                                 */
/*                        File "stat.c"                            */
/*        Normal and T Distribution Quantile Computation Functions */
/*                                                                 */
/*********************************************************************/

/*-------- COMPUTE pth QUANTILE OF THE NORMAL DISTRIBUTION ---------*/
real Z(p)
  real p;
    { /* This function computes the pth upper quantile of the stand- */
      /* ard normal distribution (i.e., the value of z for which the */
      /* are under the curve from z to +infinity is equal to p).  'Z' */
      /* is a transliteration of the 'STDZ' function in Appendix C of */
      /* "Principles of Discrete Event Simulation", G. S. Fishman,    */
      /* Wiley, 1978.    The approximation used initially appeared in */
      /* in  "Approximations for Digital Computers", C. Hastings, Jr.,*/
      /* Princeton U. Press, 1955. */
      real q,z1,n,d; double sqrt(),log();
      q=(p>0.5)? (1-p):p;  z1=sqrt(-2.0*log(q));
      n=(0.010328*z1+0.802853)*z1+2.515517;
      d=((0.001308*z1+0.189269)*z1+1.43278)*z1+1;
      z1-=n/d; if (p>0.5) then z1=-z1;
      return(z1);
    }

/*---------- COMPUTE pth QUANTILE OF THE t DISTRIBUTION -----------*/
real T(p,ndf)
  real p; int ndf;
    { /* This function computes the upper pth quantile of the t dis- */
      /* tribution (the value of t for which the area under the curve */
      /* from t to +infinity is equal to p).  It is a transliteration */
      /* of the 'STUDTP' function given in Appendix C of "Principles  */
      /* of Discrete Event Simulation", G. S. Fishman, Wiley, 1978.   */
      int i; real z1,z2,h[4],x=0.0; double fabs();
      z1=fabs(Z(p)); z2=z1*z1;
      h[0]=0.25*z1*(z2+1.0); h[1]=0.010416667*z1*((5.0*z2+16.0)*z2+3.0);
      h[2]=0.002604167*z1*(((3.0*z2+19.0)*z2+17.0)*z2-15.0);
      h[3]=z1*((((79.0*z2+776.0)*z2+1482.0)*z2-1920.0)*z2-945.0);
      h[3]*=0.000010851;
      for (i=3; i>=0; i--) x=(x+h[i])/(real)ndf;
      z1+=x; if (p>0.5) then z1=-z1;
      return(z1);
    }
```

References

[Adam 1983]
Adam, N. R. Achieving a Confidence Interval for Parameters Estimated by Simulation. *Management Science 29, 7* (July 1983), 856-866.

[Agrawal 1985]
Agrawal, S. C. *Metamodeling: A Study of Approximations in Queueing Models.* MIT Press, 1985.

[Allen 1978]
Allen, A. O. *Probability, Statistics, and Queueing Theory.* Academic Press, 1978.

[Balci and Sargent 1981]
Balci, O., and Sargent, R. G. A Methodology for Cost-Risk Analysis in the Statistical Validation of Simulation Models. *Communications of the ACM 24, 11* (April 1981), 190-197.

[Balci and Sargent 1982]
Balci, O., and Sargent, R. G. Some Examples of Simulation Model Validation Using Hypothesis Testing. *Proc. 1982 Winter Simulation Conf.,* 621-629.

[Banks and Carson 1984]
Banks, J., and Carson, J. S. *Discrete-Event System Simulation.* Prentice-Hall, 1984.

[Beizer 1978]
Beizer, B. *Micro-Analysis of Computer System Performance.* Van Nostrand Reinhold, 1978.

[Bentley 1985]
Bentley, J. Programming Pearls. Thanks, Heaps. *Communications of the ACM 28 3* (March 1985), 245-250.

[Berry and Chandy 1983]
Berry, R., and Chandy, K. M. Performance Models of Token Ring Local Area Networks. *Proc. ACM SIGMETRICS Conf. on Measurement and Modeling of Computer Systems,* 1983, 266-274.

[Birtwhistle et al 1973]
Birtwhistle, G.M., Dahl, O. J., Myhrhaug, B., and Nygaard, K. *SIMULA Begin.* Auerbach, 1973.

[Blum et al 1984]
Blum, A., Donatiello, L., Heidelberger, P., Lavenberg, S.S., and MacNair, E. A. Experiments with Decomposition of Extended Queueing Network Models. *Proc. 1984 International Conf. on Modelling Techniques and Tools for Performance Analysis*. North-Holland, 1985.

[Box et al 1978]
Box, G. E. P., Hunter, W. G., and Hunter, J. S. *Statistics for Experimenters*. Wiley, 1978.

[Bratley et al 1983]
Bratley, P., Fox, B. L., and Schrage, L. E. *A Guide to Simulation*. Springer-Verlag, 1983.

[Bux 1981]
Bux, W. Local-area Subnetworks: A Performance Comparison. *IEEE Trans. on Communications 29, 10* (Oct. 1981), 1465-1473.

[Bux 1984]
Bux, W. Performance Issues in Local-area Networks. *IBM Systems Journal 23, 4* (1984), 351-374.

[Buzen 1973]
Buzen, J. P. Computational Algorithms for Closed Queueing Networks with Exponential Servers. *Communications of the ACM 16, 9* (Sept. 1973), 527-531.

[Buzen 1976]
Buzen, J. P. Fundamental Operational Laws of Computer System Performance. *Acta Informatica 7, 2* (1976), 167-182.

[Carson and Law 1980]
Carson, J. S., and Law, A. M. Conservation Equations and Variance Reduction in Queueing Simulations. *Operations Research 28, 3* (1980), 535-546.

[Chen and Li 1985]
Chen, P.-Y., and Li, W. Retransmission Schemes for CSMA/CD Networks. *Proc. IEEE International Conf. on Communications*, 1985, 1133-1138.

[Chiu and Chow, 1978]
Chiu, W. W., and Chow, W. M. A Performance Model of MVS. *IBM Systems Journal 17, 4* (1978), 444-462.

[Chlamtac and Eisenger 1983]
Chlamtac, I., and Eisenger, M. Voice/Data Integration on Ethernet - Backoff and Priority Considerations. *Computer Communications 6, 5* (Oct. 1983), 235-244.

[Courtois 1975]
Courtois, P. J. Decomposability, Instabilities, and Saturation in Multiprogramming Systems. *Communications of the ACM 18, 7* (July 1975), 371-377.

[Courtois 1977]
Courtois, P. J. *Decomposability: Queueing and Computer System Applications*. Academic Press, 1977.

[Crane and Lemoine 1977]
Crane, M. A., and Lemoine, A. J. *An Introduction to the Regenerative Method for Simulation Analysis*. Springer-Verlag, 1977.

[Daley 1968]
Daley, D. J. The Serial Correlation Coefficients of Waiting Times in a Stationary Single Server Queue. *J. Australian Mathematical Society 8, 4* (Nov. 1968), 683-699.

[DEC et al 1982]
The Ethernet, A Local Area Network: Data Link Layer and Physical Layer Specifications. Version 2.0. Digital Equipment Corp., Intel Corp., and Xerox Corp., Nov. 1982.

[Denning and Buzen 1978]
Denning, P. J., and Buzen, J. P. The Operational Analysis of Queueing Network Models. *Computing Surveys 10, 3* (Sept. 1978), 225-261.

[Everitt 1986]
Everitt, D. Simple Approximations for Token Rings. *IEEE Trans. on Communications 34, 7* (July 1985), 719-721.

[Ferrari 1978]
Ferrari, D. *Computer Systems Performance Evaluation.* Prentice-Hall, 1978.

[Ferrari et al 1983]
Ferrari, D., Serazzi, G., and Zeigner, A. *Measurement and Tuning of Computer Systems.* Prentice-Hall, 1983.

[Fishman 1978]
Fishman, G. S. *Principles of Discrete Event Simulation.* Wiley, 1978.

[Gehani 1985]
Gehani, N. *C: An Advanced Introduction.* Computer Science Press, 1985.

[Gonsalves 1985]
Gonsalves, T. A. Performance Characteristics of 2 Ethernets: an Experimental Study. *Proc. ACM SIGMETRICS Conf. on Modeling and Measurement of Computer Systems*, 1985, 78-86.

[Hammond and O'Reilly 1986]
Hammond, J. L., and O'Reilly, P. J. P. *Performance Analysis of Local Computer Networks.* Addison-Wesley, 1986.

[Harbison and Steele 1984]
Harbison, S. P., and Steele, G. L., Jr. *A C Reference Manual.* Prentice-Hall, 1984.

[Hastings and Peacock 1974]
Hastings, N. A. J., and Peacock, J. B. *Statistical Distributions.* Wiley, 1974.

[Hughes 1984]
Hughes, H. D. Generating a Drive Workload from Clustered Data. *Computer Performance 5, 1* (Mar. 1984), 31-37.

[IEEE 1985a]
Carrier Sense Multiple Access with Collision Detection (CSMA/CD): Access Method and Physical Layer Specifications. ANSI/IEEE Standard 802.3-1985. IEEE, 1985.

[IEEE 1985b]
Token Ring Access Method and Physical Layer Specifications. ANSI/IEEE Standard 802.5-1985, IEEE, 1985.

[Iglehart 1978]
    Iglehart, D. L. The Regenerative Method for Simulation Analysis. *Current Trends in Programming Methodology; Vol. III. Software Engineering.* K. M. Chandy and R. T. Yeh (eds.), Prentice-Hall, 1978.

[Jackman and Medeiros 1984]
    Jackman, J. K., and Medeiros, D. J. Modeling and Analysis of Ethernet Networks. *Proc. 1984 Winter Simulation Conf.,* 595-600.

[Jacobson and Lazowska 1981]
    Jacobson, P. A., and Lazowska, E. D. The Method of Surrogate Delays: Simultaneous Resource Possession in Analytic Models of Computer Systems. *Proc. ACM SIGMETRICS Conf. on Modeling and Measurement of Computer Systems,* 1981, 165-174; also, *Communications of the ACM 25, 2* (Feb. 1982), 142-151.

[Jain and Chlamtac 1985]
    Jian, R., and Chlamtac, I. The P^2 Algorithm for Dynamic Calculation of Quantiles and Histograms Without Storing Observations. *Communications of the ACM 28, 10* (Oct. 1985), 1076-1085.

[Jones 1986]
    Jones, D. W. An Empirical Comparison of Priority-Queue and Event-Set Implementations. *Communications of the ACM 29, 4* (April 1986), 300-311.

[K&R]
    Kernighan, B. W., and Ritchie, D. M. *The C Programming Language.* Prentice-Hall, 1978.

[Kleijnen 1975]
    Kleijnen, J. P. C. *Statistical Techniques in Simulation.* Marcel Dekker, 1974 (Part I), 1975 (Part II).

[Kleinrock 1975]
    Kleinrock, L. *Queueing Systems. Vol, I: Theory. Vol. II: Computer Applications.* Wiley, 1975.

[Knuth 1973]
    Knuth, D. E. *The Art of Computer Programming. Vol. 3, Sorting and Searching.* Addison-Wesley, 1972.

[Knuth 1981]
    Knuth, D. E. *The Art of Computer Programming. Vol. 2, Seminumerical Algorithms.* Addison-Wesley, 1981 (2nd ed.).

[Kobayashi 1978]
    Kobayashi, H. *Modeling and Analysis: An Introduction to System Performance Evaluation Methodology.* Addison-Wesley, 1978.

[Lam 1980]
    Lam, S. S. A Carrier Sense Multiple Access Protocol for Local Networks. *Computer Networks 4* (1980), 21-32.

[Lavenberg 1983]
    Lavenberg, S. S. (editor). *Computer Performance Modeling Handbook.* Academic Press, 1983.

[Lavenberg et al 1977]
Lavenberg, S. S., Moeller, T. L., and Welch, P. D. Control Variables Applied to the Simulation of Queueing Models of Computer Systems. *Computer Performance*. K. M. Chandy and M. Reiser (eds.), North-Holland, 1977.

[Lavenberg et al 1977]
Lavenberg, S. S., Moeller, T. L., and Welch, P. D. Statistical Results on Control Variables with Application to Queueing Network Simulation. *Operations Research 30, 1* (1982), 182-202.

[Law 1983]
Law, A. M. Statistical Analysis of Simulation Output Data. *Operations Research 31, 6* (1983), 983-1029.

[Law and Carson 1979]
Law, A. M., and Carson, J. S. A Sequential Procedure for Determining the Length of a Steady-State Simulation. *Operations Research 27, 5* (1979), 1011-1025.

[Law and Kelton 1982]
Law, A. M., and Kelton, W. D. *Simulation Modeling and Analysis*. McGraw-Hill, 1982.

[Law and Vincent 1983]
Law, A. M., and Vincent, S. G. *UNIFIT: An Interactive Computer Package for Fitting Probability Distributions to Observed Data*. Simulation Modeling and Analysis Company, 1983.

[Lazowska et al 1984]
Lazowska, E. D., Zahorjan, J., Graham, G. S., and Sevcik. K. C. *Quantitative System Performance*. Prentice-Hall, 1984.

[Lazowska et al 1986]
Lazowska, E.D., Zahorjan, J., Cheriton, D. R., and Zwaenepoel, W. File Access Performance of Diskless Workstations. *ACM Trans. on Computer Systems 4, 3* (Aug. 1986), 238-268.

[Learmonth and Lewis 1973]
Learmonth, J., and Lewis, P. A. W. *Naval Postgraduate School Random Number Generator Package LLRANDOM*. Naval Postgraduate School, Monterey, California, 1973.

[Lewis et al 1969]
Lewis, P. A. W., Goodman, A. S., and Miller, J. M. A Psuedo-Random Number Generator for the System/360. *IBM Systems Journal 8, 2* (1969), 136-146.

[Little 1961]
Little, J. D. C. A Proof of the Queueing Formula L $=\lambda$W. *Operations Research 9, 3* (1961), 383-387.

[MacDougall 1975]
MacDougall, M. H.. System Level Simulation. *Digital System Design Automation: Languages, Simulation, and Data Base*. Computer Science Press, 1975.

[MacDougall 1979]
MacDougall, M. H. The Simulation Language SIML/I. *Proc. AFIPS 1979 National Computer Conf.*, 48 (June 1979), 39-44.

[MacDougall 1984]
MacDougall, M. H. Instruction-Level Program and Processor Modeling. *Computer 17, 7* (July 1984), 14-24.

[MacNair and Sauer 1985]
MacNair, E. A., and Sauer, C. H. *Elements of Practical Performance Modeling*. Prentice-Hall, 1985.

[Marsaglia and Bray 1964]
Marsaglia, G., and Bray, T. A. A Convenient Method for Generating Normal Random Variables. *SIAM Review 6, 3* (1964), 260-264.

[McCormack and Sargent 1981]
McCormack, W. M., and Sargent, R. G. Analysis of Future Event Set Algorithms for Discrete Event Simulation. *Communications of the ACM 24, 12* (Dec. 1981), 801-812.

[McNutt 1984]
McNutt, B. A Case Study of Access to VM Disk Volumes. *Proc. CMG XV International Conf. on the Management and Performance Evaluation of Computer Systems*, 1984, 175-180.

[Mendenhall and Scheaffer 1973]
Mendenhall, W., and Scheaffer, R. L. *Mathematical Statistics with Applications*. Duxbury Press, 1973.

[Melamed and Morris 1985]
Melamed, B., and Morris, R. J. T. Visual Simulation: The Performance Analysis Workstation. *Computer 18, 8* (Aug. 1985), 87-94.

[Molloy 1984]
Molloy, M. K. Collision Resolution on the CSMA/CD Bus. *Proc. 9th IEEE Conf. on Local Computer Networks*, 1984, 44-47.

[Morse 1963]
Morse, P. M. *Queues, Inventories, and Maintenance*. Wiley, 1963.

[Mudge et al 1984]
Mudge, T. N., Hayes, J. P., Buzzard, G. D., and Winsor, D.C. Analysis of Multiple Bus Interconnection Networks. *Proc. 1984 International Conf. on Parallel Processing*, 228-232.

[Mudge and Al-Sadoun 1985]
Mudge, T. N., and Al-Sadoun, H. B. A Semi-Markov Model for the Performance of Multiple-Bus Systems. *IEEE Trans. on Computers 34, 10* (Oct. 1985), 934-942.

[NBS 1985]
Proceedings Workshop on Analytic and Simulation Modeling of IEEE 802.4 Token Bus Local Area Networks. Special Publication No. 500-127, National Bureau of Standards, 1985.

[O'Keefe 1985]
O'Keefe, R. M. Comment on 'Complexity Analyses of Event Set Algorithms'. *The Computer Journal 28, 5* (1985), 496-497.

[O'Reilly and Hammond 1984]
   O'Reilly, P. J. P., and Hammond, J. L., Jr. An Efficient Simulation Technique for Performance Studies of CSMA/CD Local Networks. *IEEE Journal on Selected Areas in Communication 2, 1* (Jan. 1984), 238-249.

[Patterson and Séquin 1981]
   Patterson, D. A., and Séquin, C. H. RISC I: A Reduced Instruction Set VLSI Computer. *Proc. 8th Annual Symposium on Computer Architecture,* 1981, 443-457.

[Payne et al 1969]
   Payne, W. H., Rabung, J. R., and Bogyo, T. P. Coding the Lehmer Psuedo-Random Number Generator. *Communications of the ACM 12, 2* (Feb. 1969), 85-86.

[Randell 1968]
   Randell, B. Towards a Methodology of Computing System Design. *Proc. NATO Conf. on Software Engineering,* 1968, 204-208.

[Reeves 1984]
   Reeves, C. M. Complexity Analyses of Event Set Algorithms. *The Computer Journal 27, 1* (1984), 72-79.

[Rice 1983]
   Rice, J. R. *Numerical Methods, Software, and Analysis*. McGraw-Hill, 1983.

[Sargent 1984]
   Sargent, R. G. A Tutorial on Verification and Validation of Simulation Models. *Proc. 1984 Winter Simulation Conf.,* 115-121.

[Sauer and Chandy 1981]
   Sauer, C. H., and Chandy, K. M. *Computer Systems Performance Modeling*. Prentice-Hall, 1981.

[Schrage 1979]
   Schrage, L. A More Portable Fortran Random Number Generator. *ACM Trans. on Mathematical Software 5, 2* (June 1979), 132-138.

[Schatzoff and Tillman 1975]
   Schatzoff, M., and Tillman, C. C. Design of Experiments in Simulator Validation. *IBM Journal of Research and Development 19, 3* (May 1975), 252-262.

[Schmeiser 1982]
   Schmeiser, B. Batch Size Effects in the Analysis of Simulation Output. *Operations Research 30, 3* (1982), 556-568.

[Schwetman 1978]
   Schwetman, H. D. Hybrid Simulation Models of Computer Systems. *Communications of the ACM 21, 9* (Sept. 1978), 718-723.

[Schwetman 1986]
   Schwetman, H. D. CSIM: A C-Based, Process-Oriented Simulation Language. *Proc. 1986 Winter Simulation Conf.,* 387-396.

[Shanthikumar and Sargent 1983]
   Shanthikumar, J. G., and Sargent, R. G. A Unifying View of Hybrid Simulation/Analytic Models and Modeling. *Operations Research 31, 6* (1983), 1030-1052.

[Shoch and Hupp 1980]
Shoch, J. F., and Hupp, J. A. Measured Performance of an Ethernet Local Network. *Communications of the ACM 23, 12* (Dec. 1980), 711-721.

[Shoch et al 1982]
Shoch, J. F., Dalal, Y. K., Redell, D. D., and Crane, R. C. Evolution of the Ethernet Local Computer Network. *Computer 15, 8* (Aug. 1982), 10-27.

[Smilauer 1985]
Smikauer, B. General Model for Memory Interference in Multiprocessors and Mean Value Analysis. *IEEE Trans. on Computers 34, 8* (Aug. 1985), 744-751.

[Sreenivasan and Kleinman 1974]
Sreenivasan, K., and Kleinman, A. J. On the Construction of a Representative Synthetic Workload. *Communications of the ACM 17, 3* (Mar. 1974), 127-133.

[Stuck 1983]
Calculating the Maximum Mean Data Rate in Local Area Networks. *Computer 16, 5* (May 1983), 72-76.

[Stuck and Arthurs 1985]
Stuck, B. W., and Arthurs, E. *A Computer and Communications Network Performance Analysis Primer*. Prentice-Hall, 1985.

[Teorey 1975]
Teorey, T. J. Validation Criteria for Computer System Simulation. *Proc. Symposium on the Simulation of Computer Systems*, 1975, 161-169.

[Thomasian and Gargeya 1984]
Thomasian, A., and Gargeya, K. Speeding Up Computer System Simulations Using Hierarchical Modeling. *Proc. CMG XV International Conf.*, 1984, 845-850.

[Tocher 1963]
Tocher, K. D. *The Art of Simulation*. Van Nostrand, 1963.

[Towsley 1986]
Towsley, D. Approximate Models of Multiple Bus Multiprocessor Systems. *IEEE Trans. on Computers 35, 3* (Mar. 1984), 220-228.

[Trivedi 1982]
Trivedi, K. S. *Probability & Statistics with Reliability, Queueing, and Computer Science Applications*. Prentice-Hall, 1982.

[Wang and McGurrin 1985]
Wang, P. T. R., and McGurrin, M. F. CSMA/CD LANs with Overload Detection and Protection. *Proc. 10th IEEE Conf. on Local Computer Networks*, 1985, 61-68.

[Welch 1983]
Welch, P. D. The Statistical Analysis of Simulation Results. *Computer Performance Modeling Handbook*, S. S. Lavenberg (ed.), Academic Press, 1983.

[Zahorjan et al 1982]
Zahorjan, J., Sevcik, K. C., Eager, D. L., and Galler, P. I. Balanced Job Bound Analysis of Queueing Networks. *Communications of the ACM 25, 2* (Feb. 1982), 134-141.

Author Index

Adam, N. R. 121, 206
Agrawal, S. C. ix
Allen, A. O. viii, 81, 131
Al-Sadoun, H. B. 152
Arthurs, E. ix, 69

Balci, O. 82, 85
Banks, J. ix, 5, 6, 81, 82, 97, 126
Beizer, B. 74
Bentley, J. 243
Berry, R. 193
Birtwhistle, G. M. 4
Blum, A. 74
Bogyo, T. P. 283
Box, G. E. P. 125, 126
Bratley, P. ix, 5, 7, 105, 106, 121
Bray, T. A. 235
Bux, W. 169, 188, 192, 193
Buzen, J. P. 18, 42, 81
Buzzard, G. D. 282

Carson, J. S. ix, 5, 6, 81, 82, 97, 121, 122, 126
Chandy, K. M. ix, 193
Chen, P.-Y. 186
Cheriton, D. R. 281
Chiu, W. W. 70, 74
Chlamtac, I. 186, 250
Chow, W. M. 70, 74
Courtois, P. J. 73
Crane, M. A. 106
Crane, R. C. 284

Dahl, O. J. 277
Dalal, Y. K. 284
Daley, D. J. 102
Denning, P. J. 18
Donatiello, L. 278

Eisenger, M. 186
Everitt, D. 193

Ferrari, D. ix, 2, 4, 67, 81
Fishman, G. S. ix, 7, 11, 97, 105, 108, 120, 232, 233
Fox, B. L. 278

Gargeya, K. 74
Gehani, N. C. 213
Gonsalves, T. A. 184
Goodman, A. S. 281
Graham, G. S. 281

Hammond, J. L., Jr. 74, 188, 193
Harbison, S. P. 213
Hastings, N. A. J. 7
Hayes, J. P. 282
Heidelberger, P. 278
Hughes, H. D. 12
Hunter, J. S. 278
Hunter, W. G. 278
Hupp, J. A. 186

Iglehart, D. L. 106

Jackman, J. K. 185
Jacobson, P. A. 145, 148
Jain, R. 250
Jones, D. W. 244

Kelton, W. D. ix, 5, 6, 25, 82, 97, 106, 121, 122, 125, 126, 235
Kernighan, B. W. 213
Kleijnen, J. P. C. ix, 108, 121, 124, 125, 126
Kleinman, A. J. 12, 81
Kleinrock, L. vii
Knuth, D. E. 7, 27, 243
Kobayashi, H. vii, 2, 6, 41, 81, 94, 99, 101, 105, 106, 230

Subject Index

The MIT Press, with Peter Denning, general consulting editor, and Brian Randell, European consulting editor, publishes computer science books in the following series:

ACM Doctoral Dissertation Award and Distinguished Dissertation Series

Artificial Intelligence, Patrick Winston and Michael Brady, editors

Charles Babbage Institute Reprint Series for the History of Computing, Martin Campbell-Kelly, editor

Computer Systems, Herb Schwetman, editor

Exploring with Logo, E. Paul Goldenberg, editor

Foundations of Computing, Michael Garey, editor

History of Computing, I. Bernard Cohen and William Aspray, editors

Information Systems, Michael Lesk, editor

Logic Programming, Ehud Shapiro, editor; Fernando Pereira, Koichi Furukawa, and D. H. D. Warren, associate editors

The MIT Electrical Engineering and Computer Science Series

Scientific Computation, Dennis Gannon, editor